P9-CTQ-591

STUDIES IN
COMPARATIVE ECONOMICS 10

Studies in Comparative Economics

FISCAL
SYSTEMS

by Richard A. Musgrave

NEW HAVEN AND LONDON
YALE UNIVERSITY PRESS
1969

FOREWORD

Modern economics has been bred chiefly in Western Europe and the United States, and despite its aspiration toward generality it bears the stamp of institutions and issues characteristic of these areas.

But the economic world no longer revolves about London and New York. Dozens of new nations are struggling toward economic independence and industrial growth under institutional arrangements quite unlike those of the West. Economies of a novel type also extend eastward from central Europe to the Bering Strait and have been busily developing their own principles as a by-product of administrative experience. It is asserted that "Western economics" has only limited analytical value in these other countries.

The problem of the content and relevance of economics thus arises inescapably. Are the economic principles taught in the West really susceptible of general application? Or are they culture-bound and relevant mainly to industrial capitalist countries? Is it possible to create a general economics which would be as useful in Poland or India as in Canada or France? Or must we be content with several species of economics which will remain distinct in intellectual content and applicability?

"Comparative economics" has been regarded as a separate area of the economics curriculum, consisting of a botanical classification of national economies into a few loosely labeled boxes. But surely any course in economics is potentially comparative. A concern with comparative experience can

profitably be infused into any of the standard branches of economic study. This series is inspired by the hope that a rethinking of particular branches of economics in world perspective, combined with a bibliography of available material from many countries, may help teachers to give their courses a broader and more comparative orientation.

In pursuing this objective, we deliberately chose autonomy over standardization. Each author was left free to determine his own approach and method of treatment. The essays thus differ considerably in length, analytical as against descriptive emphasis, geographical coverage, and other respects. How far the original intent of the series has been accomplished is for the profession to judge.

We are grateful to the authors who have struggled with possibly insoluble problems, to the Ford Foundation for its support of the enterprise, and to the staff of the Yale University Press for their helpful cooperation.

The Inter-University Committee on Comparative Economics: Abram Bergson, Arthur R. Burns, Kermit Gordon, Richard Musgrave, William Nicholls, Lloyd Reynolds (Chairman)

PREFACE

The purpose of this series is to examine the functioning of economic institutions and the solution of economic tasks in a variety of settings. This is a fascinating theme applied to any area of economic study, but it is of particular interest in the field of public finance, where the interrelation between social, political, and economic forms is unusually close. How do fiscal institutions and functions change with their environment, and what similarities remain even though the setting differs?

Treated exhaustively, an investigation of this sort could readily fill many volumes, and to remain in bounds choices had to be made. Thus the broader problems of public ownership, control, and planning have been excluded, and attention focused on the fiscal system as it operates within the budget. Nor do I offer systematic comparison of specific institutions and policies in a large number of countries, with the vast array of detail that this involves. Instead, I attempt to examine the essential characteristics of fiscal systems in the context of certain key features of economic life.

Part I deals with the adaptation of fiscal systems to the requirements of centrally planned and decentralized, or market, economies. While most economies involve elements of both, we begin with the more or less polar cases, so as to bring out the nature of the difference more clearly. The fiscal sectors under the two systems are found to differ sharply, and outward similarities frequently cover up quite different functions. Yet certain basic problems persist, and it is interesting to see how they are handled in the theory and

practice of either setting. Also, it is of interest to note how the current move toward decentralized socialism is reflected in the changing tax structure of socialist countries.

Part II examines the interaction between fiscal systems and economic development. On one side, fiscal systems render an important contribution to economic development, and the nature of this contribution changes as the economy advances; on the other, the fiscal system is influenced by and must adapt itself to the structural and institutional changes that result in the course of economic development. In particular, the limitations imposed by the availability of tax handles (i.e. forms of economic activity that lend themselves to effective taxation) undergo drastic change, and the demands for public services with regard to both public consumption and capital formation similarly vary with changing income levels and stages of capital formation. Against this perspective, Wagner's law on the expanding scale of public expenditure is reconsidered, and its validity is tested empirically. On the revenue side, the changing composition of the tax structure is examined, and such familiar hypotheses as that of a declining share of indirect taxes are tested. Historical and cross-sectional comparisons are used and an attempt is made to reconcile their results.

Next, the tax structures of a number of highly developed countries are compared. Emphasis is placed on the individual income tax and the problems inherent in income tax comparisons. Other taxes are compared more briefly. While there are considerable differences in the composition of tax structures, the differences in particular taxes are less, and there is a notable drift toward greater structural similarity. Finally, the changing contexts and instruments of stabilization policy are examined, as the economy changes from the poverty level to one in which savings can be generated and on to a more advanced stage where the task is to maintain both high employment and balanced growth.

Part III deals with the role of fiscal systems in international transactions, and the problems that arise because fiscal

policy does not operate in a closed setting. Special attention is given to international tax coordination. The coordination of income and product taxes is considered from the point of view of both equity and efficiency, with recognition of the fact that conclusions may differ, depending on whether a national or a world point of view is taken, or whether concern is with the welfare of a group of countries such as the Common Market. Expenditure coordination is approached in terms of a spatial theory of social goods supply, and the issue of international income redistribution is examined as a new and potentially major branch of international public finance. Lastly, the role of stabilization policy in the open setting is considered, including the particular factors that determine the effectiveness and role of fiscal and monetary policies. Returning to the discussion of growth policy in low income countries, the constraint of foreign balance is introduced into the earlier discussion.

There is a concluding chapter in which the reader is reminded that I have offered but a sample, drawn from a wide range of problems that might have been covered. These include fiscal centralization versus decentralization, the formulation of the budget plan, the impact of governmental forms on fiscal behavior, social security and transfer systems, and the structure and management of public debt. By at least raising some of these issues, I hope that further work of this sort will be encouraged, leading toward a truly multinational and international view of fiscal issues.

Thanks are due my associates and students, who have read and commented on the manuscript, and Alan Peacock, who has been a most perceptive and helpful reader. Special thanks are also due my wife, who has stimulated my interest in the international aspects of public finance and who contributed greatly to Part III of this study. There is nothing like having an expert in the house.

R.A.M.

Cambridge, Mass.
February 1968

CONTENTS

Contents

xii

Contents

Contents

TABLES AND FIGURES

FIGURES

PART I
PUBLIC SECTOR AND
ECONOMIC ORGANIZATION

1 THE ISSUES

The proper scope and role of the public sector differ under conditions of socialism and capitalism or, broadly speaking, in a centrally planned and a market-determined economy. At the same time, certain aspects of the fiscal problem persist under various forms of economic organization. The purpose of this chapter is to explore these differences and similarities.[1] We begin with a theoretical approach to the issue and then proceed to a comparison of institutions.

1. For general reflections on the role of taxation and the public sector in various economic systems see W. Gerloff, *Steuerwirtschaft und Sozialismus* (Leipzig, 1922); Herbert Timm, "Steuern im Sozialismus," in *Beiträge zur Finanzwissenschaft und zur Geldtheorie*, Festschrift für Rudolf Stucken, ed. Fritz Voigt (Göttingen, Vandenhoeck and Ruprecht, 1953), pp. 66–93; Rudolf Goldscheid, "A Sociological Approach to Problems of Public Finance," in *Classics in the Theory of Public Finance*, ed. Richard A. Musgrave and Alan T. Peacock (London and New York, Macmillan, 1958); J. A. Schumpeter, *Capitalism, Socialism and Democracy* (New York, Harper, 1942), and "The Crisis of the Tax State," in *International Economic Papers*, no. 4 (1954), p. 5.

For general discussion of the economics of socialism see also Oskar Lange, "On the Economic Theory of Socialism," in *On the Economic Theory of Socialism*, by Oskar Lange and Fred M. Taylor, ed. B. E. Lippincott (Minneapolis, University of Minnesota Press, 1938); and Abram Bergson, "Socialist Economics," in *A Survey of Contemporary Economics*, ed. Howard Ellis (Philadelphia, Blakiston, 1948).

The Anatomy of Economic Systems

The function of the public sector is not single-purposed, but comprises a variety of subfunctions. These include provision for the satisfaction of public wants, adjustments in the distribution of income, and stable growth. Let us consider how these functions appear under various economic systems. To simplify our task, and to reduce the number of dimensions with which we must deal, we will assume throughout that the fiscal system is centralized on a national level.[2]

PUBLIC WANTS VERSUS PUBLIC PRODUCTION

In comparing the role of the public sector under conditions of socialism and capitalism, two concepts of the public sector must be distinguished. One concept hinges on the organization of production and is based on the distinction between private and public *enterprise*. This corresponds to the classical distinction between capitalism and socialism, where the size of the public sector is measured by the fraction of GNP produced by enterprises owned and managed by the government. This concept is not of central concern for our investigation and is of interest only where it bears on the fiscal function. Another concept hinges on the determination of resource use and is based on the distinction between private and public *wants*. This is the distinction that matters here, since it goes to the heart of the fiscal function. Public wants, for reasons which will presently be apparent, are wants that must be provided for through the budget and be made available free of direct charge to the user. Private wants in turn may be satisfied through price payments at the market and do not require (though permit) the budgetary mechanism. The size of the public sector, in

2. For a discussion of fiscal centralization versus decentralization, see p. 341.

this sense, depends on the fraction of output directed to the satisfaction of public wants.

To illustrate the distinction, we may readily imagine a socialist society where most goods and services are produced by government, but where the bulk of government product is sold at the market to private consumers in order to satisfy private wants. This is the case of socialism with consumer sovereignty, i.e. a production mix designed to match consumer preference, and a pattern of consumer preference that favors private wants. Or we may imagine a society where production is carried on very largely by private firms, but where a substantial part of their output is purchased by government and is made available through the budget for the satisfaction of public wants. This is the case of capitalism, with consumer preferences that favor public wants.

The size of the public sector in the sense of public production, therefore, must not be confused with the size of the public sector in the sense of resource use for the satisfaction of public wants. The two decisions are basically independent and involve quite different sets of considerations. At the same time, the organization of production has important bearing on how public goods are paid for—e.g. withholding of profits from state enterprises under socialism versus income taxation under capitalism—and hence on the revenue structure. Moreover, incentive considerations are more far-reaching in the capitalist system, where risk taking as well as work incentives must be considered. This, as we shall see, may limit the extent to which public wants can be satisfied under a system of private production.

ALTERNATIVE FORMS

In addition to the distinction between private versus public ownership and management of enterprise, there are certain other aspects of economic organization which are highly significant in shaping the function of the fiscal system.

Thus it will be useful to distinguish between economic systems according to

1. whether the basket of consumer goods produced is based on individual preferences (C_i) or directed by government (C_g);

2. whether choice among jobs is left to the individual worker with wages determined in line with the worker's marginal product (W_i); or whether the allocation of labor is determined by government through conscription (W_g), with wage payments determined as a matter of social policy;

3. whether the overall savings rate, i.e. the share of GNP directed into capital formation (public or private), is determined by individual choice (S_i) or by government (S_g);

4. whether means of production (land and capital goods) are owned and managed by individuals (O_i) or by government (O_g).

From these structural factors one may specify the anatomy of alternative economic systems; and the symbols as defined above will be used for purposes of brevity.[3] Thus, C_i, W_i, S_i, O_i define pure capitalism; C_g, W_g, S_g, O_g give orthodox socialism; C_i, W_i, S_g, O_g describe liberal socialism; C_i, W_i, S_g, O_i show the essential features of modern capitalism, and so forth. It goes without saying that the various features tend to be mixed and that our "pure forms" (in Max Weber's sense) hardly exist in the real world. Thus most socialist economies have always had substantial sectors of private

3. The reader will keep in mind that these symbols stand for the organizational feature of the economy, and hence should not be confused with the national accounting symbols as customarily used. Thus C_i and C_g refer to whether the mix of consumer goods depends on public or private preferences; they do not indicate public and private consumption expenditure. The symbols S_i and S_g refer to whether the overall savings rate is determined privately or publicly; they do not indicate public and private saving respectively.

6

ownership, especially in agriculture, and most capitalist economies have had substantial sectors of public ownership, especially in utilities and transportation. Similarly, the distinction between individual and governmental choice may not be drawn clearly but be a matter of degree, and so forth. Nevertheless, this structuring is helpful for our purposes, as it will permit us to consider how various fiscal functions—including provision for public wants, adjustment in distribution, and stabilization—depend on these four features and are performed under the various systems.

PROVISION FOR PUBLIC WANTS

The literature of public finance has had much to say, if somewhat inconclusively, about the nature of social wants and the process by which they should be provided for. To what extent may these findings be generalized and adapted to various economic systems?

TYPES OF WANTS

For purposes of this discussion, the following terminology regarding the types of wants, or goods that go to provide for them, will be used:

Types of Wants

| | Nature of Benefits | |
Basis of Want Determination	Internal	External
Individual (C_i)	Private	Social
Imposed (C_g)	Merit	Merit

Private wants are contrasted with two types of public wants, one referred to as social and the other as merit. As we shall see, the distinction between private and social wants or goods depends on whether the resulting benefit is internal or external. They are similar in that both reflect individual preferences. The distinction between the two types of public

7

wants or goods hinges on the distinction between C_i and C_g. Social wants are public wants that (like private wants) belong to the C_i group. The basket of goods, produced to satisfy such wants, is to be in line with consumer preference. Public wants of the merit type, on the other hand, are wants that reflect the preference scale of a ruling group and that are imposed on the individual consumer.

SOCIAL VERSUS PRIVATE WANTS

Let us see how the distinction between private and social wants applies to the capitalist and socialist systems.

Capitalist System. We begin with a market economy of the C_i, W_i, S_i, O_i type, where individual consumer choice determines how resources are used and where use of factor supplies is left to the free choice of suppliers. Also, suppose first that we are concerned with the satisfaction of private wants only.

The satisfaction of *private* wants involves goods that are rival in consumption. A given physical product (e.g. cake) which is consumed by A cannot also be consumed by B and vice versa. These goods may be consumed in varying amounts by particular individuals, and in line with their desire to do so at the prevailing market price. Those who do not contribute are excluded. Since such goods cannot be obtained without payment, the individual is forced to reveal his preference by bidding at the market. The process of resource allocation is performed through the pricing mechanism which (by equating marginal cost with price) achieves efficient resource use under competitive conditions. No government intervention is needed.

The same process, however, breaks down in the case of *social* wants.[4] These are wants that are satisfied by goods the

4. For further discussion see P. E. Samuelson, "The Pure Theory of Public Expenditure," *Review of Economics and Statistics, 36* (November 1954); Leif Johansen, "Some Notes on the Lindahl Theory of the Determination of Public Expenditures," *International Economic Re-*

benefits from which are "nonrival." The benefits that A derives from national defense or an antipollution program are not reduced by B's sharing therein. Such benefits are available to all members of the group, independent of individual contribution. This has two consequences. First, it changes the conditions of optimal allocation with given preferences. Marginal cost pricing with uniform prices payable by everyone will not give an efficient solution. Marginal cost of the public facility must now be equated with the sum of the prices paid by A and B; and the price payable by each must be in line with his respective evaluation.[5] Second, the auctioning system of the market ceases to bring about revelation of consumer preferences.[6] Since consumption is not conditioned by individual contributions, consumers cannot be excluded, and hence are not induced to reveal their preferences and thus contribute voluntarily in accordance with their true evaluation. National defense, the judicial system, public sanitation, are cases in point. A voting mechanism with compulsory adherence to the voting rule is needed to

---

view, 4 (1963); and J. G. Head, "Public Goods and Public Policy," in *Public Finance/Finances Publiques, 17* (1962), where an incisive discussion of the literature may be found. See also my *The Theory of Public Finance* (New York, McGraw-Hill, 1959), Chap. 5; and my "Provision for Social Goods," *The Theory of the Public Sector,* ed. J. Margolis, International Economic Association, forthcoming.

5. A possible pricing rule is such that for each consumer the ratio of his price of social goods to that of private goods equals his marginal rate of substitution of one for the other. This, however, is not the only efficient rule. Other pricing rules may be used, and the choice among them may be made on pragmatic grounds (whichever can be approximated best through the political process) provided the choice of rule is stipulated in determining the proper state of distribution.

6. Such at least is the case where large numbers are involved. With small numbers, negotiation may occur, but the result will tend to be imperfect, as is the case where the market for private goods deals with small numbers. But whereas the increase in numbers solves the problem for private goods, it leads to nonrevelation in the case of social goods and to a situation where negotiation ceases to be feasible.

force revelation of preferences and to establish the basis on which tax payments can be assessed.[7] The taxes thus assessed reflect (or would do so under ideal conditions) the consumer's evaluation of the public service. They are benefit taxes.

The market mechanism, for both these reasons, cannot deal with the provision for social wants. A tax-expenditure process is needed to allocate resources to the provision of social wants and at the same time to assign the cost to the individuals who demand that such wants be satisfied. It is in this sense that the satisfaction of social wants must be provided for through the budget. As previously noted, this does not mean that such goods must be produced by government. The crucial point is that they must be demanded by government, and given such demand, the supply side of the private market can usually respond to meet it, just as in the case of private wants.[8]

The difference between social and private wants, viewed in this fashion, does not lie in the psychology of wants or in ideological attitudes toward social versus private objectives. Social along with private wants constitute an integral part of the individual's preference system: Both are individual wants and (under pattern C_i at least) subject to consumer sovereignty. The difference, rather, lies in the externality characteristics of the goods needed to satisfy the two types of wants. It is not a matter of ideology but an objective or "technological" distinction.

Liberal Socialism. This being the case, the same dis-

7. It should be noted that even if exclusion could be applied to force the revelation of preferences, this would not be desirable. In the case of purely social wants, where A's partaking in the benefits does not interfere with B's, exclusion would be wasteful.

8. This is not to deny that there may be situations (e.g. the idea of *public* schools as a means of social integration) where public production is essential to the quality of the product, but such cases are exceptional and may be disregarded here.

10

tinction between private and social wants remains relevant for a public ownership system (O_g) provided only that C_i is maintained, i.e. allocation is to be in line with individual consumer choice. Consider the liberal type of socialism— here defined as pattern C_i, W_i, S_g, O_g—where socialist planning is in effect a substitute for the pricing mechanism, trying to reach essentially the same objectives. Here the externality characteristics inherent in the goods supplied to meet social wants pose precisely the same problem as in the capitalist setting.[9] Whereas production planning regarding the satisfaction of private wants may be tested by profit maximization in a competitive market, such a test cannot be applied to the case of social wants. As was the case for the capitalist system, a political process of decision making, designed to induce voters to reveal their preferences so that the proper supplies of such goods can be provided for, must again be substituted. While the appropriate mechanisms of resource diversion and cost allocation will be seen to differ somewhat in the capitalist and socialist settings, the same basic policy objective is involved. Provided that the socialist system accepts individual consumer preferences as a basis for production planning, the same distinction between private and social wants which was relevant in the capitalist context remains relevant in the liberal socialist setting.

MERIT WANTS

So far, we have assumed that the basket of goods (social or private) is to be supplied in line with the individual preferences of consumers. The distinction between social and private goods was derived not from basic demand features but from the technical characteristic of the goods, i.e. the degree to which externalities are present. Now it must be recognized that goods and services supplied by government frequently do not fit this picture. Western governments, in

9. Lange, "On the Economic Theory," p. 75, n. 24, recognizes this similarity but overlooks the difficulties involved.

fact, make provision for certain goods and services which generate what seem to be strictly internal benefits and which are quite capable of being subjected to the exclusion principle. Thus, low-cost housing is subsidized and the consumer is furnished with free milk rather than given cash subsidies and free choice as to how he spends them. Government, in this case, substitutes collective for individual choice, be it through budgetary provision (fully, or partially through subsidy) of "meritorious" goods (the consumption of which is assigned to particular consumers), or through regulatory devices to deter "undesirable" goods, e.g. prohibition of sale of dangerous drugs or sumptuary taxes. Such wants, which I have referred to elsewhere as "merit" (or "demerit") wants,[10] remain outside the framework of analysis as sketched in the preceding discussion of social wants.

The recognition of merit wants thus appears to involve substitution of imposed for individual choice and a clear departure from the basic principle of consumer choice.[11] While limited in scope in the Western economies, merit wants are nevertheless recognized over a considerable range. The decision to subsidize "good" products (e.g. housing) while penalizing "bad" products (e.g. liquor) is based on the proposition that the decision-making group is capable of superior judgment, be it due to better education, information, or other factors. In this, as in other respects, the modern Western economy is, in fact, a mixed C_i and C_g system, with resource allocation being based in large part, but not entirely, on consumer choice. Social forms are not, after all, designed (at least, outside the evangelist's mind) to reflect

10. See my *Theory of Public Finance*, p. 13.

11. Two alternative explanations may be offered. (1) It may be argued that intelligent choice requires knowledge of alternatives and that the necessary learning process requires temporary compulsion. (2) X may derive satisfaction from the knowledge that Y consumes milk, while he would be indifferent (or hostile) toward his consumption of beer. What appears a subsidy in kind is thus an act on X's part to satisfy his own preferences. See my "Provision for Social Goods."

polar cases of theoretical abstraction. They are designed to permit a working solution and as such may be expected to reflect mixed approaches.

Similarly, resources will be used to satisfy merit wants in the liberal socialist system, even though reliance is based primarily upon the C_i approach. There is no logical reason why option for O_g rather than O_i (public rather than private ownership of the means of production) should carry with it greater reliance on C_g than on C_i; but the cultural tradition (with both C_g and O_g stemming from the same body of thought) makes this a likely situation.

ORTHODOX SOCIALISM

What happens to the distinction between public and private wants if the assumption of consumer sovereignty is dropped and the C_g approach becomes the general rule? If wants are not to be based on individual preferences to begin with, all wants become merit wants. Also, the policy problems created by the existence of externalities which distinguished social from private goods lose much of their relevance. At the same time, this distinction remains of some (if changed) significance from the socialist (with C_g) point of view. Goods which satisfy social wants still provide benefits that are available to all within the group. Only goods which satisfy private wants permit the placing of unequal weights (in whatever pattern of inequality the planner desires) on individual consumption units. Only private goods can be used for purposes of differentiation, be it for incentive, political, or other reasons. Therefore, the distinction remains relevant, if in a somewhat different sense.

THE ROLE OF TAXATION

Remaining still within the allocation context, I now turn to the role of taxation in providing for the satisfaction of public wants. Distribution and stabilization aspects of tax policy are disregarded for the time being.

13

General Function. Here the situation differs sharply, depending on the treatment of the W and O factors. In the capitalist system, with W_i and O_i, more or less the entire income of the economy is assigned to individuals in the form of factor income. Taxes are the means by which a part of their outlay is diverted into the purchase of public goods. In the case of social goods, the cost is to be allocated through a system of benefit taxation, imposed in line with consumer preference. Merit wants are to be financed by taxes imposed so as to avoid undesirable distributional results. The nature of the taxes used and the resulting burden distribution—including the entire problem of tax shifting and incidence—are thus of crucial importance.

Consider now the corresponding problem in a socialist setting of the liberal (i.e. C_i, W_i, S_g, O_g) type. To simplify, let us assume that all capital formation is public and that there is no private saving. Moreover, let us stipulate that all goods provided by government are for capital formation or merit wants. Social wants are excluded for the time being. The basic fiscal principle is then to equate the wage bill paid out with that part of the total product that is to be available for sale to consumers at the market.[12] Since the earnings of other factors (land and capital) accrue to government to begin with, the residual adjustment is in the wage bill only. If the cost of publicly provided goods exceeds the marginal productivity earnings of nonlabor factors, wage disbursements will be less than would be imputed to labor in a competitive factor market. If the public goods share in output falls short of the wage share in factor income, the payment will be larger. These differences in public payments (relative to competitive returns) may be referred to as

12. Complications arise if private saving and capital formation are allowed for. Wage disbursements will now equal the excess of total income (or output) over public capital formation plus merit goods, plus the excess of private saving over private capital formation. The latter will be returned to the public sector through private lending.

negative and positive "social dividends"—underpayment or overpayment—or they might be considered positive and negative "taxes." The latter might be justified on the grounds (embedded, if vaguely so, in the Hobbesonian natural law tradition) that labor has individual property rights to its competitive wage income, while other factor earnings belong to the "group." This, however, seems rather far-fetched and involves an awkward mixture of capitalist and socialist terms. More about this later.

An alternative, though more clumsy, solution would be to pay money wages in line with competitive factor earnings (or for that matter at any arbitrarily set level) and then to recoup the excess via taxation. The net result is the same, but in this case the tax analogy may seem more appropriate. However, since wage payments may be adjusted initially to suit distributional objectives, there is little to choose between the two procedures. Wage payments can be adjusted with tax payments in mind or vice versa. A difference arises only to the extent that wage earners may respond differently to various ways of receiving the same net wage.

The situation is changed, however, with the introduction of social (as distinct from merit) goods. The supply of social goods is subject (at least ideally so) to determination by consumer choice. This means a cost allocation in line with consumer preferences for the satisfaction of such wants. To solicit these preferences, efficient socialism no less than capitalism must resort to budget determination by voting procedure, involving a given expenditure budget and revenue structure. In principle, this requires that the income be assigned to individuals first, and then be reclaimed by appropriate taxes. Whether such taxes are largely withheld or involve actual return flows is a matter of administrative detail; what matters is that the individual should be able to choose budget patterns on the basis of his pretax income. There is thus a sharp difference in principle between tax withholding for social goods and the concept of underpayment (relative to the marginal productivity wage) needed for the finance of public capital formation or of merit-want type goods.

Shifting and Incidence. In the capitalist setting, taxes are to be imposed to distribute the cost of public services (including social and merit goods) by an appropriate pattern, to make distributional adjustments, or to control the level of aggregate demand in a distributionally neutral fashion. In each case, it is important that the effective incidence of the tax burden be on the person designated to bear it. But the impact point of a tax need not be the point at which the final burden is borne. The tax burden may in fact be shifted, i.e. the reduction in real incomes due to imposition of a tax may not be distributed in the same fashion as the reduction in money incomes due to tax payments. Excises initially reduce the gross income of the seller, but the burden may fall on the consumer; the corporation profits tax initially is paid out of profits, but profits may be recouped from wage earners or consumers, and so forth. The makers of tax policy must thus design the tax system so as to beat the response of the market and to arrive at the desired burden distribution. The magnitude of this problem is reduced in the socialist system to the extent that prices are subject to public control rather than determined by the mechanism of the market. Hence, very little is said about the shifting problem in the fiscal literature of socialist countries.

MIXED WANTS

So far, I have dealt with the polar cases of private, social, and merit wants. The reader may feel critical of this approach. Are not elements of externality always present, varying only in degree, and do not many goods involve both private and social aspects of want satisfaction? Ladies' fashions may please (or displease) the onlooker as well as the wearer, education expenditures are beneficial to society as well as to the particular student, and so forth. Moreover, do not considerations of merit want enter as a matter of degree, either positively when "worthy" activities are subsidized, or negatively when sumptuary taxes are imposed? The theory, therefore, needs to be adjusted to consider the whole spectrum of cases.

In dealing with goods that involve a mixture of private and social want components, this adjustment leads us to translate the theory of taxation into a more general theory of subsidy. The budgetary contribution to the provision of various goods and services must then be made in proportion to the ratio of social to total (social plus private) benefits that result. The contribution will range from zero to one hundred per cent as may be required by the particular case.

Suppose that a unit of product X—e.g. educational services—satisfies both private and social wants. In Figure 1–1a we show the private component. Since individual consumers may purchase different amounts, the individual demand schedules of consumers A and B are added *horizontally* to obtain the total or market demand D_{A+B}^p. In Figure 1–1b we show the social-want component. Since both A and B consume one and the same supply, the individual schedules must now be added in vertical fashion to obtain the total demand D_{A+B}^s. The SS schedule in Figure 1–1c shows the supply schedule for X. Adding D_{A+B}^p and D_{A+B}^s vertically, we obtain D_{A+B}^{p+s}, the combined private and social demands.[13] The proper output equals OE. Of the unit cost ER, EF is paid for privately by the consumers while a subsidy equal to FR is contributed through the public budget and pays for the social good component. As shown in Figure 1–1a, A purchases OH and B purchases OL at the market

13. Alternatively, D_{A+B}^s may be deducted from SS so as to obtain a new supply schedule SS′, and output be determined by its intersection with D_{A+B}^p. The subsidy then equals the vertical distance between SS and SS′.

17

FIGURE 1–1

Mixed Goods

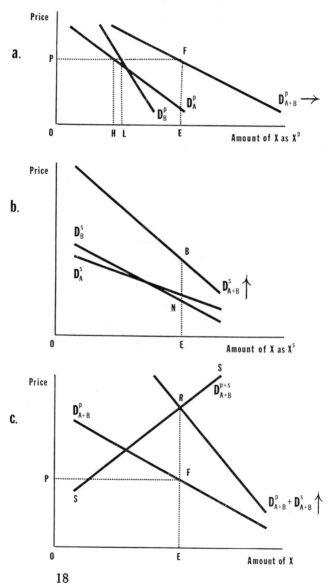

price $OP = EF$. As shown in Figure 1–1b, B's tax contribution equals EN and A's tax contribution equals NB, with EB in Figure 1–1b equal to FR in Figure 1–1c. In the limiting case of a wholly private good FR in Figure 1–1c equals zero, while in that of a wholly social good EF equals zero. Our theoretical framework, therefore, is in no way limited to the polar cases but explains the entire range of intermediate situations.[14]

A similar approach may be taken with regard to goods that involve elements of merit wants. Indeed, various goods may be rated in both dimensions, including "private" versus "social," and "individual" versus "merit" want qualities. Each case may thus be thought of as falling somewhat in a box such as shown in Figure 1–2.

In a capitalist system, one would expect most resources to be used for the satisfaction of wants located in the upper quadrants, whereas in the communist system the lower quadrants would be more important. This was brought out vividly in Khrushchev's vision of an ample supply of free goods as the economy advances toward true communism. Though exclusion can be applied and externalities do not apply, they are to be made available on a merit-good basis.[15] At the same time, our taxonomy offers no simple presumption regarding the importance of the left and right quadrants. Whereas recognition of consumer sovereignty is an ideological matter, externality is a technical issue. Whether at any given time consumer preferences emphasize goods

14. See my "Provision for Social Goods." In the case of social costs, a similar analysis calls for taxes instead of subsidies.

15. See *Program of the Communist Party of the Soviet Union*, ed. H. Ritvo (New York, The New Leader, 1962), p. 155, where it is said that "at the same time as the country advances towards communism, personal needs will be met increasingly out of public consumption funds, whose rate of growth will exceed the rate of growth of payments for labor." And again on p. 163: "At the end of the twenty years, public consumption funds will total about half of the aggregate real income of the population." Rent-free housing was to be included.

with externality characteristics depends on tastes, incomes, and available choices, rather than views of the social system. A capitalist may like to travel (hence needs roads) while a socialist may like to stay home (hence needs a private yard).

FIGURE 1–2

Spectrum of Wants

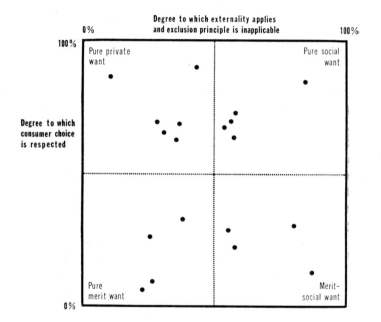

With efficient operation of both systems, there is no a priori reason why the relative importance of social goods should be more or less in one or the other setting.

INCENTIVE CONSTRAINTS

Such a relation may arise, however, through the back door of incentive constraints.

Consider a classical capitalist system (with C_i, W_i, S_i, O_i)

where all decisions are left to private choice. There would be no recognition of merit wants in this system. Ideally, consumers would provide fiscal authorities with a fair statement of their evaluation of social goods and would be assessed accordingly. There would be no special incentive issue. The payment for social goods would be a "price-payment," similar to that for private goods. But, as noted before, preferences are not thus revealed. Nor should exclusion be applied even if it were possible. A political process (usually some form of majority vote) must be interposed and mandatory taxes be assessed. These taxes in turn are usually based on a general index of economic status such as income or consumption. As a result, relative prices and tradeoffs (between leisure and goods, alternative goods, saving and consumption, hoarding and investment, etc.) are changed and the allocation process is affected.

Suppose now that the share of social goods is increased and financed by raising the income tax. This means that the net wage rate is reduced. Looking at the tax side of the picture only, it is not possible to predict whether work effort will be increased or reduced. An increase in income tax rates has both an income effect which increases labor supply and a substitution effect which reduces it. The net effect on work effort may go either way. But let us also consider the effect of increased public services. Increasing the level of public services has an income effect that is detrimental to work effort.[16] At the same time, it is without substitution effect since the supply of public services available to any one worker is not affected significantly by his work effort and tax contribution. Public goods, to him, are not an opportunity cost of leisure. The negative income

16. This assumes that public goods are substitutes for private goods in the general equilibrium of consumers' welfare. If the public goods in question are complementary to private goods (acquisition of which requires income and hence surrender of leisure), the result may not hold.

effect from the expenditure side thus counteracts the favorable effect on the tax side, and the negative substitution effect on the tax side may well carry the day.[17] Thus the scope for public provision of goods is subject to incentive constraints in a W_i system. This difficulty would not arise if labor were subject to conscription (W_g) or to other nonpecuniary pressures.

Similar considerations apply to the choice between present and future consumption and with regard to investment incentives. The former does not pose too serious a problem, as it may be adjusted for in an S_g system by substitution of public savings. This need not involve O_g, as public savings can be made available to private investment via public lending. The matter of investment incentives is not as easily met in an O_i type of system, where investment is to be private. Here a situation similar to work effort arises. These considerations, to be sure, are of relatively minor importance, as long as the share of public goods is modest and hence tax rates are low; and even at higher rate levels, much will depend on how the tax burden is distributed,[18] and on what rate levels are considered acceptable. For these reasons, there exists no rigid upper limit of "taxable capacity," or even a range that applies equally at all times and places.[19]

17. To put it differently, the resulting drop in labor supply imposes an "excess burden," as it interferes with an efficient choice between income and leisure. The excess burden arises because the work-leisure choice is interfered with, not especially because work effort is reduced. There would be an excess burden also if work effort were increased.

18. It is safe to state that the pattern of progression or regression will matter, since the substitution effect depends on marginal tax rates. But the direction of the effect is not obvious. Progressive (as against proportional) taxation involves not only higher marginal rates for the rich, but also lower marginal rates for the poor, and the net effect on work effort depends on the two reactions.

19. Colin Clark's famous 25 per cent limit for noninflationary finance is a political rather than an economic phenomenon. Colin Clark, "Public Finance and Changes in the Value of Money," *Economic Journal, 55* (December 1947), 371.

Nevertheless, we have here an interesting analytical distinction between the various systems. If consumers wish to devote a rising share of their resources to social wants, this may involve an opportunity cost in efficient factor-supply and in the functioning of the factor market as an allocative device. The critical point at which such a dilemma may arise is reached earliest in the setting of W_i, I_i, O_i, followed at some distance by W_i, I_g, O_g and last by W_g, I_g, O_g. This reasoning, however, assumes "efficient" behavior. Beyond this, some ideological biases may be expected to sneak in.

In the capitalist setting, an expansion of externality-intensive goods to greater prominence (even though required by changes in tastes, incomes, or technology) may be considered unfortunate in that it widens the range of economic activity that the market cannot handle on its own. In the socialist setting, the same development may be applauded for the inverse reason. On these grounds, the former system may be expected to be biased against externality-intensive goods and in favor of private goods; and the opposite may be expected to hold (apart from the stick-and-carrot aspect of private goods) in the socialist economy.

A high ratio of externality-intensive goods, moreover, involves a high level of tax rates. This makes it politically easier, especially in the capitalist setting, to carry out distributional adjustment. Those who favor redistribution may, therefore, also favor increased provision for social goods, and those who lean in the other direction will take the opposite view. Depending upon the balance of political forces, this intrusion of distributional considerations will tend to raise or lower the social goods share.[20]

20. See p. 86.

Adjustments in Distribution

A second function the fiscal mechanism may perform is that of adjustment in the distribution of income.[21] The significance of this function depends on how the distribution of income and wealth is determined in the first place.

In the capitalist system with W_i and O_i, an individual's income position is determined by his factor endowments, including capital and services, and the price these endowments will fetch in the market. The capital endowment in turn depends on initial endowment by inheritance as well as on subsequent accumulation. The distribution of income thus determined is then subjected to certain adjustments, whether to reduce inequality in the size distribution of income, or to improve the relative position of particular groups, e.g. the indigent, the young, or the aged. The extent to which such adjustments are desirable is a matter of continuous political debate, and appropriately so.

The technique by which a given adjustment is best secured, however, is a matter on which the economist can speak. The adjustment is made more efficiently, i.e. with a lesser burden to the economy, through a direct tax-transfer mechanism, rather than through an interference with product and/or factor prices, and with the initial distribution of income that results therefrom. Thus the fiscal operation assumes an important second function.

From an analytical point of view, the tax-expenditure budget (of the allocation branch) needed to provide for satisfaction of social wants is supplemented by a tax-trans-

21. We cannot here enter into the question whether and to what extent the allocation and distribution functions of the public sector can be separated. It remains my position that such separation is possible if carefully formulated, and is indeed essential to an operationally meaningful theory of public finance. See my "Provision for Social Goods," and n. 5 above.

fer budget (of the distribution branch) needed to provide for adjustments in distribution. The tax structure under the former should be proportional, regressive, or progressive, depending on whether (assuming preferences to be known) the income elasticity of demand for social goods equals, exceeds, or falls short of its price elasticity.[22] The tax-transfer structure under the latter will be progressive, provided the intent is to reduce income inequality. We may then think of the budget as being combined into a consolidated form where transfer payments are canceled against the two sets of taxes and only net payments are made.[23] Such net payments will be distributed by whatever pattern emerges from the nature and weight of each of the sub-budgets.

In the orthodox socialist system with O_g and W_g, the situation is very different. Inheritance is absent or quite limited, and capital is owned by government. The distribution of private income, therefore, depends on labor income. While labor (and, for that matter, capital) as a factor of production must be assigned a "competitive" shadow price for allocation purposes, this shadow wage rate need not determine the payments made to the worker. The fraction of the income that is available for distribution to individuals (i.e. after deducting the cost of capital formation and of merit goods) may be distributed among workers or households in line with what is considered proper distribution. The tax-expenditure process of the budget, therefore, is not concerned with distributional considerations; and the tax structure, needed to finance social goods, should (assuming C_i) correspond to the consumer's evaluation of benefits received.

This, however, is a very extreme view, since incentive considerations of a pecuniary kind will arise in any practicable system. In the liberal socialist system with O_g and W_i, the

22. See J. M. Buchanan, "Fiscal Institutions and Efficiency in Collective Outlay," *American Economic Review, Papers and Proceedings, 54* (1964), 230–49.
23. See my *Theory of Public Finance*, Chap. 2.

distribution of private income remains essentially a matter of wage income. Wage determination, however, comes to have an allocative function, and wages paid must be adjusted so as to attract labor to its proper uses. This does not mean that full marginal productivity wages must be paid, but that actual wage payments must involve such differentials as are needed to draw various types of labor into their proper employment. The resulting distributional pattern may not be the desired one, and thus introduces the need for redistributional measures.

But even if this is allowed for, a substantial difference between the capitalist system with O_i and the liberal socialist system with O_g remains. The distribution of wealth and of property income in capitalist countries is typically more unequal than that of labor income. Assuming the distribution of labor income to be similar to that of the socialist system—and stipulating equal distributional objectives—the function of the distribution branch tends to be of greater importance in the capitalist setting. At the same time, we must recall our earlier observation that the capitalist system with O_i and W_i must be concerned with effects upon investment as well as work incentives, whereas liberal socialism with O_g and W_i need be concerned with work incentives only. Accordingly, capitalism is left with both a greater need for and more limited degrees of freedom to undertake distributional adjustments.

STABILIZATION AND GROWTH

We now turn to the third aspect of the fiscal process, namely, its bearing on the level of employment, the stability of prices, and economic growth. Again we find that this function assumes different forms under the various patterns of economic organization.

26

CAPITALIST CASE

Much depends on the nature of national income determination, and various views of the capitalist case (involving C_i, W_i, and O_i) must now be distinguished.

Classical System. We begin with a so-called classical system, where adjustments in the rate of interest equate the level of investment with that of planned saving out of a full-employment income. In such a system, full resource utilization is automatically assured. The level of public outlays does not affect aggregate demand, whether expenditures are financed from taxes or from loanable funds. The essential requirement for the maintenance of price-level stability is a monetary policy that provides for an increase in the money supply in step with the rising demand for real balances. There is no need for fiscal policy as a stabilization device.[24]

Nor, some would argue, is there a need for growth policy. In the classical context, it might well be held that the growth rate (as determined by the allocation of resources between present and future consumption) should be left to the market, where the time preference of individual savers will be equated to the marginal efficiency of investment. That is to say, a pure case of capitalism, with C_i, W_i, O_i, and S_i, may apply. At the same time, this is not a situation that excludes public investment. Social goods characteristics may apply to capital as well as consumer goods, and externality-intensive capital goods are to be provided for in the budget. Such goods should then be loan financed, thereby diverting private saving into public investment. Social goods of the consumer goods type being tax financed, the government's budget on current account is balanced, and there occurs no public "saving" in the classical sense of tax receipts exceeding current outlays.

24. See also p. 207.

Alternatively it might be argued that even in the classical system the overall savings rate should not be left to private decision. Since government takes a longer view, the social rate of discount may fall short of the private, so that a higher rate of saving is called for. The savings rate, in other words, assumes a social goods quality.[25] Private saving must then be supplemented by public saving. An excess of tax receipts over outlays on social goods of the consumption type may be used to create a surplus in current account or public saving in the classical sense.[26] The public saving may be used in turn to finance public capital formation, or it may be made available to the market via lending to finance private capital formation. The classical case, therefore, may leave fiscal policy a factor in economic growth, while eliminating its stabilization.

Neoclassical System. The situation differs if a more realistic view is taken, in which the system does not automatically generate the proper level of demand, which secures full employment and price stability. Total expenditures may now exceed the output that can be supplied at prevailing prices, or they may fall short of full-employment output. Thus inflation or unemployment may result. This may take the form of cyclical instability or may pose difficulties of a more secular sort. Fiscal policy along with monetary policy now face the task of securing and maintaining the proper level of aggregate demand. A high level of public purchases, even if tax financed, is now expansionary, as follows from the balanced-budget multiplier. Substitution of loan for tax finance now becomes expansionary, just as sur-

25. For a discussion and summary of the literature on this point, see Otto Eckstein, "A Survey of the Theory of Public Expenditure Criteria," *Public Finances: Needs, Sources and Utilization,* National Bureau of Economic Research (Princeton, Princeton University Press, 1961).

26. See also p. 229.

plus finance becomes restrictive. Thus the rules of the game are quite different from those of the classical case.

The stabilization function now becomes a key aspect of budget policy. If properly understood, and not disturbed by the interference of "fiscal politics," it may be pursued without conflict with the other (allocation and distribution) objectives of budget policy. Expansionary action may be accomplished through transfer payments or, in the net budget, through tax reductions which are distributionally neutral; just as restrictive action may be accomplished through distributionally neutral tax increases or, in the net budget, through reduced transfer payments.

While the stabilization function is added, growth policy continues in the picture. Allowance must now be made for two effects of budgetary action. On one side, budget policy may affect the economy's capacity to produce, whether through effects on the rate of technical advancement and/or through effects on the rate of growth of capital stock. On the other side, budget policy affects the level of expenditures or of effective demand that is forthcoming. Keeping both objectives in mind, the task is now one of balancing the increments in capacity and expenditure growth. This in turn requires an appropriate mix of fiscal and monetary policies. A policy mix involving restrictive budgetary and easy monetary policies is helpful to growth, provided that monetary ease is in fact capable of securing the desired level of investment; and the reverse should be helpful in securing a high-level consumption economy. As will be noted later, further restraints with regard to the policy mix arise if balance of payment considerations are added to the picture.

In this second and more realistic view of fiscal policy in the capitalist system, the rate of growth becomes inevitably a concern of public policy. The mix of stabilization policies (fiscal and monetary) must be adjusted so as to secure balanced growth, i.e. a situation where the rate of growth of potential output is matched by the rate of growth of actual

29

expenditures. Since this balance may be reached at more than one growth rate, the proper growth path must be chosen. The realistic view of the modern capitalist system, therefore, involves S_g rather than S_i.

SOCIALIST CASE

Consider now the role of fiscal policy in a socialist system. By virtue of O_g, the decision to invest is made by government rather than individual investors. Because of this, the delicate problem of stabilization—aimed at forestalling imbalance of planned saving and investment in the capitalist system—does not arise. Socialist planning must merely see to it that the level of expenditure grows with potential output, which is a simple task. The socialist trauma, corresponding to aggregate demand instability in the capitalist system, is that of imbalance between industrial sectors. This type of instability, as we shall see, is not without its fiscal implications, but it does not pose a problem of stabilization similar to that of the capitalist system.

While the investment decision is made by public policy, this policy may be either of the S_i or S_g type. In the former case, saving originates in the private sector and is then loaned to government to finance public capital formation. In the latter, saving may all be done in the public sector, or it may be mixed. Private saving may be supplemented by public saving, either by way of increased taxation or of initial withholding of wage disbursements; or it may be curtailed by public dissaving, implemented through loan finance of government outlays on consumption.

The role of fiscal policy under the various systems, as derived from the preceding discussion, may be seen in the following bird's eye view.[27]

27. As may be noted once more, the distinction between "systems" as here drawn is designed to serve our purpose and does not claim general validity. Moreover, some readers may wish to substitute their

The Issues

Fiscal Functions and Economic Structure

Policy Functions	Capitalist	
	Classical	Neoclassical
	C_i, W_i, S_i, O_i	C_i, W_i, S_g, O_i
Provision for social wants	Needed	Needed
Provision for merit wants	None	Needed
Distributional adjustments	Not needed	Needed
Stabilization	Not needed	Needed
Optimal growth	Not needed	Needed

	Socialist	
	Liberal	Orthodox
	C_i, W_i, S_g, O_g	C_g, W_g, S_g, O_g
Provision for social wants	Needed	None
Provision for merit wants	Needed	All-inclusive
Distributional adjustments	Needed	Not needed
Stabilization	Not needed	Not needed
Optimal growth	Needed	Needed

We note the increasing complexity of the fiscal problem
as we move from the polar cases of classical capitalism or
communism to the more realistic structures of modified
systems, either on the capitalist or the socialist side. The
peak of the fiscal function is reached in the neoclassical
model, where the scope and complexity of the public sector
assumes its most challenging form. Not only are social goods
and merit wants provided for; fiscal policy also serves to implement distributional adjustment, and last but not least
plays a crucial role in determining the level of employment,
prices, and the rate of economic growth. Fiscal policy, it
appears, is an eminently capitalist art, or, hopefully, science.

---

own terminology, e.g. refer to a neoclassical system with a high degree
of redistribution as "liberal-socialist." This would reflect the position
of continental European socialist parties as illustrated by the Godesberg
Program of the Social Democratic Party in Germany. Disenchanted with
O_g, and desirous of appealing to middle-class voters, European socialism
has thus reclassified itself as C_i, W_i, S_g, O_i, plus redistribution. Similarly, the moderate left in the United States does not want this combination classified as socialist.

31

Even though the socialist expenditure budget is larger, due to the inclusion of most capital formation and opposite bias in the private-public goods choice, the fiscal problem (if we exclude the allocation of investment expenditures from this category) is a good deal simpler. At the same time, certain fiscal or, rather, quasi-fiscal operations constitute an important link in the socialist planning process, thus introducing considerations into its fiscal policy not to be found in the capitalist setting. This link is the use of taxes as a means of guiding the conduct of the socialist firm, and as a device to clear markets (assuming liberal socialism with C_i) where production plans did not properly anticipate consumer choice. The tax system thus becomes a control device, in the broader structure of economic planning, as painfully illustrated by the vast number of excise rates in the Soviet system. This aspect of tax policy may or may not be considered a fiscal function, but it constitutes a major difference in the two settings.

2 THE INSTITUTIONS

The preceding analysis suggests various hypotheses for the fiscal structures of planned and capitalist economies, which may now be tested against existing institutions.

1. Regarding the size of the public sector:

a. the fraction of resources allocated to the satisfaction of social wants should be largely independent of political systems;

b. the fraction of resources devoted to the satisfaction of merit wants might be larger in the socialist setting;

c. inclusion of most capital formation in the public sector suggests that the ratio of public purchases to GNP should be substantially higher in the socialist setting;

d. greater need for redistribution-oriented budget policies should make for a larger ratio of transfer payments to personal income in the capitalist setting.

2. Regarding the nature of the tax structure:

a. progressive income and other personal taxes should play a larger role in the capitalist tax structure;

b. profits from public enterprise should be more important in the socialist case;

c. differential product taxes as instruments of price

33

policy should play a greater role in the socialist setting.

In addition to these differences in expenditure and tax structures, the relation of budget to overall economic policy should differ greatly between the two systems.

LEVEL AND STRUCTURE OF PUBLIC SERVICES

A comparison of the size of the public sector between essentially capitalist economies has its difficulties, but fairly meaningful common denominators can be found.[1] These may include (1) income originating in government, (2) government purchases of goods and services, or (3) total government expenditures, including purchases and transfers, all expressed as a fraction of GNP or some other global measure of economic activity. Public enterprise, for this purpose, is considered part of the private sector, with only enterprise surplus or deficit appearing on the revenue side of the budget ledger. Comparison (1), as noted at the outset, is not our primary concern, but both (2) and (3) are of interest: (2) shows the extent to which resources are allocated to the satisfaction of social and merit wants, while (3) indicates the total extent of budgetary involvement in the income stream.

Comparison becomes more difficult if extended to planned economies. Government purchases of goods and services now cease to be an indicator of the extent to which the composition of output is directed toward public wants, since most production (be it for public or for private wants) is handled in this fashion. Moreover, government sales are not a reliable measure of private goods. The mere fact that consumer goods are sold at the market (free consumer choice) need not imply that the basket of goods which is offered for sale meets the basic pattern of consumer preference (consumer

1. See p. 169.

sovereignty).[2] Transfers, similarly, do not measure the extent of distributional adjustment, since factor payments are determined publicly to begin with. More generally, there is the danger that particular expenditure and revenue items, though they may appear under the same name in the budgets of capitalist and socialist countries, do in fact reflect different functions. For these reasons, overall comparisons must be followed up by reconsideration on a disaggregated basis.

In Table 2–1 we compare the structure of purchases in various typical economies. All are developed countries, so as to focus on differences in economic organization, rather than stages of development.[3] All levels of government are included, and the question of fiscal centralization versus decentralization is again left aside for the time being.[4]

As shown in lines 1 and 2, the division of total output (excluding defense) between consumption and capital formation does not differ greatly between the U.S.S.R. and non (or less) socialist countries. Nor would we expect that this should be the case, this division of the product being a matter of growth policy rather than economic organization. If capital formation is somewhat higher in the socialist setting, this may reflect the lower level of social as against private time preference.[5] As shown in lines 3 and 4, the per cent of public purchases is substantially higher in the U.S.S.R. than

2. For this difference see F. D. Holzman, *Soviet Taxation* (Cambridge, Mass., Harvard University Press, 1955), and H. Timm, "Steuern im Sozialismus," *Beiträge zur Finanzwissenschaft.*

3. This leaves open the question whether structural differences between capitalist and socialist countries at low levels of income would be the same as for the group here considered. An integration of the subject matters of our Parts I and II would be of interest.

4. See p. 341.

5. The 1960 ratio of net fixed capital formation (including increases in stock) as per cent of GNP was 27.7 for Bulgaria, 25.7 for Hungary, and 26.8 for Poland. Source: United Nations, *Yearbook of National Account Statistics, 1961* (New York, United Nations, 1962).

TABLE 2-1

Composition of Purchases*

	U.S.S.R. 1962	United States 1962	United Kingdom 1962	Federal Republic of Germany 1961	Sweden 1961
GNP excluding defense and net exports					
1. Per cent for consumption	68.5	79.5	81.7	72.1	65.9
2. Per cent for capital formation	31.5	20.5	18.3	27.9	34.1
Total	100.0	100.0	100.0	100.0	100.0
GNP excluding defense and net exports					
3. Per cent purchased privately	60.7	76.5	81.4	85.3	76.6
4. Per cent purchased publicly	39.3	23.5	18.6	14.7	23.4
Total	100.0	100.0	100.0	100.0	100.0
Investment, excluding defense					
5. Per cent purchased privately	4.3	76.8	58.2	88.4	62.7
6. Per cent purchased publicly	95.7	23.2	41.8	11.6	37.3
Total	100.0	100.0	100.0	100.0	100.0
Consumption, excluding defense					
7. Per cent purchased privately	86.6	89.3	86.6	84.2	83.1
8. Per cent purchased publicly	13.4	10.7	13.4	15.8	16.9
Total	100.0	100.0	100.0	100.0	100.0
GNP, including defense					
9. Per cent of purchases for defense	6.8	8.9	6.9	3.5	1.8
10. Per cent of purchases for other	93.2	91.1	93.1	96.5	98.2
Total	100.0	100.0	100.0	100.0	100.0

* Source: Appendix Table 1.

in the other countries. As against 39 per cent in the former, it ranges from 15 to 23 per cent in the latter. This reflects primarily the different treatment of investment. As shown in lines 5 and 6, the U.S.S.R. has 96 per cent of investment in the public category. While the ratio for the other countries varies considerably, it generally is half of this or less. The composition of consumption expenditures (lines 7 and 8), on the other hand, shows little difference. Private expenditures amount to over 80 per cent in all cases. With the exception of housing, the U.S.S.R. not only relies on the distribution of private consumer goods through direct purchases, but the division of consumer goods into those distributed through purchases and those provided for through the budget is quite similar to that of the Western countries. Moreover, there is a high degree of similarity in this respect among the U.S.S.R. and other socialist countries.[6]

This similarity is of interest but, as noted before, it does not prove that the basket of available consumer goods is adjusted wholly to the preferences of individual consumers. Rather, it means that such consumer goods as are available are distributed through the market and not in kind. In other words, the Soviet economy does not provide for the "free" supply of "private" consumer goods, i.e. of consumer goods that are rival and can be subjected to exclusion on a substantial scale. While this was the basis of commodity distribution that had been envisaged in the early stages of moneyless communism, it failed to materialize in the realities of Soviet development. Whether the mix of consumer goods sold at the market is selected with individual preferences in mind or weighted by "merit good" considerations is a different matter, and not revealed by these data. However,

6. Data on the composition of consumption for 1960 show private consumption at 90 per cent for Bulgaria, 89 per cent for Hungary and Poland, and 80 per cent for Yugoslavia, the remainder being shown under collective consumption defined as material consumption by nonproductive institutions. Source· ibid.

TABLE 2–2

Purchases as Per Cent of GNP*

	U.S.S.R. 1962	United States 1962	United Kingdom 1962	Federal Republic of Germany 1961	Sweden 1961
Private Purchases					
Consumption					
1. Retail sales to households	42.7	37.9	50.7	n.a.	n.a.
2. Housing	0.8	8.3	6.8	n.a.	n.a.
3. Other services	5.4	17.6	12.8	n.a.	n.a.
4. Food consumed on farm	6.3	0.2	n.a.	n.a.	n.a.
5. Subtotal	55.2	64.0	70.3	57.0	53.7
6. Investment	1.3	14.2	10.6	23.3	21.0
7. Total, private (5 + 6)	56.5	78.2	80.9	80.3	74.7
Public Purchases					
Consumption					
8. Health	2.8	1.3	3.5	2.7	2.6
9. Education	4.4	3.0	3.6	1.9	3.4
10. Internal security	0.8	0.7	0.7 }	6.0	4.8
11. Other, excluding defense	0.6	2.7	3.8		
12. Subtotal	8.5	7.7	11.6	10.6	10.8
13. Defense	2.4	0.5	0.2	n.a.	n.a.
14. Subtotal	11.0	8.2	11.8	10.6	10.8
15. Investment, including defense	32.5	12.7	13.0	7.0	14.5
16. Total, Public (14 + 15)	43.5	20.9	24.8	17.6	25.3
Foreign Sector					
17. Net exports	—	0.7	−6.6	2.1	—
All Purchases					
18. Total (7 + 16 + 17)	100.0	100.0	100.0	100.0	100.0

* Source: Appendix Table 1.

the relatively uniform share of public consumption suggests that resources allocated to consumption of the social goods type absorb about the same share in the U.S.S.R. as in the other countries.

In Table 2–2, various expenditure shares in relation to GNP are given. While the share of private consumption purchases (line 5) in the U.S.S.R. is on the low side of the range, it falls well within the pattern of the other countries. Such difference as remains arises largely from the low private housing share in the U.S.S.R. The private investment share in GNP (line 6) is drastically lower in the U.S.S.R., which also explains its lower share of total private purchases (line 7). The U.S.S.R. share of public consumption (line 14) is rather similar to that of the other countries, but its share of total public purchases (due, again, to the role of investment) is substantially higher (line 16).

Turning to the breakdown of public consumption purchases, we note that health and education absorb a larger share in the U.S.S.R. than in most of the other countries, while that of "other community services" is relatively low. Such comparisons must be interpreted with caution, however, since the ratios do not reflect total (public and private) outlays on these functions. While the ratio to GNP of public expenditures for health and education is higher in the U.S.S.R., countries such as the United States have a higher ratio of private purchases of such services. Indeed, if private and public outlays are combined, it appears that the health and education shares in GNP are somewhat larger for the United States. Thus, differences in the ratio of public expenditures on particular services to GNP tend to reflect differences in the way in which provision for such services is divided between the private and public sectors, rather than in the share of total resources allocated to this use.[7]

7. This important factor is emphasized by Frederick L. Pryor in *Governmental Expenditures in the Soviet Union and the United States,*

A broader comparison of public expenditure structures, including transfers, is given in Table 2–3. The higher ratio for total public expenditures in the socialist economies again results from the different treatment of investment. Not only do such outlays comprise a much larger fraction of total public expenditures in their budgets (line 7), but they again account for the much higher overall ratio of public expenditures to GNP (line 16). Social security outlays, as expected, comprise a higher share in the Western budgets (line 3). This is the case especially for Germany, where the higher level of transfer payments also gives rise to a higher overall ratio of public expenditures to GNP (line 16).

In all, the results of these comparisons are fairly well in line with our expectations. The larger size of the public sector in the socialist economies reflects the fact that investment is largely public, or O_g as against O_i in terms of our earlier model. There is no clear evidence that a larger share of resources is allocated to social wants in the socialist case. The similar shares of consumer goods sold to the individual consumer does not prove that merit goods play an equal role, as the "merit factor" may be reflected in the mix of available consumer goods sold at the market. The transfer sector, as expected, ranks larger in the capitalist economies, where the initial control over income distribution through wage policy is more limited.

TAX STRUCTURE

Turning now to differences in revenue structures, a much stronger contrast prevails. Not only does the composition of tax structures vary greatly between capitalist and socialist economies, but taxes that are listed under similar terms do in fact carry different meanings. This precludes

forthcoming; and in "East and West German Governmental Expenditures," *Public Finance/Finances Publiques*, 20 (1965).

TABLE 2–3

Public Expenditures in Socialist and Western Economies*
(includes all levels of government; purchases and transfers)

	U.S.S.R. 1962	Czechoslovakia 1960	Poland 1960	United States 1961	Federal Republic of Germany 1961	United Kingdom 1961	Sweden 1961
I. As Per Cent of Budget							
Current expenditures							
1. Education	8.7 ⎫	39.0	9.7	12.4	4.9	13.0	10.6
2. Public health	5.7 ⎭		7.1	4.5	9.9	9.8	3.4
3. Social security	11.6	8.5	11.7	16.4	31.1	18.5	23.5
4. Defense	12.5	2.9	7.4	16.5	8.9	19.6	17.9
5. Other (including interest)	8.9		7.6	30.5	37.0	29.3	28.5
6. Total, current	47.4	50.4	43.5	80.3	91.8	90.2	83.9
Capital expenditures							
7. Total, capital	52.6	49.6	56.5	19.7	8.2	9.8	16.1
8. Total expenditures (6 + 7)	100.0	100.0	100.0	100.0	100.0	100.0	100.0
II. As Per Cent of GNP							
Current expenditures							
9. Education	4.5	n.a.†	4.8	3.7	1.9	4.5	2.5
10. Public health	2.8	n.a.	3.5	1.3	3.9	3.4	.8
11. Social security	5.7	n.a.	5.7	5.0	12.2	6.4	5.6
12. Defense	6.2	n.a.	3.6	5.0	3.5	6.7	4.3
13. Other (including interest)	4.3	n.a.	3.7	9.2	14.5	10.1	6.8
14. Total, current	23.5	n.a.	21.3	24.2	36.0	31.1	20.0
Capital expenditures							
15. Total, capital	26.1	n.a.	27.5	6.0	3.2	3.4	3.9
16. Total expenditures (14 + 15)	49.6	n.a.	48.8	30.2	39.2	34.5	23.9

* Source: Appendix Table 2. Transfer payments and trust funds are included.
† Not available.

simple cross-classification, one pattern being applicable to the socialist economies and another to the Western countries. Variations within each group are slight as compared to the sharp difference between the two groups.

Such at least has been the case until recently, when decentralization of decision making has called for drastic tax reform. Leaving these changes for later consideration, I begin with the traditional system. Here (Table 2–4) receipts are divided between those derived from the national economy, and those derived from the population. The former provide much the larger part of the total. The most important component is the so-called turnover tax. Akin, in Western terminology, to a set of excise taxes, the turnover tax is imposed mostly in a single stage form and at varying rates upon a large variety of products. Next in importance is the state's share in public enterprises, supplemented by an income tax on collective farms and other revenue sources, including social insurance contributions. Taxes on the population contribute only a small fraction of total receipts. They consist largely of individual income taxes, imposed at varying rates upon different occupational groups. In capitalist economies (Table 2–5), net profits from public enterprise are a minor and frequently even negative item. All taxes are understood to be "from the population," and turnover (or turnover type) taxes are a much smaller factor in the total tax structure. Much greater importance is assigned to the individual income tax and to other direct taxes, such as the corporation profits tax. Increasingly this is found to be the case as a country reaches high levels of per capita income.

All this is quite in line with expectations. In the capitalist setting, the tax concept is basic to the operation of the public sector. The claim to income lies with the individual recipient, and taxes are the means by which part thereof is assigned to the purchase of public goods, or by which adjustments in the distribution of income are carried out. The nature of the taxes used and the resulting burden distribu-

TABLE 2–4

Structure of Budget Receipts in Socialist Economies*
(all levels of government)

	Bulgaria 1963	Czechoslovakia 1964	Poland 1964	U.S.S.R. 1964
As Per Cent of Total				
I. Receipts from National Economy				
1. Sales and turnover tax	48.9	38.6	47.1	38.3
2. Share in profits of state enterprise	16.9	20.2	23.8	32.1
3. Other	10.0	28.1	10.6	22.3
4. Subtotal (1–3)	75.8	86.9	81.5	92.7
II. Other				
5. Taxes on population	6.1	10.0	6.2	7.3
6. Other receipts	18.1	3.1	12.3	†
7. Total (4–6)	100.0	100.0	100.0	100.0
As Per Cent of GNP				
8. 1 + 2 + 5	45.0	52.9	42.2	39.3
9. 7	62.6	76.9	54.8	50.6

* Based on Appendix Table 3.
† Included in item 3.

43

TABLE 2-5

Tax Structures in Capitalist Economies, 1961[a]

(all levels of government)

	United States	Canada	France	Federal Republic of Germany	Italy	Japan	Nether-lands	Sweden	United Kingdom
1. Individual income	32.2	19.5	15.8[b]	20.6[b]	12.7	20.3	28.3[b]	52.8	35.5
2. Corporate income	16.3	16.1	6.0	14.4[c]	2.1	26.8	10.4	—	4.0
3. Death and gift, net wealth	1.8	1.5	0.7	1.5	2.1	.5	2.4	0.5	3.2
4. Property	13.2	14.2	1.0	1.6	2.0[d]	5.7	2.4[d]	—	9.5
5. Excises, sales, customs	21.4	38.2	44.8	32.7	46.6	33.1	29.3	33.8	34.6
6. Social security contributions of employees	6.6	4.9	6.9	13.5	6.3	6.4	16.1	7.4	7.3
7. Social security contributions of private employers	7.5	4.1	19.3	13.8	25.5	6.0	10.9	4.9	5.9
8. Other	1.0	1.5	5.5	1.9	2.7	1.2	.2	.6	—
9. Total tax receipts	100.0	100.0	100.0	100.0	100.0	100.0	100.0	100.0	100.0
10. Public enterprise profits as per cent of profits plus tax receipts	2.3	n.a.	n.a.	4.8	n.a.	n.a.	n.a.	8.7	1.2

a. Lines 1–9 are based on *Excise Tax Compendium*, U.S. Congress, House Committee on Ways and Means, 88th Congress, Part I (Washington, D.C., G.P.O., June 15, 1964). Line 10 added by author.

b. Includes tax on investment income.

c. Includes municipal trade tax.

d. Includes tax on land and buildings.

44

tion are thus of crucial importance. In the socialist setting, the situation differs. As shown in the preceding chapter, taxes meet a different and more limited function. Private demand may now be controlled through the level of wage payments as distinct from the accounting price of labor, and the need for distributional adjustments is more limited. No wonder, therefore, that the revenue structures should be different.

It is more surprising, perhaps, that the level of taxation (relative to GNP) in the socialist countries (Table 2–4, line 8) should be considerably higher than in the capitalist. There are a variety of reasons for this. The ratio of total budget expenditures to GNP is substantially higher in the socialist economy, due to the inclusion of most capital formation. Also, the socialist economies do not conform to our "pure" model, where the excess of output over consumer purchases is withheld at the outset, rather than being recouped (mainly from enterprises) in the form of taxation.[8] Moreover, most of the socialist economies contain substantial sectors that are essentially private, especially agriculture, and capitalist (work and profit) incentives remain a factor. Finally, taxes (or taxlike instruments) assume a planning function which they do not perform in the capitalist system.

SOCIALIST TAXATION

The pattern of socialist taxation is discussed here first in terms of the traditional Soviet system.[9] Thereafter, more

8. See p. 14.

9. For discussion of Soviet taxation, see Holzman; Gunter Hedtkamp, "Das Steuersystem im Dienste der Sowjetischen Staats und Wirtschaftsordnung," *Finanzarchiv*, N.F., *20* (1960), and Gertraud Menz, *Die Entwicklung der Sowjetischen Besteuerung unter Besonderer Berücksichtigung der ordnungspolitischen Funktionen* (Berlin, Duncker and Humblot, 1960). The latter work contains a detailed history of Soviet taxation, including extensive literature references. For a recent study of the Soviet economy, with occasional reference to fiscal problems, see Abram Bergson, *The Economics of Soviet Planning* (New Haven, Yale University Press, 1964).

recent developments in socialist taxation in line with decentralization of Soviet economies are considered.

Until recently, at least, there existed a fairly high degree of uniformity among socialist countries, which renders this a representative case.[10]

Types of Revenue. As was shown in Table 2–4, so-called taxes from the population provide only a small part of total revenue, with the bulk being furnished by revenues from the national economy. These in turn are composed largely of turnover tax and the government's share in the profits of public enterprises.[11]

In socialist terminology, these receipts are not considered taxes. They are generally regarded (together with profits left in the enterprises) as part of the "surplus value" which is created in puplic enterprises, and which belongs to the

10. For a discussion of the fiscal structures of Poland and the Deutsche Demokratische Republik see L. Kurowski and R. Szawlowski, "Das Finanzsystem und der Stattshaushalt Polens"; and E. Kaemmel, "Das Finanzsystem der Deutschen Demokratischen Republik," both in *Handbuch der Finanzwissenschaft, 3,* ed. W. Gerloff and F. Neumark (2d ed. Tübingen, Mohr, 1958).

11. Due to language limitations, it was unfortunately necessary for the author to rely on secondary sources, which are indeed ample. According to Hedtkamp, p. 185, a more detailed breakdown of tax receipts in the U.S.S.R. for 1960 was as follows:

From the Socialist Economy	*Per Cent of Total*
1. Sales and turnover tax	41.1
2. Share in profits of public enterprises	26.3
3. Income tax on collective farms and other non-state rural enterprises	2.8
4. Social Insurance contributions of firms and other receipts from socialist economy	20.8
5. Total	91.0
From the Population	
6. Individual income tax	7.3
7. Other	1.7
8. Total	9.0
9. Sum of Receipts	100.0

state as their owner. These receipts, which are also referred to as "products of the society" or "net income of the society," are not considered as a burden on the population, since they are created by the enterprises of the state.[12] The income share, which previously accrued to the "capitalist class," plus or minus the difference between wages paid and the earnings of the labor factor, is now imputed to the state. The taxes from the population, however, are considered a burden, since they are not drawn from the state's accumulation but from wages, including not only wages paid by the private sector but also those paid by public enterprise.

From my point of view, the distinction between the two groups of taxes seems a formality with little economic substance. Even if one proceeds on the assumption that capital income belongs to the state, while labor income belongs to the worker, the determination of labor income in the socialist case may be a matter of distribution policy and need not coincide with the shadow price needed for purposes of efficient labor allocation. While the two are linked by incentive considerations, considerable freedom of variation exists.

If a parallel were to be drawn with Western terminology, the income tax equivalent would equal the sum of income tax from the population plus the excess (or minus the deficiency) of labor earnings (in the sense of economic factor returns) over wage payments. As far as the overall level of taxation is concerned, the tax to GNP ratio for the capitalist systems would be matched in the socialist setting by the ratio to GNP of tax receipts plus profits of state enterprises plus factor earnings minus wages paid. But this is misleading. Since capital formation is paid for publicly in one case and privately in the other, the totals that result are not at all homogeneous. It seems better, therefore, not to compare overall tax ratios at all but to consider the shares of GNP that are devoted to particular types of public services.

12. See Menz, p. 171.

Turnover Tax. Whether the turnover tax is to be classified as a tax or not, its administration clearly presents a technical tax problem in any sense. Misleadingly referred to as a turnover tax, the Soviet system of indirect taxation does not provide for a multiple-stage tax on gross receipts, but consists of a bundle largely made up of single-stage taxes on consumer goods. The tax is imposed for the most part on the distributor but sometimes also on the producer. It is generally levied on an ad valorem base and may be related to retail price, wholesale price, or margins, depending on the product. Rates are differentiated widely by industry, quality, and region, with a considerable degree of decentralization in administration. In the late fifties the shoe industry, for instance, had 1,443 different rates, and the cotton industry, nearly 1,000.[13] In some cases the tax base is adjusted further so as to respond to cost differences of individual firms. Rates, expressed as per cent of retail price (including tax), are as high as 90 per cent on some items and, while they have been declining, still average over 40 per cent. There appears to be some tendency for luxuries to be taxed more heavily than necessities, but many exceptions are made to this rule.

Why is such a cumbersome sales tax structure needed, involving so vast an array of complex rate differentials? Various explanations have been suggested.[14] One is that monthly reports on turnover tax are valuable as they provide data on output and sales which are needed for production planning. The tax would serve this purpose better, however, if it were imposed more largely on the producer. Another is that differential rates are used to make profitability of firms a better index of efficiency. Since the difference between assigned factor costs and prices varies by firms and industries, such rates serve more nearly to equalize profit margins between firms of equal efficiency. Thus corrected,

13. Ibid., p. 179.
14. Ibid., p. 209.

profit margins provide a control over the performance of individual firms and industries. Finally, while the basket of consumer goods produced may have been selected on a "merit basis," its distribution must be such as to clear the market. The sales prices that result will be determined by consumer preferences, and relative prices may not be in line with relative costs, assuming factor inputs into various products to be assigned the same cost. Differential tax rates are needed to equalize the two.

Moreover, although the market basket may have been aimed at serving consumer preferences, there may have been planning errors. Differential rates may then reflect corrections for planning errors in adapting supply and demand, errors that once embedded in the system are not readily changed thereafter. But apart from this, they provide intended corrections, forming an inherent part of the way in which cost and prices are set in the planning process.

Apart from the matter of differential rates, we again face the puzzling question of why so high a turnover tax rate is needed. The planning function, served by differential rates, could surely be met by a much lower average rate level. For any given total division of output between consumer goods sold at the market and other outputs (capital formation and public goods) not thus disposed of, this would make it necessary, however, to make other arrangements to keep private demand for consumer goods in line with goods available for purchase at the market. Comparison of the turnover tax approach with two alternatives is illustrated in Table 2-6.

In all cases, tax receipts must suffice to pay for capital and social goods. The turnover tax case, illustrating the present arrangement, is shown in column 1.[15] In column 2 the turn-

15. To simplify, we disregard factor shares other than labor and assume that there are no profits in the initial situation of case 1. These can be readily introduced and do not change the nature of the argument.

TABLE 2-6

Alternative Taxes under Socialism
(money values)

	Turnover Tax (1)	Income Tax (2)	Profits Tax (3)
Wages originating in consumer goods industries for sale at market	60	60	60
Wages originating in capital goods industries	30	30	30
Wages originating in industries producing social goods	10	10	10
Total wage income	100	100	100
− Income tax	—	40	—
Disposable wage income and consumer expenditure	100	60	100
− Factor cost of consumer goods	60	60	60
− Turnover tax	40	—	—
Profits	—	—	—
− Profits tax	—	—	40
Profits after tax	—	—	—
Price index of consumer goods	100	60	100

over tax is replaced by an income tax, or an equivalent reduction in the wage bill paid out to workers, and consumer
goods prices are reduced. In column 3, the turnover tax is
replaced by a profits tax. Money wages and consumer goods
prices remain unchanged, profits emerge and are taken up
through profits tax.

If the turnover tax has been considered the more attractive alternative, the reasons are not difficult to guess at.
The higher nominal wage share has certain psychological
(political and incentive) advantages over alternative 3,
which leaves a higher profit share, and alternative 2, which
requires higher direct taxes or lower wages. Anti-infla-
tionary measures are accomplished less painfully by increases
in turnover tax than by nominal wage reduction, and differential turnover tax rates may be used for price adjustments. Finally, there remains a substantial private sector,
where wages are not subject to close public control, so that
alternatives 2 and 3 would have to be combined to replace
the turnover tax.

Profit Share in State Enterprises. The other major
revenue source is the budgetary share in the profits of state
enterprises. The planning of net prices and costs (including
differential turnover tax rates) provides a margin of planned
profit in state enterprises, achievement of which is taken to
reflect a standard level of managerial efficiency. About one-
third of planned profits are retained by the enterprise with
two-thirds absorbed in profits tax, the annual rate depending on the scope of planned capital investment. If total
profits exceed planned profits, a certain fraction of the
excess, now above 50 per cent, is also retained by the firm.
This retention, however, is subject to certain conditions,
designed to assure that the gain in profits reflects increased
efficiency. It is allocated to the Director's Fund, with 50 per
cent to be used for increasing production, the remainder
being available for capital expansion such as housing and
for workers' welfare. The profits tax is thus a residual claim-

ant, absorbing such profits as are not needed as an incentive to management or to overall firm efficiency.

The function of profits after tax in this system is to induce efficient management. Unlike its role in the capitalist system, its main use is not to allocate capital between industries, which is done as a part of the overall production plan. Rather, net profits remaining in the firm may be looked upon as a supplementary wage to workers in the form of housing or other goods, and to management in the form of prestige gained from plant expansion. Also, it provides a further source of funds for capital formation.

Other Taxes. Corresponding to the government's profit share in state enterprises, other enterprises are subject to income taxation of their own. Thus, a rate of 25 per cent is imposed on the profits of consumer cooperatives. Producer cooperatives are subject to steeply progressive rates, assessed in relation to margins (profit/sales) and ranging up to 90 per cent. This again serves as an important control function, as well as to curtail the comparatively high profitability of such firms.

Collective farms are also subject to income tax. The tax is based on gross receipts, after deducting costs incurred for purchases from other firms. The tax is thus essentially on value added. The rate in 1960 was 12.5 per cent and may be differentiated regionally.

Income Tax. Direct taxes on the population account for only less than 10 per cent of total tax revenue. The income tax is paid by workers and other employees, tradesmen, and by others with independent income. Employees of state enterprises are covered, along with employees in the private sector, even though their wages are set by public policy in the first place. Taxpayers are divided into categories, subject to quite different rate schedules, giving the Soviet income tax a highly schedular character. Workers and employees are subject to the lowest tax, with a maximum bracket rate of only 13 per cent and a substantial tax-free minimum. Even highly paid employees benefit from this low rate, so that the income tax is not used as a redistributional device *within* this group.[16] Tradesmen organized in co-operatives pay an additional 10 per cent. Artists and writers are subject to the same rates as workers and employees but are permitted no family allowance. Taxpayers in independent professions, tradesmen not in cooperatives, and landlords are subject to substantially higher rates, ranging up to 80 per cent. The income tax is thus used as a redistributional device *between* occupational groups rather than income brackets. One purpose, it appears, is to render certain occupations more attractive than others, and thereby to influence the sectoral allocation of labor resources.

The tax is of only minor revenue importance, however, and its primary function may be to control earnings from sources other than state enterprises. Beginning with 1960, a plan for annual reduction in the income tax and exemption of low paid groups was initiated, and its eventual disappearance has been promised. How rapidly this will be possible in a setting where the private sector is expanding rather than contracting remains to be seen. Moreover, recent developments to be noted presently point to a reversal of this trend.

Agricultural Tax. While collective farms are subject to income tax corresponding to the profit share in state enterprise, other agricultural income is subject to a land tax, based on acreage. This tax applies to the private farms of peasants working in collective farms, as well as independent farmers and workers engaged in agricultural side activities.

16. By the same token, the problem of disincentive effects is only minor. The incentive effects of wage rate policy, however, are more or less the same as those of tax policy, and the two cannot be separated in the socialist setting. For emphasis on the incentive aspect, see Bergson, pp. 123, 187, 190.

Rates again differ with the groups involved and are much the highest for independent farmers. While the private agricultural sector may be "taxed" to some extent by setting low procurement prices for agricultural products, the retained product escapes turnover tax, so that an additional form of taxation is needed to reach it from the consumption side. Such is provided through this agricultural tax.

Other taxes involve a tax on bachelors, a tax on horses owned by independent farmers, a tax on livestock kept by urban residents, and various local taxes, including a property tax on land and real estate.

New Directions. Current developments in the socialist countries foreshadow some far-reaching changes in the traditional system. These are a reflection of the ongoing changes in the structure of socialist planning and decision making. While these changes proceed along different lines in various countries, especially in connection with fiscal reform, a common direction does emerge.[17] This is that economic decision making is to be more decentralized, and that the scope for independent action by the managers of state enterprises is to be increased. The price structure is to be adapted to a new set of relative prices, which more nearly reflect relative costs, including the opportunity cost of capital; and prices are to be permitted to respond more readily to changing market conditions. More independence is to be given to the enterprise as a decision unit. Increased attention is to be paid to incentives for managers and workers to operate efficiently, and new success indices, including profit maximization, are

17. For a general discussion of these problems, see, for instance, Julius Branik, "The Budget and the Distribution of National Income," and other papers contributed to the Prague Congress of the International Institute of Public Finance (1967), published in *Public Finance/Finances Publiques, 23* (Spring 1968). The same paper contains literature references to changing fiscal policies in the U.S.S.R., Poland, the German Democratic Republic, Hungary, Bulgaria, Romania, and Czechoslovakia.

to be stressed. Remuneration of workers is to be differentiated more sharply in line with contribution to output, thereby increasing incentives and the allocative function of the labor market.

Two of these changes are of immediate fiscal importance. One is that in line with emphasis on incentives, private consumption is to be raised in relation to social consumption. The other is that there is to be increased reliance on internal finance out of retained earnings. For both reasons, the size of the budget in relation to national income will shrink, a smaller part of capital formation being channeled through the budgetary process.

While these directions are fairly clear, it remains to be seen just how the structure of investment is to be determined. On one side, the intention is to encourage enterprises to expand where they find it profitable, i.e. to decentralize the investment decision to the firm level. On the other, the central plan is to continue as an important or even basic determinant of the structure of investment. Two lines of demarcation between private and public investment are under discussion, but neither points to a clear solution.

One suggestion has been that enterprises should make day-to-day investment decisions in their particular sphere, while it remains for the plan to determine "basic" investment, or to call for "major" changes in the structure of investment. Basic investment, in this sense, is to include budgetary provision for social overhead capital, as it does in the capitalist countries. Major changes are not as readily defined. Will the plan set overall investment quotas for various industries and let firms compete for their share within this quota? What form will this competition take, and how broadly or narrowly will the industry blocks be defined?

The other suggestion has been that the plan should control long-run economic development, while the market should determine short-run adjustment. This formulation, while attractive at first sight, is less operational than the preceding one. Capital investment, by its nature, involves a long-run decision, and it would make little sense to leave short-lived assets to the firm while delegating longer-lived ones to the plan. The long run, after all, results from a sequence of current decisions, and long-run plans must be reflected in short-run investment patterns.

These problems, it should be noted, are rather similar to those discussed in more or less capitalist countries. Here also the budget has the function of providing for social overhead capital, and in countries such as France there is the further task of coordinating investment planning by firms, if informally so, by setting guidelines that project the overall development of the economic structure. One is tempted, therefore, to say that little difference remains between the two systems, but this would be going much too far. The state ownership of enterprise remains a crucial difference, and profits in the two systems do not play identical roles, even though the manager, acting for the state, may be instructed to behave as if he were the manager of a private firm.

Turning to the fiscal implications of the new system, we find that it will involve not only a reduced size of the budget, but also fundamental changes in the structure of taxation. The importance of the turnover tax is to be greatly reduced and a flat charge (of 5 per cent or more) on capital is to be the core of the new tax structure. In addition, new forms of tax will be imposed on profits, differentiated in some countries between the share going to personal payments and that going to investment. These new forms, in effect in some cases and still on the drafting boards in others, show a great deal of ingenuity. Indeed, the Western fiscal expert, who is frustrated by so little improvement in his tradition-determined tax system, may envy his socialist colleagues for the sweeping scope of the reforms they are about to undertake. However, closer consideration suggests that the range of choice may not be as wide as appears at first sight. Both macro and micro constraints present themselves and need to be noted.

Let us postulate that the economy is to grow at a certain rate, say 5 per cent. With a given marginal capital output ratio, a given ratio of investment to total output is required. Thus the needed level of total investment is determined.[18] We then determine how much of this is to be internally financed, and hence the amount with which enterprises must be left after paying for labor, materials, and taxes. Given product prices and wage rates, and hence internal funds before tax, we know what the total amount of taxes thereon must be to yield the desired amount of retention. With the total amount of enterprise taxation given in this fashion, the problem is only what form this taxation should take.

In particular, what should be the division between that part which is to be in the form of a flat charge on capital, and that part which is to be in the form of profits tax? This, of course, is not only a technical fiscal question, but goes to the heart of resource allocation and the role of profits as an index of efficiency. Ideally, capital should be charged with a cost (over and above recovery of investment outlay) equal to the marginal efficiency of investment in the economy. No investment should be undertaken if its return is less. If the charge on capital (which is a cost and deducted in measuring profits) is less, the profit rate does not serve as an index of efficiency. More-capital-intensive firms will be more profitable than less-capital-intensive firms, assuming equal wages to be paid for equal labor; and the investment structure will be

18. It is interesting to note that the theoretical formulation of these problems is very similar for both capitalist and socialist countries. See, for instance, Robert Solow, "A Contribution to the Theory of Economic Growth," *Quarterly Journal of Economics, 52,* no. 1 (February 1956); and M. Kalecki, *An Outline of the Theory of Socialist Growth* (Varsava, PWN, 1963).

biased toward long-lived assets. Setting the charge against capital at the proper level is thus a crucial step in capital allocation; and the proposed rate of 5 per cent, it would seem, is rather on the low side.

Having thus determined the capital charge and deducted it to obtain profits, the required level of profits taxation is given by the excess of such profits (plus depreciation) over the desired level of internal finance. Thus the level and composition of enterprise taxation are determined by the macro variables in the system, in particular the growth target, and the decision to impose a charge on capital to account for capital cost. Profits taxation will then be the higher, the lower is the part of investment that is to be financed internally.

There remains the question of how the profits tax may be adapted as an incentive device, designed to induce managers and workers to perform in a more efficient fashion. In the Hungarian system, for instance, profits are to be allocated between (1) a share for bonus remuneration to workers and managers, and (2) a share for investment, and different tax treatment is applied to each share. The former is to be taxed progressively so as to avoid too sharp a rise in wages above the average increase, and the latter is taxed at a flat rate. The hope is that both labor and management will be interested in maximum profits and that the wage earners will be interested in economizing the use of labor so as to distribute profits among a smaller number. Moreover, a penalty tax is to be placed on additions to the labor force. In Czechoslovakia, there is to be an 18 per cent tax on profits and wages, which tax is to be paid out of profits. This arrangement again is designed to keep management from raising wages and attracting more labor unless the enterprise is highly profitable.

These provisions have their specific purposes and are understandable in the particular transition setting. But they run the risk of giving conflicting incentives. On one side the enterprise is encouraged to maximize profits and to expand, but on the other it is not to increase its working force. One wonders whether it would not be better, after the adjustment difficulties are overcome, to rely on a simpler system, which taxes profits by a general profits tax but leaves the pursuit of efficiency more largely to the process of profit maximization.

Somewhat similar problems arise on the wage side of the picture. If there is to be a given amount of investment and of social consumption, resources available for private consumption are determined; and with given wages and a given savings rate, this determines the permissible level of disposable income and hence the required level of income or wages tax. The chance that the desired level of consumption will just match consumer expenditures with a zero tax on wages is very slight. Thus, a wages tax (or income tax) will be needed, and this quite apart from the distributional function such a tax may have.

This reasoning implies that wages are given by allocational considerations, so that the needed adjustment in income paid to the workers cannot be made to begin with by adjusting the division of total income between wages and profits, i.e. by determining the wage rate. The latter solution, as previously noted, was possible (theoretically, at least, though not applied in practice) in the more fully centralized system, where a distinction could be drawn between the amount paid to workers and the shadow price of labor, or the true economic (opportunity) cost at which labor is entered (or should be entered) into the economic calculation of the plan. Given a market system where firms can bid for labor by offering a higher wage rate, this rate must be set according to the value of the factor's marginal product, so that the wage rate ceases to be an instrument for adjusting the share of private consumption in output.

This then leaves the question of whether a gross receipts tax might not be used for this purpose, thus restoring the turnover tax (i.e. the socialist single-stage but multiple-rate excise system) to a major place in the picture. The answer is yes, provided that the tax will be reflected in reduced real wages which, with downward rigid money wages, means higher prices. In this form, the turnover tax (or, better, a value-added tax) is a meaningful alternative to an income tax; but, of course, its distributional implications differ. It should be noted here that this function of the turnover tax will be contingent on its being shifted to consumption; and more broadly, that the whole problem of tax shifting will become an issue in the socialist setting as prices are made flexible in the course of market adjustment.

Before turning to the distribution issue, a further word about the requirement of macro stability. As decision making is decentralized sufficiently, the socialist economy will come to pay the price of a decentralized system, that is, the risk of potential macro instability. The more the investment decision is left to the managers of the enterprises, the less certain it will be just how high the level of investment will be the next year. This will be the case especially if a form of capital market is created by which profits retained in one enterprise may be transferred to investment in another. Similarly, the larger the share of consumption which goes through private outlays rather than social consumption, the greater will be the uncertainty regarding the level of consumer expenditures. And this will be the case especially if private savings (and hence the possibility of dissaving) become a factor. Thus the whole problem of stabilization policy—of the planned use of budget deficit and surplus—will emerge as a new aspect of socialist finance. On the tax side, there will be a need for flexible tax policy, and one of the new questions to be considered is which tax should serve this stabilizing function.

Finally, the fiscal system will come to have a greater bearing on the interpersonal distribution of income. As various writers have pointed out, there is to be greater emphasis on the incentive function of earnings, and this is to result in a much wider range of income differentials. This poses the question of how income distribution will compare in so-called capitalist and socialist countries. To be sure, in capitalist countries the distribution of property income is more unequal than that of labor income; thus, if the distribution of labor income in both economies were the same, the distribution of total income would still be more equal in the socialist setting. But it should be remembered that wage income in Western countries is over twice as large as capital income, so that the weight of capital income is limited, and that there has been an increasing trend toward equalizing adjustments. Moreover, the distribution of wage income is already more unequal in some socialist than in some capitalist countries. Increased differentiation of wage income in the socialist economies, therefore, could lead to a situation where their distribution of income would be as or more unequal. Indeed, this is quite possible if one looks at the distribution of consumption rather than of income, since upper income saving in the capitalist setting is a substitute in large part for state saving in the socialist setting, leaving capitalist distribution of consumption less unequal than that of income. In all, these prospects are startling to contemplate if one thinks of the traditional ideologies of left and right, and the communist dream (postponed further by socialist necessity) of income (or consumption?) distribution according to need. And as socialist distribution becomes less equal, the redistributive function of progressive income taxation (raising problems of conflicting incentive considerations) will enter the arena of socialist finance as well.

In all, it appears that as the allocation and distribution mechanism of the socialist economy is decentralized, its fiscal structure will become more similar to that of the capitalist systems. Socialist public finance will lose some of its older problems. The association of the budget with the structure of production and investment will become less intimate and complete, and the role of the fiscal mechanism with regard to the creation of a "socialist capital market" will pose new challenges. Tax concern with effects upon incentives, especially managerial incentives, will become more important; the issue of tax shifting will rear its ugly head; problems of stabilization, of Keynesian economics, will arise; and before too long, there may also be concern with correction of interpersonal distribution via progressive income taxation.

CAPITALIST TAXATION

Capitalist taxation stands in sharp contrast to the traditional forms of socialist taxation, as evidenced by the Soviet pattern. As shown in Table 2–5, public enterprise profits (line 10) now play a small role only. Nearly the total net product, looked at from the income side, is assigned initially to private income recipients. Thus, nearly the entire budgetary resource-use must be matched by tax (or loan) withdrawals from the private sector of production and income. With the initial distribution of income given by the market, the pattern of taxation, supplemented by transfers, now becomes the strategic instrument for adjusting the state of distribution. Accordingly, the stage is set for a much heavier reliance on progressive income and wealth taxation, as well as for high social security taxes.

All this is reflected in Table 2–5 where the tax structures of various Western countries are summarized. At the same time, the composition of these tax structures shows more variation than was to be found for the socialist group in Table 2–4. The contribution of income taxes (individual and corporate) ranks highest in Sweden with 53 per cent, followed by about 48 per cent in the United States and Japan, and less in the Netherlands. Italy and France are the lowest, with 15 and 22 per cent respectively. These two countries, in turn, show an excise, sales, and customs share of about 45 per cent, as against 21 per cent in the United States and 34 per cent in Sweden. Another source of difference arises from the weight of social security contributions, ranging from 33 per cent in Italy to less than 10 per cent in Canada. These variations reflect differences in a variety of factors, such as the extent of resource transfer to public use, attitudes toward tax equity, the pattern, scope, and method of distributional adjustment, the balance between industry and agriculture, the size and legal form of business organization, the extent to which the tax structure is used for regulatory purposes, and so forth.

These are familiar matters to which I shall return later. Obviously, the problems of tax policy are more complex in a setting where almost the entire revenue is drawn from taxpayers who are private agents, be they individuals or corporations, rather than from state enterprises whose legal structure and policies are more or less subject to public control. One important difference, as previously noted, arises from the natural desire of the private taxpayer to escape his tax burden, either by minimizing actual payments through tax avoidance (making the best of legally permitted loopholes) or evasion (illegal noncompliance with the law), or by adjusting price and production policies in such a way as to pass on the burden of such tax payments as have been made. All this must be allowed for, since distributional objectives of tax policy must relate to the de facto rather than the statutory or impact distribution of the tax burden.

Taxes may be imposed on a variety of bases, including income and expenditures associated with the production of current output, other transactions, the holding of assets, transfers by gift or bequest, and so forth. But whichever base is chosen, the final tax burden must be borne by an individual or household, be it as income recipient, consumer, heir, or in some other form. The task of designing an equitable tax structure, therefore, is to arrive at an equitable distribution of the tax burden among *individuals*. This involves requirements of horizontal equity, demanding that people in equal position be treated equally; as well as requirements of vertical equity, demanding that people in unequal positions pay different burden shares.

The problem of vertical equity, or progressivity, in the tax-transfer structure is not subject to scientific solution, but has to be solved in terms of social values regarding equality (or inequality) as a goal of policy. Rather, it is the implementation of horizontal equity that poses most of the technical difficulties in the design of the tax structure. The basic task is one of defining an index of equality. This may take the form of income, interpreted in the sense of consumption plus accretion during a given period. Or it may take the form of consumption. In either case, the logical means of taxation is a personal tax, be it assessed on income or expenditure at the household level.

Where income is chosen as the proper base, the logical conclusion points to a single tax system, consisting of an individual income tax only. Implementation of such a tax, however, would require inclusion of a wholly comprehensive income base, including retained earnings of corporations (to be imputed to the shareholder), other capital gains, imputed income, gifts and bequests, and so forth.[19] Actually, tax structures in Western countries fall far short of such a pattern, and by no means all the revenue is obtained from the income tax.

Partly this reflects the simple fact that tax structures come about by political process rather than analytical design, and partly the explanation may be found in the interaction between the horizontal and vertical dimensions of the equity issue. By maintaining a truncated income concept (especially due to exclusion or preferential treatment of capital gains), the redistributional bite of highly progressive rate structures is dulled, especially toward the upper end of the income scale; and by combining the income tax with a substantial sales tax component, the overall mix is again rendered less

19. For further discussion and literature references on the structure of a "good" income tax, see p. 180.

progressive. To be sure, it might be argued that the index of equality need not be defined in terms of income only, but that a double standard of income and consumption taxation may be chosen. There is no objection to this in principle, but the logical form of consumption tax, in this case, would be a personalized expenditure tax which, analogous to the income tax, could be adapted to the position of the tax-paying unit.[20]

Equity considerations aside, we have noted also that tax policy in the capitalist setting must be more concerned with incentive effects than is the case in the socialist system. Effects on investment as well as work incentives must be allowed for, and may modify tax policy objectives which are arrived at in the equity context only. Thus, much of the debate on tax policy deals with various incentive devices— such as accelerated depreciation, the investment credit, deductions for saving, and so forth—and their implications from both an economic policy and equity point of view. Finally, tax policy in the capitalist setting must serve the needs of economic stabilization, which imposes further requirements of built-in flexibility and adjustability of the tax system. After all is said and done, one is left with a complex set of multiple objectives, which does not lend itself to a simple, single-model solution.

20. For an analysis of tax structure problems in Western countries see: For the United States: Joseph A. Pechman, *Federal Tax Policy* (Washington, D.C., The Brookings Institution, 1966). For Canada: *Report of the Royal Commission on Taxation* (Carter Commission) (Ottawa, Queens Printer, 1966). For the United Kingdom: A. R. Prest, *Public Finance in Theory and Practice* (3d ed. London, Weidenfeld and Nicolson, 1967). For Germany: *Gutachten zur Reform der Direkten Steuern,* Schriftenreihe des Bundesministeriums der Finanzen, *9* Bonn, Stollfuss, 1967). As a general source for many countries, see also Gerloff and Neumark, *Handbuch der Finanzwissenschaft, 3.*

PART II
PUBLIC SECTOR AND
ECONOMIC DEVELOPMENT

3 THE THEORY OF PUBLIC EXPENDITURE DEVELOPMENT

Public expenditures play an important role in the functioning of the economy, whether at a relatively low or high level of income. However, there is good reason to expect that this role will change in the course of development, as the budgetary function is adapted to the changing needs of the economy. The purpose of this chapter is to examine this changing role, thereby exploring what might be called a theory of public expenditure development.

DETERMINANTS OF EXPENDITURE DEVELOPMENT

The determinants of expenditure development, it must be admitted at the outset, are not only economic. Other forces, referred to here as conditioning and social factors, must be considered as well.

DETERMINANTS

The changing needs of the economy relate to both the allocation and distribution aspects of expenditure policy, but the former is of primary interest in this connection, as it deals with the "proper" share of public resource use in the course of rising income. More specifically, the problem may be defined as follows: Let us assume that society divides resource use between private and public goods (as defined in Chapter 1) in an efficient pattern. That is to say, the total output of consumer goods is divided between private (internal-benefit intensive) and social (external-benefit intensive) goods, depending on consumer preferences, and the output of capital goods is similarly divided between private and public so as to secure the most productive use. Public goods are provided (paid for) through the budget but, as noted before, this does not involve the question of whether such goods are produced by private or by public firms. The problem now under discussion, therefore, applies equally to both a capitalist and a socialist setting. We now add the heroic assumption that the conditioning and social factors (as noted below) remain constant and ask ourselves this question: As per capita income rises due to increasing productivity, either because of a rising capital–labor ratio or for other reasons, what will happen to the public goods share in total output? The answer will then depend on the income elasticities of demand for private as against public consumer goods; and on the appropriate mix of the capital stock between private and public investment goods as the stock increases.

Regarding the distribution function of budget policy, a similar question may be asked. As per capita income rises, is there an increasing or decreasing need for distributional measures, depending on (1) changes in the existing distribution of income, and (2) changes in the need to secure a given pattern of distribution? The resulting hypotheses, as we shall see, will differ depending on the stipulated objectives of distribution policy.

Going beyond economic factors as here defined, allowance must be made for certain conditioning factors which will greatly affect the results achieved by the operation of our economic forces. Among these conditioning forces, changes in technology and demographic factors are of primary importance.

Changes in technology will affect the preferred mix of public and private goods, in both the capital and consumer goods sector. New consumer goods, created by technological innovation, may call for either public or private provision, thereby changing the mix of the preferred basket of goods. Similarly, new production techniques may call for a change in the mix of public and private capital goods. Changes in demographic factors also may affect demand patterns and hence the appropriate output mix. Increased demand for education, for instance, is a lagged effect of an increased birthrate, and so forth.

Finally, allowance must be made for the political, cultural, and social factors that determine the environment in which budget policy operates and that affect the underlying value judgments or the political weights attached to them. With changing political institutions and attitudes toward the public sector, the resource allocation between public and private uses may come to approximate more closely, or move away from our model of efficient resource use. Political biases and rigidities may enter the picture. Wars may play a major role in determining what are acceptable levels of taxation, and displacement effects may arise as military expenditures decline at the end of a war. Changes in the climate of social philosophy may be reflected in changing distributional objectives and the budgetary functions that are performed in this area.

The dividing lines between these categories of economic, conditioning, and social forces, to be sure, are not clear-cut, nor are they wholly independent of each other. At the same time, this grouping will provide a framework within which specific hypotheses regarding expenditure development can be formulated and perhaps tested. In particular, they will permit us to isolate the allocation issues which are of primary interest to the economic analyst.

VERIFICATION

Even if the conceptual distinctions can be drawn, it remains difficult to verify hypotheses regarding the role of our economic factors. If we consider the change in the expenditure share for any one country over, say, the last hundred years, this change may be related to economic development as measured by rising per capita income. But rising per capita income was not the only influence on budget policy during this period. The other factors, including conditioning and social forces, entered as well, and their influence cannot be separated neatly from that of our economic factors.

Nor are we better off if the comparison is drawn between a cross section of countries with differing current levels of per capita income. Here all countries are subject to the same general set of contemporary influences broadly defined, but strong political and social differences remain at any point in time. These differences influence the structure of the public sector and blur such differences as result from varying levels of per capita income.

It follows that the relationships between per capita income and fiscal structure that are obtained from the historical view may well differ from those revealed by the cross-section approach. Low income countries today do not operate under the same technical, political, and value conditions as prevailed in the past when now developed countries were at similar low levels of income. Attitudes toward growth, changed communication, the demonstration effect of affluence and welfare measures abroad, the conflict of political ideologies, all make for basic differences in the historical setting. These factors, in both their historical and sectoral dimension, affect the fiscal structure along with differences in the level of per capita income. Hence a variety of patterns may be expected to emerge, and the verification of hypotheses regarding the role of our economic factors will be difficult. Nevertheless, let us consider the proposition that these factors play an important role—i.e. that the efficient structure of the public sector varies with the stages of economic development as measured by the growth of per capita income—and examine what hypotheses may be established on that basis.

Economic Factors

Economic factors, which are our **primary** interest, will be considered first. As previously suggested, a distinction is drawn between the allocation and distribution aspects. The former deals primarily with the share of public purchases of goods and services in GNP, while the latter deals primarily with the role of transfer payments.

ALLOCATION ASPECTS

Wagner's Law. Ever since Adolph Wagner expounded his law of the "expanding scale of state activity," [1] econo-

1. See Adolph Wagner, *Finanzwissenschaft* (3d ed. Leipzig, Winter, 1883), *1*, 63, and *Grundlegung der politischen Oekonomie* (3d ed. Leipzig, Winter, 1892–94), pp. 892–906. See also Herbert Timm, "Das Gesetz der Wachsenden Staatsausgaben," *Finanzarchiv*, N.F., *21* (1961), 201–47.

While there is no explicit statement in Wagner that the law of expanding scale relates to the share rather than the absolute level of public expenditures, occasional reference to "quotas" suggests the former. It is evident, however, that Wagner is concerned not only with the scope of public expenditures for the provision of social goods and redistribution but that his law includes the expansion of public enterprise as well. Indeed, much of his emphasis is on the latter aspect. The operation of more and more industries is seen to involve social considerations. Public control being too difficult, public operation becomes necessary. This blurs the issue, since the determinants of resource allocation to the satisfaction of social wants are quite different from those that involve the choice between public and private production management. See p. 4.

Recognizing various expenditure functions, Wagner distinguishes between expenditures for protection and expenditures for social and welfare purposes. The latter in turn are broken down into general administration, economic administration, and education. The major element of expansion is foreseen in education and in the general area of legal administration and protection.

mists have speculated on its validity and the underlying causes. These causes may be economic or political, but it is the former that are of primary interest here.

The proposition of expanding scale, obviously, must be interpreted as postulating a rising *share* of the public sector in the economy. An absolute increase in the size of the budget can hardly fail to result as the economy expands. To focus on the economic factors that support the hypothesis of a rising share or ratio of public expenditure to GNP, let me repeat the mental experiment I wish to make: Holding constant conditioning and social forces, I now follow the development of a country from low to high per capita income in the course of capital accumulation. In such a setting, what will happen to the share of income that, assuming efficient resource use, is to be channeled through the public budget?

This question cannot be answered for public expenditures at large. In our model of efficient resource allocation between public and private goods, there is no presumption that alternative public expenditures are more closely substitutable for each other than are public and private outlays. Hence the growth of public expenditures as a whole is not a dependent variable by itself but must be reduced to its components if prediction is to be made. Later on, when I consider the role of social and conditioning factors, attention will be given to the hypothesis that, in fact, *total* public expenditure levels are a function of the acceptable level of *total* tax rates. In this case, public goods as a group become substitutes for private goods as a group and the total level of public expenditures (as distinct from, or in addition to, specific expenditure items) becomes a meaningful dependent variable. This, however, is not the case in my present model, where resource allocation between alternative public and private uses is made on an efficient basis.[2]

2. To avoid misunderstanding, I restate the point more fully. In the model, here referred to as following a hypothesis of "efficient"

Theory of Expenditure Development

As Wagner pointed out to begin with, the course of *particular* types of public expenditures must be considered. But his choice of categories—protection, general administration, economic administration, and education—is not entirely suitable here. While the distinction between defense and civilian functions is accepted, civilian expenditures must then be examined by economic categories, i.e. public capital formation, public consumption, and transfers. What reason is there to expect that the share of any of these in GNP will vary in some systematic fashion as the level of per capita income rises?

Capital Formation. Given the division of total output between consumption and capital formation, the share of public capital formation in total output depends on the appropriate mix of capital goods.[3] Those that are externality-intensive must be supplied publicly, while others (the benefits of which are primarily internal) may be provided for privately.

consumer behavior, choices are made between outlays on public goods $G_1 \ldots G_J$, and private goods $P_1 \ldots P_J$, so as to maximize welfare from both. In such a world, utility is defined as $U = U(G_1 \ldots G_J, P_1 \ldots P_J)$ and resource allocation to public goods as a whole can be determined only as the sum of specific allocations to $G_1 \ldots, G_J$.

In an alternative model, here referred to as following a "political" behavior hypothesis, it is assumed that people dislike a high tax rate, so that the utility function assumes an additional term. Utility is now defined as

$$U = U\left(G_1 \cdots G_J, P_1 \cdots P_J, \frac{\Sigma G_1 \cdots G_J}{\Sigma P_1 \cdots P_J}\right)$$

where the last term is negative. This we take to be the basic formulation underlying the "tax resistance" aspect of the Peacock-Wiseman model, as discussed below. See p. 90.

3. This argument relates to public capital formation in a mixed rather than a socialist economy. In the latter, capital formation is by definition public, although investment planning must continue to distinguish between internality- and externality-intensive types of capital assets.

The literature on economic development suggests that public capital formation is of particular importance at early stages of development. Transportation facilities must be provided to open up the country and to link natural resources with the market. Road, rail, and port facilities are required as prerequisites to productive capital formation in the private sector. Improved agricultural techniques require irrigation. Use of machinery demands minimal technical skills, and so forth. All these are types of investment the benefits of which are largely external, and which must therefore be provided publicly, either by local or central government. As the economy develops and a larger flow of savings becomes available, the capital stock in private industry and agriculture must be built up. The basic stock of social overhead capital has now been created and additions are made at a slower rate. The structure of social overhead capital, similar to public utilities, becomes a declining share of net capital formation.[4]

As was stressed throughout Chapter 1, the proposition that public goods must be provided for publicly means that they must be financed through the budget, not that they must be publicly produced. Now it should be noted that the facilities for private capital accumulation are limited at early stages of development, as is entrepreneurial talent. For these reasons public production of certain capital goods may be necessary, even if benefits are of the internal type. This in turn may lead to budgetary provision (in the sense of tax rather than price financing) of such goods.[5] At a later stage,

4. For support of this thesis, see R. Nurkse, *Problems of Capital Formation of Underdeveloped Countries* (Oxford, Basil Blackwell and Mott, 1958), pp. 58–67; W. Arthur Lewis, *The Theory of Economic Growth* (Homewood, Ill., R. D. Irwin, 1955), p. 211; P. N. Rosenstein-Rodan, "Problems of Industrialization of Eastern and Southeastern Europe," *Economic Journal, 53* (June 1943), 202–11.

5. The reader might rightly feel that allowance for this factor is not compatible with the spirit of our "efficient" model and that it should be reclassified as a conditioning or political factor.

the institutions for private capital formation become more developed and provision of such capital goods may be left to the private sector. Considerations of this sort offer a second reason why the share of publicly provided capital goods may fall.

This hypothesis is reasonable, but it covers only movement along the earlier to middle stages of economic development. There may well be periods, at a later stage, when the public component of net investment is again rising. As per capita income rises, budget patterns are changed. Private goods which demand complementary public investment may come to the fore, and this in turn may raise the share of public investment. Thus the fiscal systems of European countries will be burdened heavily in the next decade by a greatly increased need for highway facilities, due to the fact that the rise of consumer incomes will permit widespread use of automobiles. The development of urban concentration in conjunction with industrialization calls for municipal programs involving large public investment. Increased need for skilled labor places higher demands upon education and the need for human investment. In high income countries such as the United States, the development of urban slums and the migration of higher income population to suburbia calls for urban redevelopment and expanded commuter facilities, and so forth. At the same time, the changing private consumption patterns also call for complementary private investment, so that the net effect on the public share depends on the particular case.

In short, the ratio of public to total capital formation may be expected to be high at early stages and to decline at least temporarily after the "take-off" is reached. At the same time, there may well be periods at later stages of development when the ratio of public to total capital formation rises. Much depends on the particular stage of income and its capital requirements, and there is little reason to expect a continuous trend to prevail.

Apart from the composition of capital formation, it should be noted that the ratio of total (public plus private) capital formation to GNP tends to rise with economic development. This will counterbalance a possible tendency for a declining ratio of public to private capital formation and tend to maintain the ratio of public capital formation to GNP.

Consumption. Turning now to public consumption, the basic question is whether the income elasticity of demand for public consumer goods is in excess of unity.[6] That is to say, will the demand for consumer goods the benefits of which are highly externality intensive, and which therefore are publicly provided, absorb an increasing share of income as per capita income rises?

In line with an expanded Engel's law, the share of consumer outlays going into private expenditures on the basic needs for food, shelter, and clothing declines as income rises. But there are also certain public services which meet basic needs such as protection and other rudimentary functions of government. Much the same argument can be made regarding these, so that no simple presumption regarding the changing ratio of private to public outlays emerges on these grounds. Nevertheless, there seems to remain a case for the primacy of private expenditures at very low levels of income when food, shelter, and clothing are all that can be provided. As some slack develops, resources may be applied to satisfy secondary needs, and these will call for a larger public goods share, i.e. education, health facilities, safety, and other items which fall on the borderline of the division between consumption and capital formation. Considerations such as these suggest a rising public to private consumption ratio over the early stages of economic growth, but the case appears less clear than with regard to capital formation.

6. Price elasticity of demand will enter as well if the relative prices of public and private goods change as per capita income rises. Since there is no reason to expect a systematic relationship of this sort, the problem is primarily one of income elasticity.

Theory of Expenditure Development

Over subsequent stages, prospects for a rising ratio of public to private outlays are again strengthened by the hypothesis that the pattern of private consumption, which develops at rising levels of per capita income, includes an increasing share of goods, utilization of which requires complementary public services. In the affluent society, a rising share of consumer expenditures flows into "adult toys" for leisure time use, such as pleasure cars, motorboats, and other durables serving luxury consumption. These toys are frequently such as to require substantial public outlays to provide the requisite facilities for their use, either in the form of public investment in high-speed roads, marinas, parks, and so forth, or in the form of services such as traffic patrols, park services, or weather reporting.

Furthermore, the increasing complexity of economic organization, which goes with economic growth, may generate a new set of basic public services which are of a remedial sort.[7] The emergence of corporations and large enterprises necessitates the services of regulatory agencies such as the Interstate Commerce Commission and the Securities and Exchange Commission, and the antitrust activities of the Justice Department. Higher population density raises the need for traffic patrols; advancing industrialization calls for measures to counteract air and water pollution, and so forth. These activities clearly make for an increased absolute level of public activity, but they need not make for a rising public share. The development of remedial activities is not limited to the public sector but has its counterpart in private services. Thus private swimming pools are needed as public beaches become overcrowded. Residences are moved to suburbs as cities deteriorate, and so forth. Thus the rising need for remedial output does not necessarily make for a rising public share, since remedial needs may also call for increased supply of private goods. The scope of merit goods, a final

7. See my *Theory of Public Finance*, p. 189.

aspect of the allocation problem, will be examined briefly after considering the distribution function.

Next the changing weight of transfers in the distribution of income is examined. The combination of tax and transfer policies serves to rearrange the distribution of income as determined by factor returns and endowments in the market. Let us suppose first that the distribution of factor earnings does not change with the rise of per capita income and that the goal of redistributional policy remains constant.

Much depends in this case on how the goal is defined. If (1) the purpose is to reduce inequality, as measured by, say, a Lorenz coefficient, to a certain level, the transfer share in total income will remain unchanged (and the absolute level of transfers will rise) as per capita income rises. The same holds if redistribution aims at providing each family with a given minimum income but the minimum is defined as a fixed percentage of average income. The case differs if (2) the purpose of distributional adjustments is not the reduction of inequality per se, but assurance of an absolute minimum standard of living as determined by an objective criterion such as nutritional requirements. The requisite ratio of transfers to total income (and, indeed, the per capita level of transfers) will now fall as per capita income rises.

It is evident, without further pursuit of this, that the relationship between the transfer share and the level of per capita income depends on the objective of the distributional adjustment; but since assurance of an absolute minimum standard is at least part of the picture, the transfer share may well fall with rising income.

Certain considerations may be added which qualify this expectation. Even though distributional objectives are held constant, the objective need for distributional measures may change with economic development. Thus, the distribution of factor income may become more equal, due to wider distribution of human investment and of property ownership, thereby reducing the need for distributional measures.[8] Or urbanization and increasing interdependence may raise economic risks, thus increasing the need for social insurance, both with regard to unemployment and old age.

Finally, there are the questions of whether society can "afford" any desired degree of redistribution, and of how this relates to the level of income. It is frequently said that low income countries are handicapped in their growth policy by pressures for welfare measures copied from more advanced countries. If the private savings rate is reduced by equalizing transfer measures, the growth rate may be retarded. And even if the desired savings rate is restored through public saving, other disincentive effects might result. Redistribution may thus involve a cost in terms of growth. But as per capita income rises, growth becomes less urgent. The social cost of redistribution, therefore, declines and (contrary to our earlier hypotheses) the transfer share may be expected to rise.

There must be added the complicating fact that redistribution need not involve transfer payments. It may take the form of financing general expenditures by progressive taxation which, in principle, is equivalent to a combination of benefit taxation with a progressive tax-transfer scheme.[9] It may also take the form of subsidies in kind, thus again raising the previously mentioned case of merit wants.

MERIT WANTS

There is no evident presumption as to why public expenditures for the satisfaction of such wants should rise or fall, relative to GNP, as per capita income increases. Having provided for the proper state of distribution by tax-transfer measures, why should there be more reason to interfere with

8. See p. 24.
9. See my *Theory of Public Finance*, Chap. 2.

consumer choice at low income levels, where the choice may be between better clothing and more adequate food, than at high ones, where the choice may be between a second car and a motorboat?

Posing the question in this way is to answer it in the negative, but this may not be the right way of putting it. In practice, merit wants tend to be associated closely with redistribution. Public expenditures for low-cost housing or free hospitalization for the needy combine redistributional objectives with the substitution of imposed for free consumer choice. The imposition of public choice typically relates to the consumption of "necessities," suggesting a basically different view of redistribution. Putting it in extreme form, let us assume a social philosophy which postulates that everybody should consume a certain amount of basic necessities, such as food, clothing, and shelter, but that the distribution of income available for discretionary use is of no social concern. This would suggest that such items would be provided to everyone through the budget; but since they are purchased privately by consumers with higher incomes, public provision may be limited to the lower end of the income scale. If the relevant concept of necessities is defined in absolute terms, this reasoning suggests a falling share of merit wants with rising per capita income. However this may be, it is evident that the prevalence of merit-type expenditures complicates the interpretation of expenditure trends, as it extends the operation of distributional objectives beyond the transfer and into the purchase category.

While these speculations yield no unique hypothesis for the development of the total expenditures share, something can be said about each of the major categories. There is reason to expect that the public share in total capital formation will be relatively high at early stages of development, with less predictable fluctuations thereafter, and that the ratio of transfers (including expenditures for low-income-oriented merit goods) will tend to decline with rising income. Also, there may be a tendency for the ratio of public to private consumption to rise with rising income. Intuition does not tell us how these three trends may be expected to compound into changes in the overall public expenditure to GNP ratio. Moreover, these economic forces are not readily verifiable since they operate concurrently with other variables which may be of equal or greater importance. To these we now turn.

CONDITIONING FACTORS

So far, we have disregarded certain conditioning factors of change which have important bearing on the efficient expenditure share and which operate on both the numerator and denominator of the expenditure ratio. These can readily be incorporated into our economic model.

DEMOGRAPHIC CHANGE

Demographic factors are an important determinant of the level of public expenditures, and the share of public expenditures in total outlay. Both changes in absolute population size and in age structure are relevant.

Beginning with absolute population increase, suppose first that the level of per capita income is not affected. Such an increase will call for absolute expansion of basic public services and an increased level of expenditures thereon. While this would not be the case if public goods were indeed available for joint consumption by the entire group, many of the goods and services in question are available to subgroups (e.g. residents of particular cities) only, or represent mixed goods and services the cost of which is not independent of the number of consumers served (i.e. fire protection). But though there is a strong presumption that the absolute level of public expenditures rises with population, effects on the public expenditure share are less obvious. Much will depend on the location pattern of the growing population, the bearing of density on service costs, the presence of economies or diseconomies of scale, and so forth. While it seems likely that a more crowded world will need to spend a larger share of its output on public goods than did Robinson Crusoe and his friend Friday, the case is not as clear-cut. Increased density may involve economies as well as diseconomies in the use of public services.

Changes in the growth rate of population also affect the population structure, and changes in age composition call for varying allocations to particular public services. Thus the ratio of school expenditures to GNP, current and especially capital, is closely related to the ratio of school age children to population; a high ratio of aged calls for a larger share of retirement assistance, and so forth. Moreover, increased life expectancy raises the return on investment in education and thus justifies larger outlays. Economies of scale are again a factor in determining the effects of such changes on expenditure shares, and may operate as either a strengthening or a dampening factor.

TECHNOLOGICAL CHANGE

Next, there is the impact of technological change upon the public expenditure share, a crucial factor especially in the historical approach to expenditure growth. As technology changes, new products become available and the mix of desired goods changes. Depending upon the nature of the technical change, the relative importance of externality-intensive or social goods may change as well. The invention and rise of the automobile provides the most startling illustration. Highway construction in response to the rise of the automobile in the United States was one of the major factors of expansion in state finances during the interwar years, and a similar experience is now in the making in Europe. Similarly, it is not unreasonable to expect that the future share of public expenditures in GNP will be affected greatly by the development of space technology and by the extent to which related needs can be met privately or must be provided for through the public budget. The implications of changing military technology provide another illustration. Thus technical change will result in unpredictable departures from such basic relation between the expenditure to GNP ratio and per capita income as would prevail under constant technology.

Also there is the problem of statistical bias which arises from differential productivity gains. If, as has been suggested, productivity gains have been greater in the production of private than of social goods, use of an undeflated expenditure to GNP ratio will overstate the gain in the public expenditure share.[10] This may have been the case at a time when public purchases were highly labor intensive, while technical change has been capital saving. Over recent decades, the opposite may hold, as defense purchases have become a large share of the budget and defense industries have been subject to the most rapid technical change.

SOCIAL, CULTURAL, AND POLITICAL FACTORS

A quite different set of factors, noneconomic in nature, which cannot be readily incorporated into the economic model but nevertheless have important bearing on the expenditure ratio, remain to be considered. Changes in cultural values and social philosophy affect the extent to which distributional adjustments are desired, and may bear also on the degree to which demand is directed at public as against private goods. Changes in political structure, moreover, alter the effective demand (distribution of votes) for

10. See Suphan Andic and Jindrich Veverka, "The Growth of Government Expenditures in Germany since the Unification," *Finanzarchiv*, N.F., *23* (January 1964), 178.

public goods, and hence affect expenditure levels. War finance interrupts the steady path of fiscal development and may have profound aftereffects.

SOCIAL CHANGE

The growing sense of social responsibility for the welfare of individuals, which characterized the course of political thought during this century, greatly increased the demand for transfer programs, and acceptance of a larger role of the state reduced political resistance to the allocation of resources for the provision of public goods. These changes have occurred at different speeds in various countries—witness the quarter-century lag in the United States pattern behind that of Europe—but the general trend has been similar throughout. Undoubtedly it deserves major weight in explaining the rising public expenditure share during this century.

Changes in political structure were equally favorable. Transition from authoritarian to representative government strengthened the effective demand for social goods, as did the subsequent democratization of representative forms of government through the broadening of suffrage. Since redistribution through tax-transfer programs was more difficult to achieve than through finance of public services by progressive taxation, the expansion of public services served in part as a means of implementing redistributional measures.

But this may not be a continuing process. At a time when the budget to GNP ratio was relatively low, the voting block comprised by the low and lower-middle income groups could readily place the burden of increased outlays upon the high income minority.[11] The turning point in this process may well have been reached in the postwar period. With a rising budget to GNP ratio, revenue needs come to exceed the tax base available in the high income brackets, and

11. See K. Wicksell, *Finanztheoretische Untersuchungen* (Jena, Fischer, 1896), p. 122; reprinted in Musgrave and Peacock, *Classics in the Theory of Public Finance*, p. 95.

additional expenditure programs come to be financed increasingly by drafts on taxpayers in the middle to lower income groups, where the tax base broadens out with the income pyramid. The impact of the marginal tax dollar moves down the income scale as the average budget to GNP ratio rises. The voting constellation changes, and it becomes more difficult to find a majority in favor of expanding budgets.

A final factor in the politics of fiscal expansion relates to the built-in revenue response to economic growth. The faster the economy grows, the greater will be the "fiscal dividend" or built-in revenue gain with constant rates of tax. Given the asymmetry of political behavior which shows voters more eager to reduce rates than they are willing to raise them, a rising absolute level of public expenditures becomes permissible as the economy grows. But this need not imply a rising expenditure to GNP *ratio*. Such will be the case only if the income elasticity of tax yield exceeds unity, i.e. if the tax structure is distinctly progressive over the relevant income range, or if the tax base increases as a component of GNP.[12]

WAR AND SOCIAL DISTURBANCE

It remains to consider the role of war and of major social disturbances such as the great depression of the thirties. Such events may have a profound effect on the timing of expenditure growth, causing sharp temporary departure from underlying trends; beyond this, they may have a lasting effect on the trend line itself.

Figure 3–1 shows three possible patterns of influence. We assume throughout that during a war the displacement required by the increase in war expenditures is spread between

12. In the Germany of the fifties, for instance, yield elasticity of the personal income tax was very high because a rising share of personal income moved above the initially relatively high exemption level. Given a low exemption level, such as in the United States, the GNP elasticity of income tax yield is but slightly above 1, and that of the total tax structure will be close to 1 if viewed in the secular context.

FIGURE 3-1

Public Expenditure Patterns
War and Postwar

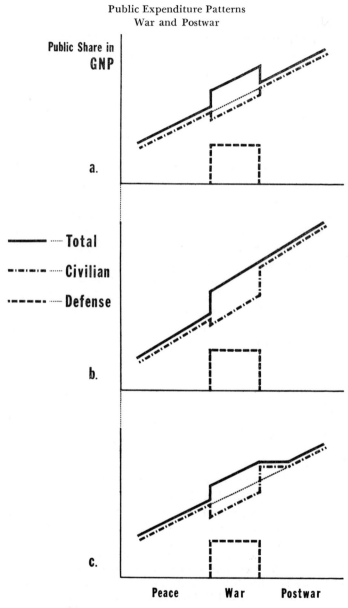

88

public and private civilian uses. Thus, total public expenditures rise sharply, but the increase is below that of war expenditures. This is more realistic than to assume that the entire replacement is in civilian public or in private expenditures.[13]

Our primary interest is in the postwar development, and here the three models differ. In case *a* we assume that civilian public expenditures resume their old growth path after the war. In case *b* we assume that the wartime trend of total public expenditure increase is maintained, with a postwar upward shift in the level of civilian public expenditures. In case *c* we assume a temporary postwar rise in civilian public expenditures which, however, continues only until the old trend line is reached. The long-run effects are thus similar to case *a*, leaving the level of civilian and total public expenditure as it would have been in the absence of war. There is no permanent displacement effect. Such effect only arises in case *b*, where there has been a permanent displacement of private by civilian public expenditures.

Which of these patterns (or combinations thereof) applies depends on public attitudes toward tax and expenditure policies. Our earlier model of efficient expenditure determination would suggest pattern *a*. The temporary displacement of resources for peacetime use would be spread between both civilian and public peacetime uses, and the longer run pattern would not be changed. Pattern *c* may be considered a qualified version of pattern *a*, as the filling of backlog needs results in a temporary increase in the public service level.

Pattern *b* requires a different explanation. Political behavior may be such that the voting public (or the ruling group) is unwilling or hesitant to accept an increase in tax

13. By marking the vertical axis as public expenditure share in GNP but relating the argument to tax rates, we assume that tax and expenditure rates will move together. This is proper for the trend line, which is our major concern. During the war, the rate of debt finance is likely to increase, which may reduce dampening effects on civilian public outlays.

rates. There is a bias against public and in favor of private goods. As noted before, this is not in line with our efficient behavior model, but it may nevertheless reflect the actual situation. Now a war comes along and, considering the urgency of the need for defense outlays, a threshold effect results. The resistance to higher taxes is overcome, and once overcome, the threshold of resistance is moved to a higher level. Thus, civilian public expenditures fill the gap after the war, and the public expenditure share is permanently raised.

In addition, it may be that wars or other major events in the history of a nation, such as the great depression, lead to a reassessment of social values or change in the power balance of political groups. This may result in a changed pattern of preferences for public and private wants and may lead to an increase in the public expenditure share. Discontinuous changes in preference pattern, associated with wars and other social disturbances, may thus have been a major factor in the cultural-political environment which determines expenditure choice.

Both these factors—the threshold effect and the change in preferences—help to explain case b and both are noted by Peacock and Wiseman in explaining their displacement effect, to which they ascribe a central role in determining expenditure increase.[14] Following case b, these forces are said to have a lasting effect on expenditure levels. Without national crisis, the tax rate threshold would not have been broken, and the change in philosophy would not have occurred. This does not exclude the temporary operation of such forces, in line with pattern c, where a temporary shift in tax threshold may explain the willingness to meet backlog needs. But the more important point, made by these authors, is that pattern b may explain a lasting rise in expenditure levels.

14. See Alan T. Peacock and Jack Wiseman, *The Growth of Public Expenditure in the United Kingdom,* National Bureau of Economic Research, (Princeton, Princeton University Press, 1961), pp. 24 ff.

4 EMPIRICAL EVIDENCE ON EXPENDITURE DEVELOPMENT

We now consider what empirical evidence there is to support the hypothesis of a rising expenditure share. Beginning with a historical (time trend) view, we examine the course of public expenditures in the United Kingdom, the United States, and Germany, covering the period from 1890 to date. Over this period, per capita real income rose sharply —nearly quadrupling in the United States—and the question is whether there was a corresponding expansion of the public sector.

HISTORICAL VIEW

The share of the public sector will be measured broadly as the ratio of public expenditures to GNP,[1] and total ex-

1. The proper expression depends on what is to be measured. If purchases only are included in the numerator, the national product total is the proper denominator. Depending on whether or not depreciation of public assets is included in purchases, gross or net national product provides the appropriate base; and depending on whether or not government purchases are subject to indirect taxes, market price or factor cost is called for.

If transfers to persons only are included in the numerator, the appropriate choice of denominator would be personal income. If both transfers to persons and firms are included, national income must be used.

If transfers and purchases are combined into a total expenditure

91

penditures (including all levels of government) are considered.[2]

TIME TRENDS[3]

As shown in Table 4–1, total public expenditures (col. 1) as per cent of GNP increased sharply in all three countries, the rise from 1890 to date being from 7 to 33 per cent in the United States, 9 to 38 per cent in the United Kingdom, and 13 to 44 per cent in Germany.[4] Plotted in Figures 4–1 to 4–3, the same data—with reference years chosen so as to omit wartime peaks—reveal a rather steady pattern of increase in the expenditure to GNP ratio. On the overall basis at least, Wagner's law well meets the test of Western economic development during the last three-quarters of a century.

---

figure, no very satisfactory definition of expenditure share is possible; but looked at from the income side, total tax revenue may be related meaningfully to gross or net national product.

2. This leaves open the question of how expenditure growth is affected by and affects the degree of fiscal centralization. For a discussion of the "concentration process," see Peacock and Wiseman, *Growth of Public Expenditures in the United Kingdom,* Chap. 6. Also, see p. 344 below.

3. For time trend studies of government expenditures see M. Copeland, *Trends in Government Financing,* National Bureau of Economic Research (Princeton, Princeton University Press, 1961); S. P. Gupta, "The Size and Growth of Government Expenditures" (doctoral dissertation, University of York, England, 1965); and "Public Expenditures and Economic Growth," *Public Finance, 22,* no. 4 (1967); Ursula K. Hicks, *British Public Finances 1880–1952* (London, Oxford University Press, Home University Library, 1954); Richard A. Musgrave and J. M. Culbertson, "The Growth of Public Expenditures in the United States 1890–1948," *National Tax Journal, 6,* no. 2 (June 1953); Peacock and Wiseman; Andic and Veverka, "Growth of Government Expenditures in Germany," *Finanzarchiv, 23* (1964).

4. We do not claim that the data here presented are strictly comparable, as certain conceptual differences arise regarding both the expenditure and GNP definitions.

Moreover, this picture is not changed greatly if civilian and defense expenditures are considered separately. The upward trend in the ratio of defense expenditures to GNP is accompanied by a parallel and, with the exception of the United States, even steeper increase in the ratio of civilian expenditure to GNP. As shown in Table 4–1 (cols. 2 and 7) and in the figures, the hypothesis of a rising public share is borne out for the two components separately as well as for the total. While the civilian ratio rises at a different pace for the various countries—witness the lag in the United States ratio up to the recent past—the general picture is nevertheless fairly uniform. The parallel rise of both ratios suggests that the taxable capacity constraint was not sufficient to restrain the increase in civilian functions in the face of rising priority needs for defense; going further, it suggests that the displacement effect of rising defense needs included both civilian public and private resource use.

Continuing the disaggregation, Table 4–1 gives a breakdown of the civilian expenditure increase among the major functions. A fairly uniform pattern emerges. General governmental expenditures defined to include law, order, and administration have expanded at over twice the rate of GNP, but have remained a small factor in the total picture. The ratio for expenditures on environmental and economic services shows a somewhat faster rise. For all three countries, however, the big factor of increase is in the social service category, defined here to include education, welfare programs, social insurance, and housing. This is the case especially for the later decades, but even for the period as a whole this category accounted for a large part of the increase in the total civilian expenditure to GNP ratio, more precisely, 82 per cent for the United Kingdom, 66 per cent for the United States, and (with 1913 as base) 72 per cent for Germany. Apart from defense, which accounts for nearly 50 per cent of the gain in the United States, the rise in the overall expenditure to GNP ratio has been due primarily to

TABLE 4-1

Government Expenditures by Functions as Per Cent of GNP
(all levels of government)

| | Total | Defense | Public Debt | Civilian | | | |
| | | | | Law, Order, and Administration | Economic and Environmental Services | Social Services | Total (4-6) |
	(1)	(2)	(3)	(4)	(5)	(6)	(7)
United States[a]							
1890	7.1	1.4	0.7	1.2	2.0	1.8	5.0
1902	7.9	1.5	0.5	1.1	2.1	1.9	5.1
1913	8.5	1.1	0.4	0.9	2.6	2.1	5.6
1922	12.6	1.9	1.9	0.9	3.6	3.5	8.0
1927	11.7	1.2	1.4	0.8	3.6	3.2	7.6
1932	21.3	2.8	2.3	1.6	6.0	6.3	13.9
1940	22.2	2.3	1.7	1.2	7.2	6.9	15.3
1948	23.0	8.4	2.0	0.9	3.4	6.2	10.5
1957	28.5	10.7	1.5	0.9	5.1	8.0	14.0
1962	33.2	10.6	1.7	1.0	6.3	11.0	18.3
United Kingdom[b]							
1890	8.9	2.4	1.6	1.7	1.3	1.9	4.9
1900	14.4	6.9	1.0	1.4	2.5	2.6	6.5
1913	12.4	3.7	0.8	1.6	2.2	4.1	7.9

Year							
1923	24.2	3.2		7.1	2.0	3.4	8.5	13.9
1929	23.9	2.7		6.6	1.7	3.4	9.5	14.6
1932	28.6	2.8		7.1	1.9	3.9	12.9	18.7
1938	30.0	8.9		4.0	1.9	3.9	11.3	17.1
1950	39.0	7.2		4.4	3.7[c]	5.7	18.0	27.4
1955	36.6	9.6		4.2	2.3	4.3	16.3	22.9
1963	38.0	6.5		3.3	n.a.	n.a.	n.a.	28.2
Germany[d]								
1891	13.2		2.5		n.a.	n.a.	n.a.	9.9
1901	14.9		3.3		n.a.	n.a.	n.a.	11.5
1913	14.8	3.3		0.7	2.4	2.2	5.1	9.7
1925	25.0	3.6		0.2	4.3	2.7	14.3	21.3
1929	30.6	3.9		0.6	4.2	3.2	19.3	26.7
1932	36.6	2.7		1.2	5.6	3.3	24.8	33.7
1950	40.8	6.5		0.8	4.6	4.6	24.2	33.4
1958	44.1	5.2		0.9	4.0	6.1	27.9	38.0

a. For sources see Appendix Table 4. Includes minor items not listed separately.

b. See Peacock and Wiseman, *Growth of Public Expenditures*, p. 190.

c. Column includes overseas services, which were 0.1 per cent or less prior to 1950, 1.5 per cent for 1950, and 0.5 per cent for 1955.

d. Based on Andic and Veverka, "Growth of Government Expenditures in Germany," *Finanzarchiv*, N.F., 23 (January 1964), 241–42 and 258.

the growth of social services. This reflects in particular a growing redistributional concern, rather than a rising demand for social goods as such. It appears that the underlying forces of social and political change greatly outweighed any

FIGURE 4–1

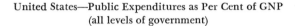

United States—Public Expenditures as Per Cent of GNP
(all levels of government)

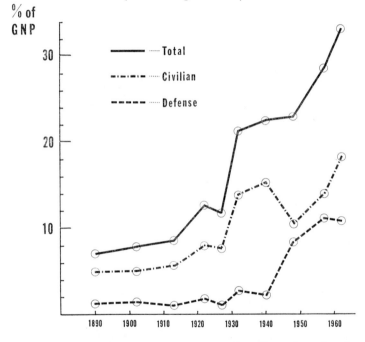

tendency, such as suggested in our earlier discussion, for the transfer share to fall with rising per capita income.

The rise in the relative importance of social services, which make heavy use of transfer payments, suggests a considerable increase in the importance of transfer payments relative to public purchases. As shown in Table 4–2 and in Figures 4–4 to 4–6, this was not strongly so. In the case of

Evidence on Expenditure Development

the United States and the United Kingdom, the increase in
the transfer to GNP ratio roughly matches that of the
civilian purchases to GNP ratio, and only in Germany does

FIGURE 4–2

United Kingdom—Public Expenditures as Per Cent of GNP
(all levels of government)

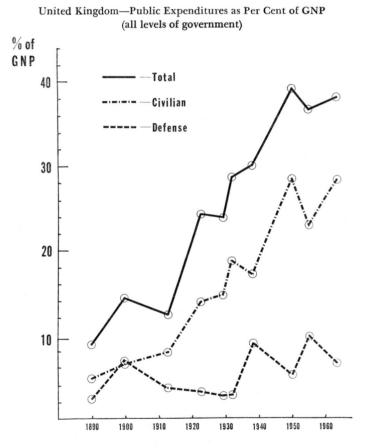

the rise in the transfer ratio outstrip that in the public purchase ratio. The expansion in the social service share, it
appears, included a substantial component of welfare serv-

FIGURE 4–3

Germany—Public Expenditures as Per Cent of GNP
(all levels of government)

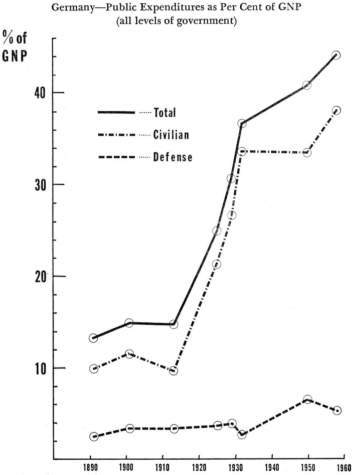

ices or merit goods. Redistribution took the form of provision for certain service levels, rather than of cash grants.

Turning now to a breakdown in government purchases between consumption and capital expenditures, data for the United Kingdom show both to have grown at about the same rate. Capital outlays fluctuate around 20 per cent of the total, with the ratio somewhat lower for civilian than for defense purchases.[5] For the United States, capital outlays as a percentage of total state and local expenditures similarly move between 20 and 30 per cent, with no visible trend during the last fifty years.[6]

INCOME ELASTICITIES

The same data are rearranged in Table 4–3 to show income elasticities for various expenditure functions, as well as marginal propensities to spend thereon. As may be seen from the table, the income elasticity of total expenditures before 1929 was substantially higher in the United Kingdom and in Germany than in the United States, but United States elasticity was higher thereafter. Reflecting the same catching-up process, we note that elasticities in the United Kingdom and Germany were higher in 1890–1929 than from 1929 to date, while the United States shows the opposite pattern.

Looking at the matter in terms of marginal propensities to spend, the United States ratio is again much the lowest for the early period, but closer to that of the other countries after 1929. The German ratio is the highest throughout. The different nature of the two indicators is brought out by noting that in the post-1929 period the income elasticity for the United States was much above that for Germany, whereas the German marginal propensity to spend was much above that of the United States. The difference may be traced to the much higher initial level of the average expenditure ratio for Germany.

Considering civilian expenditures only, the United Kingdom shows nearly the same income elasticity, for the period

5. See Peacock and Wiseman, p. 81.
6. See U.S. Bureau of the Census, *Historical Statistics on Governmental Finances and Employment* (Washington, D.C., G.P.O., 1962), p. 38.

TABLE 4-2

Government Expenditures by Economic Category as Per Cent of GNP at Factor Cost
(all levels of government)

	Purchases			Transfers	Interest on Public Debt	Total
	Military (1)	Civilian (2)	Total (3)	(4)	(5)	(6)
United States[a]						
1890	0.4	5.5	5.9	0.1	0.4	6.4
1902	1.0	5.3	6.3	0.2	0.1	6.6
1913	0.5	5.5	6.0	0.9	0.1	7.0
1923	0.7	6.7	7.4	1.3	1.4	10.1
1929	1.3	7.4	8.7	0.9	1.0	10.6
1932	2.9	12.8	15.7	2.6	2.1	20.4
1940	2.4	13.1	15.5	3.0	1.4	19.9
1948	4.9	9.6	14.5	4.7	1.9	21.1
1963	10.5	13.5	24.0	7.0	1.6	32.6
United Kingdom[b]						
1890	2.3	4.3	6.6	0.7	1.6	8.9
1900	7.0	5.7	12.7	0.9	1.0	14.6
1910	3.4	6.8	10.2	1.6	0.9	12.7
1920	8.4	7.9	16.3	4.5	5.4	26.2
1928	2.8	9.6	12.4	5.1	6.7	24.2
1933	2.7	10.1	12.8	7.5	5.5	25.8

	1	2	3	4	5	6
1938	8.9	10.8	19.7	6.3	4.0	30.0
1955	9.4	13.3	22.7	9.7	4.2	36.6
1963	6.5	16.0	22.5	12.2	3.3	38.0
Germany[c]						
1881	2.5	6.8	9.3	n.a.	0.7	10.0
1891	3.3	8.7	12.0	0.4	0.8	13.2
1901	3.4	9.4	12.8	0.9	1.2	14.9
1907	3.5	10.8	14.3	1.0	1.2	16.5
1913	3.6	8.6	12.2	1.9	0.7	14.8
1929	1.0	15.1	16.1	13.9	0.6	30.6
1932	1.5	17.6	19.1	16.2	1.2	36.5
1950	5.5	14.9	20.4	19.5	0.8	40.7
1955	4.1	15.2	19.3	18.7	1.0	39.0
1958	4.4	16.2	20.6	22.5	0.9	44.0

a. For sources see Appendix Table 5.

b. Figures for 1890–1955 based on Peacock and Wiseman, pp. 80–82. For 1963 col. 1 excludes expenditures on civil defense; col. 2 includes debt interest paid by local authorities; col. 3 includes housing subsidies; col. 4 is exceptionally high due to large capital grants to public companies to write off debt.

c. Col. 1 from Andic and Veverka, p. 261; it is assumed that totals for defense given there are for goods and services. Col. 2 equals col. 3 minus col. 1. Cols. 3 and 4 from Andic and Veverka, p. 252. Col. 4 equals the percentages for transfers and subsidies given there, minus col. 5 of this table. It includes "other transfers and subsidies," not shown separately in col. 5. Cols. 5 and 6 from Table 4–1. For col. 4, figures for 1881–1907 are estimated independently. They include social security transfers and may be less inclusive than those for later years.

as a whole, as it does for total expenditures. The marginal propensity to consume for civilian expenditures, at the

FIGURE 4-4

United States—Civilian Purchases and Transfers as Per Cent of GNP
(all levels of government)

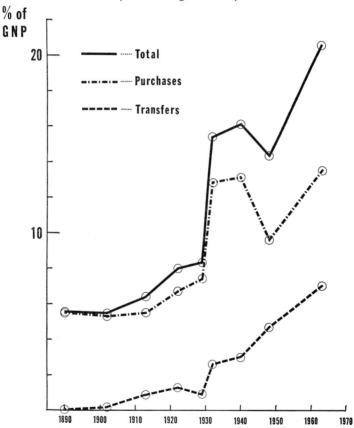

same time, is less than for total outlays and remarkably stable. For the United States, the elasticity of civilian expenditures in the post-1929 period is below that for total

FIGURE 4–5

United Kingdom—Civilian Purchases and Transfers as Per Cent of GNP
(all levels of government)

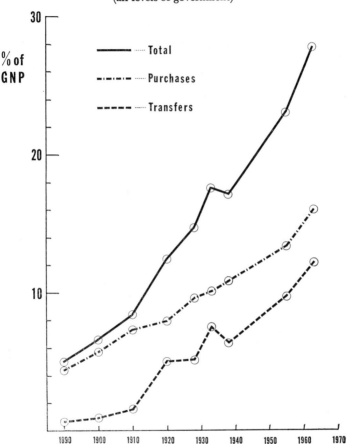

outlays. If transfers are excluded and purchases for civilian programs only are allowed for, elasticities are reduced. This is the case especially for Germany, where propensities to spend now are highly stable.

In all, the picture is one of general advance in the expend-

FIGURE 4-6

German—Civilian Purchases and Transfers as Per Cent of GNP
(all levels of government)

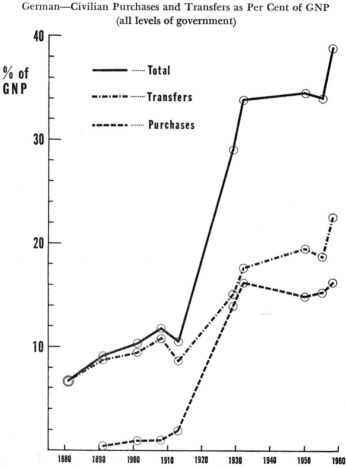

iture to GNP ratio, including military as well as civilian functions, with welfare expenditures accounting for a large share of the latter's gain. The rising ratio includes goods and services expenditures as well as transfer payments, and though timing differs in the various countries, the similari-

TABLE 4–3

Government Expenditures in Relation to GNP

	Total Expenditures		Civilian Expenditures		Civilian Purchases	
	Income Elasticity	Marginal Propensities to Spend	Income Elasticity	Marginal Propensities to Spend	Income Elasticity	Marginal Propensities to Spend
	(1)	(2)	(3)	(4)	(5)	(6)
United States[a]						
1890–1963	4.8	.30	3.5	.21	2.4	.13
1890–1929	1.5	.10	1.7	.09	1.4	.07
1929–1963	3.5	.34	2.4	.23	2.0	.13
United Kingdom[b]						
1890–1955	4.5	.39	4.4	.29	3.5	.14
1890–1928	3.7	.32	4.4	.29	3.1	.12
1928–1955	1.7	.41	1.3	.29	1.5	.15
Germany[b]						
1891–1958	3.7	.48	4.3	.44	1.7	.17
1891–1929	3.0	.38	3.8	.37	1.6	.17
1929–1958	1.9	.53	1.6	.47	1.1	.17

a. Based on expenditure figures in Appendix Table 5.
b. For sources see notes to Tables 4–1 and 4–2.

ties in overall results are rather impressive for the seventy-year period.

It remains to return to the role of war expenditures. Such expenditures have introduced sharp fluctuations into the otherwise more or less steady upward course of the public expenditure to GNP ratio. Traditionally the share of public expenditures has reached peak levels during war periods, and over the years these peak levels have tended to rise. Moreover, the aftermath of war has become increasingly expensive, as defense expenditures have continued to absorb a larger share of the budget even in postwar periods. These tendencies are illustrated for the United States and the United Kingdom in Table 4–4, where the fiscal implications of World Wars I and II are compared.

The table shows that the GNP share of civilian expenditures has tended to rise over the span of major war periods, but the nature of this relationship is by no means simple. Clearly the evidence supports the hypothesis that wars lead to temporary peaks in the total expenditure to GNP ratio. Beyond this, the evidence is compatible with the view that war results in a lasting displacement of private expenditure, because war either has raised the acceptable level of tax rates or has increased expenditure needs.[7] At the same time, the data are also compatible with the view that the effects of war are primarily temporary, involving an immediate displacement of private and civilian public expenditures but without much lasting effect on the rising trend of the public expenditure to GNP ratio.[8]

The United States pattern, as traced in **Figure 4–1**, shows a gradual upward trend of the civilian ratio, interrupted by a sharp rise in the first half of the thirties, a fall in the first half of the forties, and a return to the trend curve in the

7. See Peacock and Wiseman.
8. See p. 89.

TABLE 4-4

Public Expenditures During Two World Wars
(all levels of government)

	As Per Cent of GNP				As Per Cent of Total		
	All	Military	Debt	Other	Military	Debt	Other
United Kingdom[a]							
1913	12	4	1	7	30	7	63
1918	52	42	6	4	81	11	8
1922	28	4	8	16	14	30	56
1938	30	9	4	17	30	13	57
1943	74	17	9	48	23	12	65
1948	41	8	5	28	20	11	69
1955	37	10	4	23	26	12	62
United States[b]							
1913	7	1	—	6	16	5	79
1919	50	22	1	27	44	2	54
1922	12	2	2	8	15	15	70
1938	21	2	2	17	10	9	81
1944	51	41	1	9	80	2	18
1948	21	8	2	11	35	9	56
1955	38	12	1	25	42	5	53

a. Source: Peacock and Wiseman, *Growth of Public Expenditures*, pp. 88, 165, and 190.
b. Source: U.S. Bureau of the Census, *Historical Statistics of the United States* (Washington, D.C., G.P.O., 1960).

fifties. The rise in the thirties reflects a precipitous drop in GNP with rigid public expenditure levels, sustained thereafter by rising GNP and expenditure functions under the New Deal. The decline during the war reflects the lag in civilian public expenditures, giving way to defense during the war. Thereafter, the rise resumes and by the late fifties the ratio is again in line with the slowly upward-curving trend since 1890. The defense ratio, in turn, shows a sharp increase from 1940 to 1950, thus accounting for much the larger part of the increase in the overall ratio over the last three decades.

In reading the chart, it must be kept in mind that short-run fluctuations and war peaks are omitted. Yet, the pattern suggests war and cold-war displacement of public expenditures for civilian uses, as much or more than a war-induced increase in postwar civilian expenditure ratios. War, it would seem, brings with it temporary interruptions in the rising trend of the civilian expenditure ratio, rather than causing a lasting displacement of private expenditures, which otherwise would not have occurred. While the breaching of conventional tax limits by war finance is undoubtedly a factor in permitting an abrupt increase in the short-run level of postwar civilian expenditures, the basic forces for long-run expenditure increase may have been much the same with or without war. The more immediate impact of war, it appears, is in the displacement of civilian by military public outlays, rather than in the displacement of private by total public outlays.[9] Moreover, war in the

9. As we read them, the patterns for the United Kingdom and Germany suggest much the same story. Gupta plots annual logarithmic values for total per capita government expenditures and income for various countries. While the value of these results is limited for our purpose since the total is not broken between defense and civilian expenditures, they may nevertheless be noted here.

For the United States Gupta shows the trend line of the thirties to lie above that of the twenties, and with a steeper slope. The trend line for 1949 to 1961 shows a further upward shift, but the slope is again

modern economy tends to be accompanied by an increase in total output, so that the displacement need is less than the increase in military outlay.

If this interpretation is correct, the Peacock-Wiseman displacement thesis becomes a factor of short-run timing rather than long-run trend.[10] But it is the latter that is the essence of historical development, and not the former. To be sure, Peacock and Wiseman do not limit their thesis to war but include the effects of social upheavals (e.g. the great depression) as well. Thus, it may reduce to the proposition that the rise in the expenditure to GNP ratio must have causes, which causes may erupt into expenditure changes of a discontinuous rather than steadily pressing sort. This is surely correct, especially with regard to the welfare component of the expenditure structure, a factor that we found to be the major driving force behind the rise of the civilian expenditure ratio. Yet hidden behind it there are the basic forces of egalitarianism, rooted back in the nineteenth and indeed the close of the eighteenth century; and beyond it, there may be at work an Engel's law type of development process, making for an expansion of the public sector as per capita income rises.

---

similar to that of the twenties. It appears that depression and war combined have had little effect on the slope, or even the level of the longer run trend.

For the United Kingdom the development is broken into three trends, 1896–1910, 1923–37, and 1947–62. Each of the successive lines lies above the other and shows a reduced slope.

For Sweden where the factor of war expenditures was less important, we find a more or less linear trend, and the long-run elasticity of the overall ratio is again fairly similar to that of the other countries.

10. As noted before, Peacock and Wiseman emphasize both the short- and long-run aspects of displacement. See p. 90.

CROSS-SECTION VIEW

Let us now review the problem in cross-section terms.[11] The relationship between the size of the public sector and per capita income is examined for a group of 30 to 40 countries, representing a wide range of per capita income. Averages for the years 1953 and 1958 are used to obtain a representative picture for the mid-fifties.[12] Since the size of the public sector involves both expenditure and tax considerations, overall tax as well as expenditure ratios will be considered.

TOTAL CURRENT EXPENDITURE RATIO

Unfortunately, comparable data on total expenditures are not available for all levels of government, so that current expenditure data have to be used.[13]

11. W. Arthur Lewis and A. M. Martin, "Patterns of Public Revenue and Expenditure," *The Manchester School of Economic and Social Studies, 24* (September 1956), 203–44; H. T. Oshima, "Share of Government in Gross National Product for Various Countries," *American Economic Review, 47* (June 1957); J. G. Williamson, "Public Expenditure and Revenue: An International Comparison," *The Manchester School, 29* (January 1961), 43–56; H. H. Hinrichs, "Determinants of Government Revenue Shares Among Less Developed Countries," *Economic Journal, 75* (September 1965); and Hinrichs, *A General Theory of Tax Structure Change During Economic Development* (Cambridge, Mass., Harvard Law School, 1966), Chap. 2; and Gupta.

12. For details regarding the sample and sources, see Appendix Table 6.

13. The data on current expenditures and tax revenue in the United Nations *Yearbook of National Accounts Statistics* which are here used include all levels of government. The data on total expenditures given in the United Nations *Statistical Yearbook* are generally available for central government only.

An attempt to construct a total (current plus capital) expenditure series was made by adding capital expenditures for central government to current expenditures for total government. The result, applicable to a smaller sample, is shown in equation 27 and is less satisfactory than that for equation 1, which allows for current expenditures only.

Evidence on Expenditure Development

As shown in equation 1 of Table 4–5, the ratio of current expenditures to GNP is related positively to per capita income. The R^2 is .57 and the coefficient is significant at the 55 per cent level. The picture seems in full support of the rising-share hypothesis. But more careful inspection throws doubt on the matter. As shown in equations 2 to 4, the relationship becomes much weaker if the countries are divided into high and low income groups. The relationship breaks down for the low (per capita income below $300) and high (per capita income above $600) groups taken by themselves, and it appears that the good fit for the total group merely reflects a difference in the average levels at the two ends of the scale.

TOTAL TAX REVENUE RATIO

A similar picture emerges if the ratio of tax revenue to GNP is considered. This is not surprising, since tax revenue is highly correlated with expenditures.[14] As shown in equation 5, per capita income is a good predictor of T/GNP if the group as a whole is considered. The correlation coefficients for both simple correlation (Table 4–6) and rank correlation (Table 4–7) support the same conclusion. The fit is improved, as shown in equation 6, if per capita income is used in logarithmic form. Equally good results are obtained if both variables are placed in logarithmic form, where the coefficient now shows the income elasticity of the tax to GNP ratio. As required by Wagner's law, the elasticity is well in excess of zero.

But as with current expenditures, the result deteriorates when countries are divided by income groups. As shown in

14. The correlation coefficients between E_c/GNP and T/GNP for our sample are 0.919 for the total sample; 0.836 for countries with per capita income below $300; 0.858 for below $600; and 0.398 for above $600. For a similar point see both H. T. Oshima and J. G. Williamson.

In the same vein, the results are very similar whether total *tax* revenue or total revenue (including nontax revenues such as fees or monopoly profits) are used. See equations 6 and 28 in Table 4–5.

111

TABLE 4-5

Regressions on Current Expenditures and Revenue*

(figures in parentheses are ratio of regression coefficient and standard error)

Equation	Sample		R^2
1	H	$E_c/GNP = .1198 + .000095Y_c$ $\qquad\quad\ (10.42)\ \ \ (6.63)$	.57
2	H	$E_c/GNP = .1116 + .000055Y_{c<300}$ $\qquad\quad\ (5.08)\ \ \ (0.47)$	.015
3	H	$E_c/GNP = .0972 + .000149Y_{c<600}$ $\qquad\quad\ (0.53)\ \ \ (2.66)$	.271
4	H	$E_c/GNP = .2719 - .000020Y_{c>600}$ $\qquad\quad\ (8.73)\ \ \ (0.79)$	.049
5	A	$T/GNP = .1365 + .000076Y_c$ $\qquad\quad (10.530)\ \ (6.4360)$	.52
6	A	$T/GNP = e^{-3.6896}\ Y_c^{.3369}$ $\qquad\quad\ (-14.90)\ \ (8.1373)$	.64
7	A	$T/GNP = .1029 + 0.0002806Y_{c<300}$ $\qquad\quad\ (4.862)\ \ \ (1.777)$	.16
8	A	$T/GNP = .8420 + .0000301Y_{c<600}$ $\qquad\quad\ (5.3494)\ \ (5.8415)$	.58
9	A	$T/GNP = e^{3.685}\ Y_{c>600}^{-.0535}$ $\qquad\quad\ (3.675)\ \ (-.378)$	.01

10	A	$\dot{\mathrm{Log}}\,(\dot{T}/G\dot{N}P) = 19.087 - 11.7752\log Y_c + 2.1212(\log Y_c)^2 - 0.1215(\log Y_c)^3$ $(-3.1530)(3.2337)(-3.2129)$	.71
11	F	$T/GNP = .2918 - .3947\,Ag/GNP$ $(16.839)(-6.4669)$	.54
12	D	$M/GNP = .2679 - .0000269\,Y_c$ $(7.16504)(-.5873)$	.01
13	D	$T/GNP = .1906 + .0005742\,M/GNP$ $(6.217)(.5346)$	.06
14	D	$T/GNP = .1152 + .001015\,M/GNP + .0001046\,Y_c$ $(4.417)(1.313)(5.348)$	.45
15	D	$T/GNP = .1424 + .0001018\,Y_c$ $(8.881)(5.174)$	.44
16	D	$T/GNP = .1544 + .0005453\,M/GNP$ for $Y_{c<600}$ $(4.376)(.437)$	.10
17	D	$T/GNP = .07081 + .000182\,M/GNP + .03341\,Y_{c<600}$ $(2.804)(.245)(5.874)$	.62
18	D	$T/GNP = .07504 + .0003353\,Y_{c<600}$ $(4.174)(6.076)$	.64
19	D	$T/GNP = .0747 + .000270\,Y_{c<300} + .0649\,M/GNP$ $(3.00)(2.12)(1.04)$	.16
20	I	$(E_c - D)/GNP = .0989 + .000077\,Y_c$ $(6.03)(4.17)$	.392
21	I	$(E_c - D)/GNP = .0539 + .000197\,Y_{c<300}$ $(3.81)(2.52)$	.388

113

TABLE 4-5 (*cont.*)

Regressions on Current Expenditures and Revenue*

(figures in parentheses are ratio of regression coefficient and standard error)

Equation	Sample		R^2
22	I	$(E_c - D)/GNP = \underset{(4.63)}{.0489} + \underset{(5.71)}{.000233Y_{c<600}}$	.715
23	I	$(E_c - D)/GNP = \underset{(7.06)}{.2837} - \underset{(1.98)}{.000063Y_{c>600}}$	.246
24	B	$S/NY = e^{\underset{(-3.170)}{-2.172}} Y_c^{\underset{(6.024)}{.665}}$	.53
25	B	$S/NY = \underset{(.58158)}{.007481} + \underset{(5.30654)}{.00001984Y_{c<600}}$	.62
26	B	$S/NY = \underset{(6.6357)}{.2154} - \underset{(-2.9424)}{.0000745Y_{c>600}}$	.42
27	K	$E_T/GNP = \underset{(5.98)}{.1867} + \underset{(2.51)}{.000109Y_c}$	.327
28	A	$R/GNP = e^{\underset{(6.075)}{-3.258}} Y_c^{\underset{(7.676)}{.2841}}$	.61

* For details see Appendix Table 6. All levels of government are included. E_c is current expenditures; T is total tax revenue; Y_c is per capita GNP; A_g is income originating in agriculture; D is defense expenditure; S is social security expenditures. E_T is total (current plus capital) expenditure; R is total (tax plus nontax) revenue; M is import share.

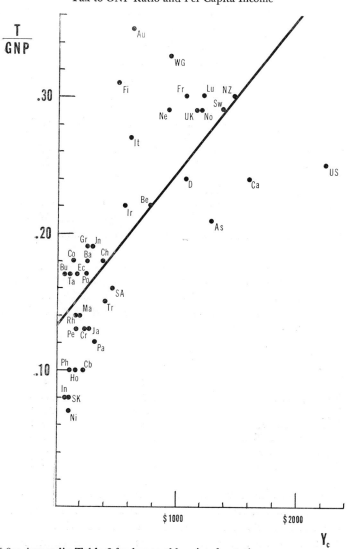

FIGURE 4-7

Tax to GNP Ratio and Per Capita Income*

* See Appendix Table 6 for key to abbreviated notation.

Figure 4–7, the observations fall largely into two groups. One includes low income countries, with per capita income under, say, $400, and is composed mainly of Asian, African,

TABLE 4–6

Correlation Coefficients*

	Y_c	Ag/GNP	T/GNP
T/GNP	0.7236	−0.6488	—
	(6.4627)	(5.1148)	
R/GNP	0.6998	n.c.	0.9800
	(6.0384)		(30.3573)
$(R - D)/GNP$	0.1606	n.c.	0.3860
	(0.9058)		(7.3298)
Ag/GNP	−0.6732	—	n.c.
	(5.4532)		
T_{id}/T	−0.6172	0.6400	−0.6164
	(4.9616)	(4.9973)	(4.8250)

* Figures in parentheses are t values; n.c. means not computed.

and South American countries. The other, following a substantial gap in which observations are sparse, includes high income countries, defined as countries with per capita incomes in excess of $600 and, for the most part, of $1,000.

TABLE 4–7

Rank Correlation Coefficients

	R	t
T/GNP and Y_c	0.8183	9.0043
T_{id}/T and Y_c	−0.4615	3.3311
$Imp./GNP$ and Y_c	0.0484	0.2741
Ag/GNP and T/GNP	−0.6648	5.3398
Ag/GNP and T_{id}/T	0.6344	4.9242
T_{id}/T and T/GNP	−0.6332	5.1798

These include Western European countries, the United States, Canada, Australia, and New Zealand. Throughout, there is a tendency for South American countries to lie low relative to the trend line, whereas European countries lie

116

FIGURE 4-8

Tax to GNP Ratio and Agricultural Share in GNP*

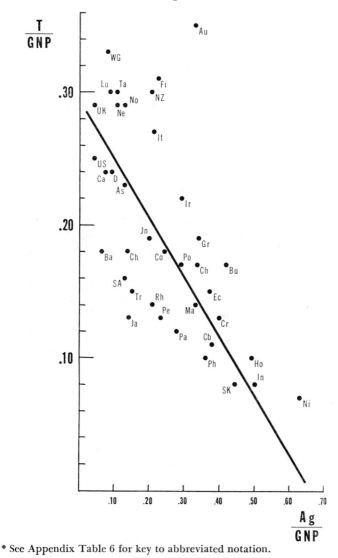

* See Appendix Table 6 for key to abbreviated notation.

high thereto.[15] Explanation of symbols used to denote countries will be found in Appendix Table 6.

Beginning with the lowest income group, including countries with incomes below $300, the relationship (equation 7) between the tax ratio and per capita income breaks down, and the regression coefficient becomes insignificant. The fit is restored if countries with per capita incomes up to $600 are included (equation 8), but again collapses if only the high income group, including countries with per capita incomes above $600, is included. The regression coefficient (equation 9) again becomes insignificant and such relationship as remains turns negative. As shown in Figure 4–7, this reflects the fact that relative to the trend line, the ratios for Austria, West Germany, and Finland are very high, while that for the United States is very low.

The good fit obtained for the sample as a whole is therefore misleading. It does not reflect a continuous tendency, but rather a comparison between the averages for the low and high income groups. The response of the tax-to-GNP ratio to rising per capita income varies over the income range and the question of whether better results may be obtained with a nonlinear relationship arises. Using logarithmic form for both the T/GNP ratio and per capita income, and a binomial function, we find (equation 10) that the R^2 is increased. The coefficients remain significant, though at a lower level. We now find that the elasticity of the T/GNP ratio over the relevant range first rises with rising income, then declines, and eventually turns negative.[16] This is not implausible. At very low levels of income, influences related to the income elasticity of demand for public services may be outweighed by those related to the availability of tax handles. As will be noted presently, lack

15. See also Gupta, p. 189, and Joergen R. Lotz and Elliott R. Morss, "Measuring Tax Effort in Developing Countries," International Monetary Fund, *Staff Papers, 14* (1967).

16. This follows Gupta, p. 65.

of availability of tax handles may be an important limiting factor to the size of the public sector at low levels of income. But as the economy develops, these restrictions become less severe, and the size of the public sector can respond more freely to rising levels of GNP.

TAX CONSTRAINTS AND OPENNESS

In line with this proposition, it has been suggested that the openness of the economy may be an important factor in explaining the size of the public sector. In explaining this hypothesis, we find that the import share (as shown in equation 12) bears little relation to per capita income and that (equation 13) it does not prove a significant determinant of the T/GNP ratio for the sample as a whole. The fit is greatly improved if per capita income is added as an explanatory factor (equation 14), but the import coefficient remains insignificant. Indeed nothing is gained (as shown by comparison with equation 15 which applies to the same sample) if the import ratio is added as an explanatory variable to per capita income. Moreover, the import ratio remains insignificant if the experiment is limited to the low income group. This is the case for the subgroup below $600 (equations 16–18) as well as for the subgroup below $300 (equation 19).[17]

Further attempts may be made to obtain a fuller explanation of the T/GNP ratio by introducing additional variables bearing on the availability of tax handles, such as degree of monetization, size of production or sales establishments, division between industry and agriculture, and so forth. Similarly, political factors, such as degree of govern-

17. This finding differs from that of Hinrichs, "Determinants of Government Revenue Shares," *Economic Journal*, 75 (September 1965), 456–557. Hinrichs, using a larger sample, finds that the import share is a significant determinant of the T/GNP ratio at low income levels. For a somewhat similar conclusion, see also Lotz and Morss, "Measuring Tax Effort," who prefer to measure openness in terms of an export rather than an import ratio.

mental centralization may be introduced.[18] Provided these variables are not themselves closely related to per capita income, this may permit the construction of a more sophisticated, "multivariable" law of expenditure growth.

INDEX OF DEVELOPMENT

So far, per capita income has been used as one index of development. Considering the difficulties inherent in establishing comparability by converting per capita income into dollars,[19] an alternative standard of comparison may be tried. One such standard, especially useful for our subsequent consideration of tax structure, is the fraction of national income originating in the agricultural sector. Use of this variable (equation 11 and Figure 4–8) does not change the picture greatly. This is not surprising, since, as shown in Table 4–6, there is a high inverse correlation between per capita income and the ratio of agricultural to total income.

EXPENDITURE COMPONENTS

Leaving these overall comparisons, it remains to be seen whether the rising-share hypothesis is borne out better if expenditures are broken down between civilian and defense. As noted before, it is only through the tax-constraint factor that total expenditures constitute a meaningful de-

18. For attempts along these lines, see Joergen R. Lotz and Elliott R. Morss, "The Influence of Selected Factors on Tax Levels in Developing Countries," unpublished manuscript; and Richard Thorn, "The Development of Public Finances During Economic Development," *The Manchester School, 35* (January 1967), 19–53.

19. The capita income figures here used are translated into dollar terms on the basis of parity exchange rates as calculated by the United Nations. While these are superior to official exchange rates for our purposes, this conversion, as has been noted by many writers (e.g. see Gupta, p. 50) still leaves much to be desired. While Gupta prefers the ratios estimated by Rosenstein-Rodan (see P. N. Rosenstein-Rodan, "International Aid for Underdeveloped Countries," *Review of Economics and Statistics, 43,* no. 2 [May 1961]), substitution of these ratios for the United Nations ratios has little effect on the overall results.

pendent variable in the analysis. Our dependent variable is thus redefined as the ratio of current nondefense expenditures to GNP. For the sample as a whole, the relationship to per capita income (equation 20) is now much weaker than before (equation 1), when total current expenditures were included. This suggests that tax restraint is a significant factor, rendering public expenditures for civilian and defense purposes relatively close substitutes, and leading to displacement of the former by the latter. This result is weakened, however, by the findings for subgroups. As shown in equations 21–23, the fit for civilian expenditures only is better than for the corresponding findings for total expenditures (see equations 2–4). This is the case especially for the group of countries up to $600 per capita income. The relationship for the high income groups nevertheless remains least satisfactory and negative.

Another expenditure component which may be singled out is social security expenditures. As shown in equations 24–26, the ratio of such expenditures to national income is related positively to per capita income, the fit being substantially better with regard to subgroups than for total expenditure. This is in line with the evidence previously encountered in the historical approach.

A more detailed cross-sectional analysis by expenditure categories cannot be undertaken here. An earlier study of sixteen low income countries in the mid-fifties showed a fair degree of rank correlation between the ratio of total public expenditures to GNP and per capita income.[20] At the same time, little systematic relationship was left if only "basic" expenditures (civil administration, health and education) were included, while omitting other items (defense, social security, public debt, and agriculture). Disaggregating further, the ratio to GNP was found to be fairly constant for administrative and economic expenditures and more variable for education, while the widest fluctuations appeared

20. See Lewis and Martin.

with regard to public health outlays. The authors explain the absence of an expected positive association between the basic expenditure ratio and per capita income by emphasizing the relatively high cost of public servants at an early stage of development, resulting in a relatively high expenditure share at a low level of income.

The theory of expenditure growth remains a fascinating but somewhat elusive problem. Even if economic factors only are considered, it is difficult to arrive at an expenditure law. Inferior goods are the exception in the public as well as in the private sphere, so that there is every reason to expect a positive association between the absolute levels of public outlay and per capita income. But matters are far from obvious once the ratio of expenditure to GNP is considered. Disaggregation is needed as hypotheses differ with regard to capital, consumption, and transfer outlays, and the weights of these components are subject to change, so that the overall pattern is left in doubt.

Moreover, noneconomic factors such as changes in technology and population are of great importance. Together with changes in social and political climate and the upheavals caused by war, they may well outweigh the effects of rising per capita income. If a historical approach is taken, per capita income rises concurrently with changes in these variables, and it is difficult to separate one from the other. With a cross-section approach, changeover time is eliminated, but countries with widely differing cultural, political, and social settings are compared. In neither case does the evidence isolate the effects of changing per capita income in a neat fashion, so that economic hypotheses regarding the effect of changes in per capita income are not easily verified.

Taking the historical approach, it is evident (exemplified here for the United States, the United Kingdom, and Germany) that the expenditure to GNP ratio, along with per capita income, has risen over time. This holds for the over-all ratio, as well as for various categories, such as civilian and defense outlays, or purchases and transfer payments. The driving force in the rise of the civilian expenditure to GNP ratio has been the growing importance of social services, pointing to change in social and political climate as a decisive causal factor in expenditure development.

The picture is less conclusive when viewed in cross-section terms. Using a sample of countries including a wide range of per capita income levels, the share of the public sector as measured by the ratio of total current expenditures to GNP is associated positively with the level of per capita income, and very similar results are obtained if a tax revenue to GNP ratio is used instead. But this relation disappears and a more complex pattern emerges once the sample is divided into low and high income groups. Taking a per capita income of about $300 as the dividing line, the relation breaks down for the low group. Similarly, it becomes much weaker and even turns negative for high income countries with per capita incomes above $600.

Moreover, the fit worsens for the group as a whole if defense is excluded and civilian expenditures only are allowed for. This suggests that the unwillingness of the public to exceed a conventional level of taxation leads to the displacement of civilian public expenditures by defense outlays. But this conclusion is weakened by the further finding that civilian expenditures give the better fit if the countries are divided into high and low income groups.

It remains to reconcile our cross-section view, which denies Wagner's law for the upper end of the income scale, with the historical view, which supports it. Various explanations are possible. The historical result may reflect the time trend of political and social forces which made for a rising expenditure share, whereas the cross-section results may be primarily a reflection of our economic factors. This is in line with our earlier suggestion that there is no clear reason why economic factors should make for a rising expenditure to GNP ratio over higher levels of income. At the same time, one can hardly interpret the cross-section result as reflecting purely economic factors. Different circumstances, such as varying severity of the aftermath of war, may have resulted in a negative relationship, even though basic economic factors would have tended to support the hypothesis of a rising ratio. While this is possible, it gains no ready support from inspection of the scatter of high income countries shown in Figure 4–7. The evidence remains puzzling and in need of further explanation, including greater emphasis on what we have called the noneconomic factors.

5 THEORY OF TAX STRUCTURE DEVELOPMENT

I now turn to the development of the tax structure, beginning again with speculative observations and proceeding to empirical evidence in both historical and cross-section terms. As in the case of expenditures, I distinguish between economic factors and the broader forces of social and political change, which also shape tax structure development. The in-between category of conditioning factors, noted in the analysis of expenditure development, is here assimilated with the economic factors.

ECONOMIC FACTORS

Economic factors bear on tax structure development in two ways. As the structure of the economy changes with economic development, the nature of the tax base changes as well, and with it the "handles" to which the revenue system may be attached. Moreover, as discussed in Chapter 7, the economic objectives of tax policy vary with the stages of economic development, as do the economic criteria by which a good tax structure is to be judged. On both counts, the effects of development upon the tax structure are more a function of institutional change and less in the nature of an inherently economic matter, as was the case with regard to expenditure change.

EARLY PERIOD

The economic structure of low income countries imposes severe limitations on the structure of the tax system.[1] The predominance of agriculture and the difficulty of reaching it through income taxation make land taxes vitally important. Presumptive methods of assessment and even taxes in kind are called for. Subject to periodic review, the physical output from particular parcels of land can be determined on a presumptive basis by land surveys; and translation into value terms can be linked annually to changes in the prices of agricultural products.[2] Moreover, it has also been suggested that an effective system of self-assessment might be established by requiring the owner to sell at the declared price.[3]

Outside agriculture, the organization of early manufacturing in small-scale establishments limits the effective base for

1. For general discussion of taxation and economic development in low income countries, see Ursula K. Hicks, *Development from Below: Local Government and Finance in Developing Countries of the Commonwealth* (London, Oxford University Press, 1961); B. Higgins, *Economic Development, Principles, Problems and Policies* (New York, Norton, 1959), Chap. 23; Lewis, *Theory of Economic Growth;* Alan R. Prest, *Public Finance in Under-developed Countries* (London, Weidenfeld and Nicolson, 1962); *Fiscal Policy for Economic Growth in Latin America,* Joint Tax Program of the Organization of American States (Baltimore, Johns Hopkins Press, 1965); *Government Finance and Economic Development,* ed. Alan T. Peacock and Gerald Hauser, Organization for European Cooperation and Development (Paris, 1965); *Readings on Taxation in Developing Countries,* ed. R. M. Bird and O. Oldman (Baltimore, Johns Hopkins Press, 1965), where an extensive bibliography on the subject is given; and Hinrichs, *General Theory of Tax Structure Change,* Chaps. 3–7.

2. See Haskell Wald, *Taxation of Agricultural Land in Underdeveloped Economies* (Cambridge, Mass., Harvard University Press, 1959). Also see Chap. 10 in *Fiscal Policy for Economic Growth in Latin America;* and Part V in *Readings on Taxation in Developing Countries.*

3. See A. Harberger, "Issues of Tax Reform for Latin America," in *Fiscal Policy for Economic Growth in Latin America.*

manufacturing excises to certain major products which are produced in larger establishments. The fluid and atomistic structure of retail outlets bars effective retail sales taxation, not to mention the application of turnover or multiple-stage sales tax systems.[4] More feasible is the use of pricing policies of public enterprises as a revenue source. This is the case especially where the sale or manufacture of liquor and tobacco products is publicly operated, but it frequently extends over a wider area, including transportation, public utilities, and some phases of manufacturing.

Personal income tax, to the extent that it can be applied at all, has to proceed on a highly schedular, nonglobal basis. The tax is assessed separately on distinct sources of income and not as a personal tax on total income received. As a result, progression is largely ineffective. Wage income is assessed more readily than business income, but the large share of self-employment in total employment renders broad application unworkable. Effective taxation is typically limited to the wage income of civil servants and employees of large firms. Determination of business income is exceedingly difficult. In the absence of adequate accounting practices, income has to be determined on a presumptive basis, e.g. by applying stipulated margins to estimated sales. The tax payable by the individual firm is thus a function of its sales. This suggests that the income tax is in effect a sales tax, with ad valorem rates varying with the average margin of the industry. But even this approach is troublesome, because the sales basis cannot be readily established, and further presumptive rules (e.g. square frontage of establish-

4. For a discussion of sales taxation see John Due, *Taxation and Economic Development in Africa* (Cambridge, Mass., M.I.T. Press, 1963); Richard Goode, "Taxation of Savings and Consumption in Underdeveloped Countries," in *Readings on Taxation in Developing Countries;* J. M. Naharro, "Production and Consumption Taxes and Economic Development," in *Fiscal Policy for Economic Growth in Latin America;* and Douglas Dosser, "Indirect Taxation and Economic Development," in *Government Finance and Economic Development.*

127

ment or number of workers) are needed.[5] Similar limitations apply to corporation taxes, where effective taxation is again limited typically to a few large and frequently foreign-owned firms. Since upper incomes are largely from capital sources, failure effectively to assess capital income becomes a severe flaw in the equity of the tax structure.[6]

It is possible, to be sure, to design a system of theoretically interlocking taxes—including levies on income, expenditures, and net worth—which would induce taxpayer compliance.[7] Thus assuming income to be known, underreporting for expenditure tax purposes raises liability under a net worth tax, and vice versa. Given the true base for any two of the three taxes, the true base for the third can be determined, and so forth. Ironically, however, such self-checking systems include highly complex taxes, and the very lack of administrative skills that renders the checks so essential also renders such schemes unrealistic. While existence of a net worth tax will strengthen the administration of an income tax with regard to capital income, a country with a highly inefficient income tax will hardly do much better in administering a net worth tax, and so forth. This is the case especially since taxpayer compliance is only half the problem. Tax collector compliance tends to be equally weak, the more so the more complex the tax system. It is advisable, therefore, not to place excessive demands on administrative skills and to minimize opportunities for discretion and collusion.

Finally, it is essential to construct a system that will enforce fines for underreporting and prosecute offenses, rather

5. See Part III in *Readings on Taxation in Developing Countries;* and Chap. 6 in *Fiscal Policy for Economic Growth in Latin America.*

6. Difficulties of securing an appropriate coverage of capital income is indeed the main theme of the discussion in *Fiscal Policy for Economic Growth in Latin America,* p. 402.

7. See B. Higgins, Chap. 23; N. Kaldor, Chaps. 18 and 19 in *Readings on Taxation in Developing Countries;* and Chap. 3 in *Fiscal Policy for Economic Growth in Latin America.*

than accept them as a normal and inevitable feature of the social scene. Without this, effective tax administration is impossible. Indeed, one wonders whether income taxation in high-compliance Western countries could survive if courts were as unwilling to support enforcement as is typically the case in low income countries. Of all the so-called cultural factors, this is surely the most important.

Given these difficulties, the strategy of tax structure development should be adjusted accordingly. Recognizing the limitations in bookkeeping, administration, and judicial support, the task is to strengthen such revenue sources as (1) permit direct (voluntary) assessment, or the application of clear-cut presumptive standards; and (2) lend themselves to administrative devices that minimize the opportunities for evasion by the taxpayer and collusion stemming from discretion by the tax collector. This involves more extensive reliance on commodity taxes than is ideal, and also calls for administrative devices that seem clumsy compared to those of efficiently administered tax structures in advanced countries.[8] But this is not the relevant comparison. The results of such taxes will be more equitable and efficient in the low income setting than those obtained from premature application of tax technologies transferred from advanced countries. A system of commodity taxes on luxury items (defined relative to living standards) in particular may prove a more effective means of progressive taxation, and one more in line with the objectives of development, than an ineffective attempt at progressive income taxation.

One bright spot in the search for identifiable tax bases is in the foreign trade sector. Most imports and exports are visible and readily identified, especially where the movement of goods converges on a few major ports, so that smuggling is limited to a minor role. Compliance require-

8. The literature on taxation and economic development does not offer an abundance of helpful suggestions in this respect, and hence is of limited use to the practitioner.

ments are reduced to a minimum, and there is relatively little scope for discretion by the official. Moreover, imported consumer goods in low income countries are frequently luxury or semi-luxury items, since manufactured articles are largely obtained through imports while basic food and shelter requirements are met at home. Thus commodity taxes based on imports tend to be acceptable or even desirable on equity grounds. Exports, similarly, afford a convenient handle for the taxation of domestic production.[9] Export taxes, or profits from state export monopolies offer a convenient and politically effective way of imposing a gross receipts tax on the domestic producer, especially in the agricultural sector. The rice export monopoly in Burma, which in fact appropriated the profit formerly made by British exporters as public revenue, is a good illustration of this.

LATER PERIOD

As economic organization develops, production and sales establishments become larger and more permanent and the scope of indirect taxation may be broadened. Concentration of employment in larger establishments and decline of the rural relative to the industrial sector render personal income taxation more manageable. As the operation of private firms is rationalized and accounting practices improve, effective taxation of business income becomes feasible. The administration of income tax as a globalized personal tax on income becomes possible. Thus there is good reason to expect that economic development will bring with it an increase in the share of direct taxes.

As the system advances into that of a highly developed, pecuniary economy, a much wider range of tax bases be-

9. See Richard Goode, George E. Lent, and P. D. Ojha, "Role of Export Taxes in Developing Countries," International Monetary Fund, *Staff Papers, 13* (1966), and Part VI of *Readings on Taxation in Developing Countries.*

comes available. The great bulk of income and output now moves through the market, and transactions are valued in money terms. The income-expenditure flows may be tapped at almost any point, and revenue be diverted to the treasury. The tax imposition may be on firms or households, on expenditures or receipts, on products or factor inputs, on flows or on stocks, and so forth.

There remain, to be sure, differences in the ease with which various taxes can be administered, and various components of the tax base can be reached. But these limitations are minor compared with the severe restrictions that prevail in low income countries. A wide range of possible tax bases is now available. The choice among them is open, and the incantation of "administrative difficulties," especially in effective taxation of capital gains, is more often a pretext for avoiding comprehensive taxation than a justified cause for rejecting tax reform.

It must not be concluded from this, however, that tax policy and administration have become a bed of roses. The development of the modern economy, while creating a wealth of feasible tax bases, also generates an enormous complexity of legal and institutional forms in which income is received or outlays are made. This complicates the task of securing equal treatment of taxpayers in essentially equal positions but engaging in different types of economic activity and subject to different legal forms. The rise of the widely held public corporation becomes a central factor in the tax structure. The problem of depreciation, the importance of capital gains, the complexity of estate and gift arrangements, need only be noted to illustrate the host of technical problems that must be met. Where the tax official of old may have worried about how to assess an elusive herd of cows, the tax collector of today's developed economies worries about how to assess a no less elusive flow of capital gains, or how to check tax evasion devices such as holding companies or trust arrangements. Tax planners in the advanced economy do not lack tax bases, but they are plagued by the knotty and never ending task of adapting the tax statutes to the changing subtleties of the economic structure, and of competing with the inventiveness of the taxpayer in creating new forms of tax avoidance.

POLITICAL AND SOCIAL FACTORS

So much for economic factors underlying tax structure development. As in the case of expenditure policy, political and social forces must be considered as well. History testifies to a close interaction between changes in political setting and in tax structure;[10] and standards of tax equity, closely linked with the social philosophy of the time, have always been a major factor in the choice of appropriate tax instruments. The rise of egalitarian philosophy, in particular, has been the driving force behind the rise of progressive taxation.[11]

Tax structure development over the modern period has been dominated by the rise of direct, and especially income, taxation. With the transition from feudal to capitalist patterns of social stratification, income emerged as a welcome substitute for property as a tax base, and subsequently it became accepted increasingly as the most representative index of economic or social status and of fiscal capacity. At the same time, income offered the most feasible base on which

10. On this point see J. A. Schumpeter, "The Crisis of the Tax State," *International Economic Papers,* no. 4 (1954).

11. It is interesting in this connection to note the hope, expressed in the Communist Manifesto some 120 years ago, that progressive taxation (along with public education) would lead to the destruction of capitalism! (See Karl Marx and Friedrich Engels, "The Communist Manifesto," in *Handbook of Marxism* [New York, International Publishers, 1935], p. 46.) In fact, both developments have done much to strengthen the structure of modern capitalist society.

to construct "personal" taxes and to which to apply progressive rates. Consumption taxes, imposed on manufacturing, on wholesale or retail sales, did not permit adjustment to family size, nor could they be an effective instrument of progressive taxation. While progression could have been achieved by limiting the tax base to a relatively small set of luxury items, this would have limited greatly the revenue-raising ability of consumption taxes. If, on the other hand, a large tax base was retained by taxing more or less all consumer goods, the resulting burden distribution would be regressive. Thus the search for progression had to be met by the income tax.

The historical association between income and progressive taxation, as against consumption and regressive taxation, has been a basic factor in tax-structure development, but it is not inevitable in principle. Theoretically at least, a personal tax on spending may be imposed with personal exemptions and progressive rates, and thus assume many of the features of the individual income tax.[12] This, however, requires a high level of administrative sophistication, which was hardly available at the earlier stages of income tax development.

Just as the historical image of consumption taxes as regressive is not inevitable, so there has been a basic change in the progressive nature of income taxation. The income tax traditionally has been in the nature of a class tax, imposed on a relatively small number of high income taxpayers only. In the United States of 1939, for instance, the income tax exemption (married taxpayer) was over four times per capita income, and only 5 per cent of the total population was covered by taxable returns. But World War II brought a transformation of the income tax into a mass tax, paid by practically all income recipients. Exemptions were cut to

12. See N. Kaldor, *An Expenditure Tax* (London, George Allen and Unwin, 1955).

less than one-half of per capita income, and 73 per cent of the population came to be included in the base.[13] This change was especially dramatic in the United States, but to a lesser extent it occurred also in most other industrialized countries. Thus the effective significance of income tax progression was broadened out, or, indeed, moved from the upper to the middle and middle-lower end of the income scale. Originally an instrument of penalizing extreme wealth and redistributing income away from the upper end of the income scale, it later became a means of securing a broad revenue base. As the lower to middle income range had to be drawn upon to meet revenue needs (this being, after all, where most of the tax base lies), the income tax became a means of avoiding regressive and applying progressive taxation over this income range.

This very change in the nature of income tax also suggests a political realignment in the direct versus indirect tax debate. Not only does the middle and lower income voter become more hesitant to vote new programs as the marginal tax dollar shifts downward, but he also grows weaker in his allegiance to income and his opposition to consumption taxes as the nature of the income tax changes. This is but another aspect of the change in fiscal politics, which emerges as the overall tax to GNP ratio rises and which should provide the basis for a long-overdue reappraisal of the sociology of fiscal politics in the Wicksell-Goldscheid-Schumpeter tradition.[14]

13. See Richard Goode, *The Individual Income Tax* (Washington, D.C., The Brookings Institution, 1964), pp. 224 and 320. The per cent refers to numbers of taxpayers and dependents covered by taxable return as a per cent of population.

14. See K. Wicksell, *Finanztheoretische Untersuchungen;* and J. A. Schumpeter, "Crisis of the Tax State"; as well as Rudolf Goldscheid, *Staatssozialismus oder Staatskapitalismus* (Vienna, 1917), and translated excerpts from Goldscheid's "A Sociological Approach to Problems of Public Finance," in Musgrave and Peacock, *Classics in the Theory of Public Finance.* See also my *Theory of Public Finance,* p. 37.

Finally, the implications of increasing fiscal centralization must be noted. Whereas this aspect has no simple bearing on expenditure ratios, it is of immediate and obvious importance for the tax structure. The progressive income tax by its very nature is better suited for national administration. Distributional adjustments through progressive taxation cannot readily be applied on a regional basis but require national coverage. Capital income is derived from various parts of the nation and must be collected in a single return for global assessment. Decentralized taxation would thus involve all the difficulties encountered in the tax treatment of foreign-source investment income, not to speak of the distortion in regional capital allocation due to differential rates. For these and other reasons, progressive income taxation has to be applied largely at the national level, with regional income taxes limited to relatively low flat rates. Property and sales taxation, on the other hand, are handled more readily at the local level. Thus the use of income taxation has been associated with the movement toward decentralization of public finances, and income taxes provide a larger revenue source in the more centralized countries.

The shift from indirect to direct taxation that has characterized modern tax structure development is, however, only the latest phase in a much longer development. Seen over the longer course of history, tax structure development began with direct rather than with indirect taxes.[15] The ancient world (Athens and Rome) relied on direct taxes imposed primarily on subjugated groups and mostly regressive in character. Medieval Europe relied on direct taxes in the gross product of land, and the same pattern is found in Asia and the Near East. The use of indirect taxation arose only with the dissolution of traditional society. The development of nation states, the rise of industry, and the expansion of trade led to the growth of internal indirect taxes, strength-

15. See the discussion by Hinrichs, *General Theory of Tax Structure Change,* Chap. 5

ened by the continued growth of taxes on external trade. The older forms of direct taxation such as the land tax thus declined in importance, and indirect taxes became the mainstay of the revenue structure. Only with the beginning of this century or the close of the last was there a renewed shift to direct taxation in the form of income tax, based on the increasingly pecuniary nature of economic life and the new alignment of social forces, making for changes in the balance of power and calling for progressive taxation.[16]

The time trend of social and political forces has been of paramount importance in the development of modern taxation and may be expected to have profound effects on the historical course of tax structure change. At the same time, the results of our cross-section approach may be expected to differ from the historical pattern. The social and political environment in which low income countries of today operate differs greatly from that which prevailed when today's high income countries were at correspondingly low levels. The demonstration effect is applicable to tax policy as well as to consumption patterns, and current ideas of equity have popular appeal at low as well as high levels of per capita income. Modern forms of direct taxation may thus be associated with lower levels of income in the cross-section rather than in the time-series approach. At the same time, the relationship between per capita income and the availability of tax handles will have changed little, thus making for a general similarity of pattern under the two approaches. It remains to be seen which of these forces was the decisive factor.

16. For a sweeping model of tax structure development, centered around the changing shares of direct and indirect taxes, see ibid., Chap. 6 and Appendix. Though highly stimulating as a first approach to the problem, it seems doubtful whether the dichotomy of direct and indirect is the best basis for historical analysis. The difficulty of proper classification, substantial even within today's tax structure, is greatly compounded in the case of historical comparisons ranging over long periods of time.

6 EMPIRICAL EVIDENCE ON TAX STRUCTURE DEVELOPMENT

Turning now to the empirical aspects of tax structure development, we begin again with the historical view, to be followed by a cross-section appraisal.

HISTORICAL VIEW

Tax structure development in the United Kingdom, the United States, and Germany over the last 80 years is summarized in Table 6–1 and depicted further in Figure 6–1. The picture is one of striking increase in the income tax share. But there are sharp differences in timing. In the United Kingdom, the increase was largely completed prior to World War I, followed by a modest further rise in the thirties. Germany acquired a high income tax share even earlier, with sharp fluctuations but no significant long-run trend in the share over the last fifty years. In the United States, the final result was similar, but with a substantial lag. Beginning with World War I, the rising importance of income tax culminated in a dramatic expansion in World War II and has held its own since then. By the end of the period the direct (individual and corporation income) tax share in the United States exceeded that of the other countries. Tax structure development in Japan also follows a similar pattern. Covering a period spanning a much wider range of economic development, the share of income taxes

137

TABLE 6–1

Development of Tax Structures

(all levels of government, excluding social security taxes; taxes as per cent of total)

	Individual Income Tax and Death Duties	Corporation Profits Tax	Excise and Sales Tax	Customs	Property	Other	Total
United States[a]							
1890	—	—	22.2	25.4	49.0	3.4	100.0
1902	0.3	—	21.0	18.1	50.2	10.4	100.0
1913	—	1.5	16.1	13.8	57.6	11.0	100.0
1922	27.5		16.3	4.4	41.3	10.5	100.0
1932	6.7	8.7	18.9	4.0	54.9	6.8	100.0
1940	11.4	9.5	30.1	2.5	32.0	12.5	100.0
1950	33.1	20.2	23.5	0.7	13.0	9.5	100.0
1960	36.6	17.5	18.8	0.8	12.2	14.1	100.0
United Kingdom[b]							
1880	16.2	—	27.6	17.8	23.9	14.5	100.0
1890	18.0	—	27.6	15.5	24.3	14.6	100.0
1900	21.3	—	21.8	14.0	25.3	17.6	100.0
1910	32.3	—	18.1	12.0	26.1	11.5	100.0
1920	27.7	13.8	14.7	8.4	10.6	24.8	100.0
1930	39.6	0.3	16.8	11.4	16.5	15.0	100.0

Year									
1940	39.1	6.0	15.9		17.5	13.3		8.2	100.0
1950	38.2	6.0	18.4		20.2	7.2		10.1	100.0
1960	40.3	3.7	16.2		20.5	10.6		8.7	100.0
Germany[c]									
1881	32.2	—		39.1			28.7		100.0
1891	27.1	—		43.5			29.4		100.0
1901	24.5	—		45.5			30.0		100.0
1914	35.9	1.8	30.1		15.8	15.2		3.0	100.0
1926	22.7	3.3	38.7		5.8	14.3		16.7	100.0
1931	21.3	10.4	31.6		8.0	17.6		18.2	100.0
1939	26.1	7.4	32.6		7.9	15.5		8.5	100.0
1951	17.9	7.4	48.2		3.4	10.9		12.2	100.0
1960	24.8	8.5	43.4		4.1	13.4		5.8	100.0

a. See Appendix Table 7.
b. See Appendix Table 8.
c. See Appendix Table 9.

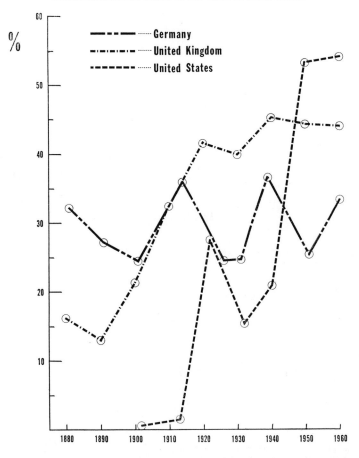

FIGURE 6–1

Income and Profit Taxes as Per Cent of Total Taxes

rose from 1.5 per cent in 1888 to 14 per cent in 1908, 27 per cent in 1921, 64 per cent in 1941, and 52 per cent in 1961.[1]

As with expenditure development, dramatic changes in the tax structure occurred mainly in wartime, in association

1. See *General Theory of Tax Structure Change*, Hinrichs, p. 51.

with the sharp increase in the overall tax to GNP ratio. But again there is the question of whether these changes in tax structure (in the sense of changing shares contributed by various taxes) were basically the result of war, or whether they reflected structural trends that would also have come about in its absence. Our interpretation is along the latter lines. More basic than its wartime timing, the rise of the income tax share reflected structural changes in the economy, as well as the social and political trends toward redistribution that have characterized the last half century or more.

The rise in the income tax share tapers off notably toward the end of our period and may experience a future decline. This reflects the increase in marginal rates that resulted as a rising income tax share was compounded with a rising tax to GNP ratio. The combination of a favorable social climate with an as yet low overall tax to GNP ratio, which had facilitated the spectacular rise in the income tax share, thus disappeared. And in this process there occurred the already noted change in the nature of income tax. Whereas only a few decades ago it was a tax on the rich, based on only a small percentage of income earnings, it then became a mass tax, including practically all earners. Per dollar of revenue, the distributive impact of today's income tax, therefore, differs much less from that of a sales tax than it did in the earlier phases of its modern history.[2] The income tax share has thus lost much of its attraction as a redistributive device and bids to become the major object of taxpayer resistance.

As the importance of income taxation increased in the United Kingdom and the United States, that of property taxation declined. Again, this decline sets in at an earlier date in the United Kingdom than in the United States, but

2. In the United States, the percentage of population covered by income tax returns rose from 4 per cent in the 1930s to 57 per cent in the mid-forties, and now exceeds 75 per cent. See Goode, *Individual Income Tax*, p. 320.

141

the basic pattern is the same. Excise and sales taxes similarly declined in relative importance. The patterns differ sharply only with regard to customs duties. Whereas the revenue significance of custom duties remained relatively constant in the United Kingdom, it had dropped sharply in the United States and Germany by the end of World War I and had become insignificant after World War II.

Social security taxes have been excluded from Table 6–1. While the rise of such taxes during recent decades played a considerable part in pushing up the overall tax to GNP ratio, they are not readily dealt with in the present context, as the allocation of such taxes to the direct or indirect group, as noted below, is a debatable matter.[3] While the shares are affected little if employee contributions are counted as direct while employer contributions are treated as indirect, this is a rather arbitrary division.

CROSS-SECTION VIEW

We now turn to a cross-section view of the relationship between tax structure and economic development. As before, use is made of samples of 30 to 40 countries, with the data for each country representing an average of its position during the decade of the fifties.[4] Again, all levels of government are included. Since the ratio of total tax revenue to GNP has already been discussed in Chapter 4, it will not be reconsidered here. Rather our focus is now on changes in the composition of the tax structure.

SHARE OF INDIRECT TAXES

The first hypothesis to be tested is that the ratio of "indirect" to total taxes is related inversely to per capita

3. See p. 174.

4. For details, see Appendix Table 6. Symbols used to denote countries in Figures 6–2 to 6–9 are also given in Appendix Table 6.

income. In the cross-section setting, this may be expected to hold because the economic structure of low income economies is not suited to the imposition of direct taxes, while indirect taxes (including custom duties) can be imposed more readily. At the same time, the inverse relation should be less marked than in the historical approach, where the time trend of rising income coincides with the rise of egalitarian philosophy and its expression in progressive (i.e. direct) taxes.

For purposes of this investigation, we use the United Nations definition of indirect taxes which includes customs duties, excises, sales and property taxes.[5] Payroll taxes (employer and employee) are now included in total taxes and thus implicitly assigned to the direct share. The dependent variable is defined as T_{id}/T, where T_{id} stands for indirect and T for total taxes. The T_{id}/GNP ratio, while important and interesting, is left for later consideration, as it is better explained in terms of its components T_{id}/T and T/GNP, to which our behavior hypotheses relate.

As shown in equations 29 and 30 of Table 6–2, the T_{id}/T ratio is related negatively to per capita income for the sample as a whole. The results with regard to both R^2 and t values are inferior to those of the earlier equations, relating T/GNP to Y_c. Nevertheless, the coefficient for Y_c is significant for both a linear and logarithmic fit, with the latter somewhat better. This pattern is reflected also in Figure 6–2 and in the correlations of Tables 4–6 and 4–7.

As with the T/GNP ratio, it is again of interest to break down the sample between countries with incomes above and below \$600. The coefficient remains significant for low income countries (equation 31), although the R^2 is greatly

5. See United Nations, *Yearbook of National Account Statistics* (New York, United Nations, 1966). An alternative source (section on Public Finance in United Nations, *Statistical Yearbook* [New York, United Nations, 1965]) gives a more detailed breakdown of taxes but includes central government only.

TABLE 6–2

Regressions on Tax Structure*

(figures in parentheses are ratio of regression coefficient and standard error)

Equation	Sample		R^2
29	A	$T_{id}/T = \underset{(23.457)}{.6333} - \underset{(-4.850)}{.0001689 Y_c}$	.39
30	A	$T_{id}/T = \underset{(25.269)}{4.986} e^{-.1761} \underset{(-5.348)}{Y_c}$	.43
31	A	$T_{id}/T = \underset{(15.19927)}{.6803} - \underset{(-7.36896)}{.0000347 Y_{c<600}}$	.19
32	A	$T_{id}/T = \underset{(6.4644)}{.5012} - \underset{(-1.099)}{.0000662 Y_{c>600}}$	.10
33	F	$T_{id}/T = \underset{(11.463)}{.3732} + \underset{(6.0396)}{.6974 Ag/GNP}$	.52
34	F	$T_{id}/T = \underset{(7.039)}{.3875} + \underset{(3.994)}{.6709 Ag/GNP_{c<600}}$	.35
35	F	$T_{id}/T = \underset{(7.504)}{.4603} - \underset{(-.6442)}{.3748 Ag/GNP_{Yc>600}}$	.19
36	B	$T_{id}/(T - T_s) = \underset{(16.914)}{.6905} - \underset{(-4.249)}{.000172 Y_c}$	.42
37	A	$T_{id}/T = \underset{(15.232)}{.7602} - \underset{(-4.825)}{1.131 T/GNP}$	.39

			R²
38	A	$T_{id}/T = .7220 - .0000989Y_c - .00651T/GNP$ $\quad\quad (14.025) \quad (-2.040) \quad\quad (-2.000)$	.44
39	A	$T_{id}/GNP = e^{-1.40}\, T/GNP^{.5584}$ $\quad\quad\quad\quad (2.7799) \quad\quad (7.0435)$	.56
40	A	$T_{id}/GNP = e^{-3.20}\, Y_c^{.1437}$ $\quad\quad\quad\quad (5.199) \quad (3.177)$	.21
41	D	$CD/T = e^{1.79}\, Y_c^{-.663}$ $\quad\quad\quad (7.0312) \quad (-4.425)$	.39
42	G	$T_{cp}/T = .01705 - .00000180Y_c$ $\quad\quad\quad (6.208) \quad\quad (-.5254)$	.01
43	G	$T_{cp}/T = .01318 + .0000959Y_{c>600}$ $\quad\quad\quad (.3337) \quad\quad (3.12738)$	.48
44	G	$T_p/T = .1981 + .000137Y_c$ $\quad\quad (7.574) \quad (5.622)$	.47
45	G	$T_p/T = .04204 + .0000639Y_c + 1.137T/GNP$ $\quad\quad (.9888) \quad\quad (1.6441) \quad\quad (4.2499)$	.66
46	C	$T_y/T = .1725 + .0000899Y_c$ $\quad\quad (4.573) \quad (2.3869)$	.21
47	B	$T_s/YN = .06369 + .000052Y_c$ $\quad\quad\quad (4.468) \quad (3.195)$	.25

* For sources see Appendix Table 6. Symbols: T = tax revenue; Y_c = per capita GNP; CD = custom duties; Ag = value added by agriculture; M = imports; T_{cp} = corporation tax revenue; T_p = personal tax revenue; T_y = income tax revenue; T_s = social security tax revenue; YN = national income.

145

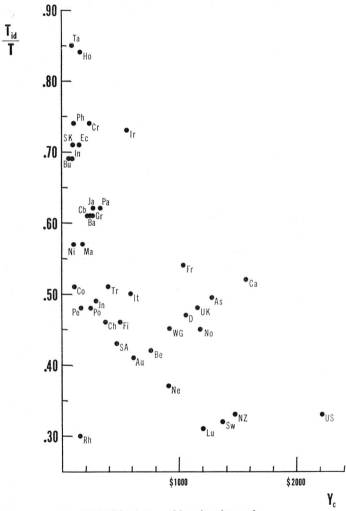

FIGURE 6–2

Indirect Tax Share and Per Capita Income*

* See Appendix Table 6 for key to abbreviated notation.

reduced. For the high income countries (equation 32) the results become insignificant. This parallels our finding in the expenditure discussion, if for different reasons. If the availability of tax handles places a constraint on total expenditures in the low income countries, it may be expected to do so even more with regard to the tax structure mix. This constraint again loosens as per capita income rises, and in high income countries the composition of the revenue structure becomes a free policy choice.

As may be expected, the relationship with T_{id}/T becomes positive (equation 33 and Figure 6–3) if the agricultural share in GNP is substituted for per capita income as the index of development. As previously seen in Table 4–6, the two indices are related negatively to each other. Both explanatory value and significance of the regression are superior to those obtained with the per capita income variable. This holds for the sample as a whole, but especially so for the low income group (equation 34). While use of the agriculture to GNP ratio made little difference in explaining the overall tax to GNP ratio, it is now of considerable help.

As noted before, social security taxes have been included in total taxes and been classified as direct. This classification is dubious but, as shown in equation 36, exclusion of social security taxes from total taxes makes little difference. The result is very similar to that of equation 29, where social security taxes are included. Note also that indirect taxes are here defined to include custom duties along with domestic excises. If custom duties are excluded, correlation with Y_c disappears.[6] This is as may be expected since (for the sample as a whole) the ratio of imports to GNP is not related to per capita income, and internal excises and customs duties are close substitutes for each other.[7]

6. This result is emphasized by Douglas Dosser in his "Indirect Taxation," in *Government Finance and Economic Development*.

7. This result holds for the entire sample as well as for small and large countries separately. The correlation coefficients of T_{id}/T and

FIGURE 6–3

Indirect Tax Share and Importance of Agriculture*

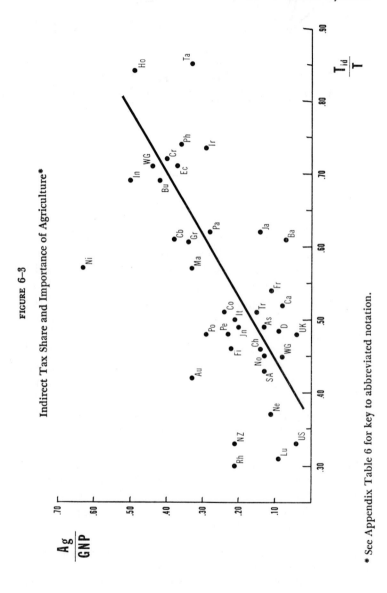

* See Appendix Table 6 for key to abbreviated notation.

Evidence of Tax Structure Development

A second hypothesis regarding T_{id}/T suggests that it should be related positively to the T/GNP ratio, or to the overall level of tax rates. The proposition is that direct taxes are given initial preference but that indirect taxes are resorted to increasingly after direct tax rates have reached higher levels. This hypothesis is not borne out. The coefficient (equation 37) is negative, although the T/GNP ratio is as satisfactory (or unsatisfactory) a predictor of T_{id}/T as was Y_c. The basic relationship between T_{id}/T and T/GNP may be U-shaped, and the stage of tax structure development to which the rising phase applies may as yet lie in the future. A second look at high income countries made 20 years hence may give a different result. An attempt to combine both variables (equation 38) is also unsuccessful. Since Y_c and T/GNP are highly correlated (see Table 4–6), little is gained in explanatory value, and the significance of the coefficients is reduced.

So far our concern has been with relating T_{id}/T to Y_c and T/GNP. While this is the more meaningful approach, brief reference is made to an alternative formulation where the ratio of indirect taxes to GNP, or T_{id}/GNP, is used as the dependent variable. As may be expected, T_{id}/GNP is related significantly (equation 39) to T/GNP, of which it forms a substantial part, but its relation to Y_c (equation 40) is not significant.

CUSTOMS DUTIES

The role of customs duties is of particular interest, due to the previously noted hypothesis that openness creates tax handles and thus permits higher taxation. As may be expected, the ratio of customs duties to total tax revenue (equation 41) is related negatively to Y_c, but, as shown in Figure 6–4, this once more reflects the difference between

---

Y_c are -0.015 for the sample as a whole; -0.43 for countries with income below \$600; and -0.28 for countries with incomes below \$300.

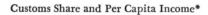

FIGURE 6–4

Customs Share and Per Capita Income*

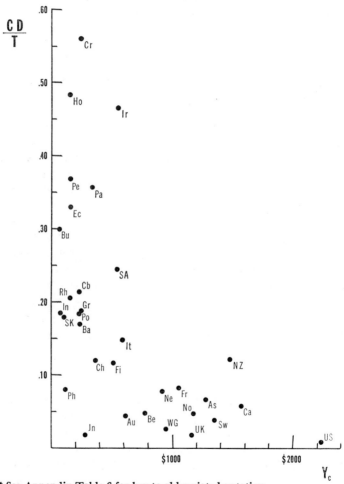

* See Appendix Table 6 for key to abbreviated notation.

FIGURE 6–5

Ratio of Imports to GNP and Per Capita Income*

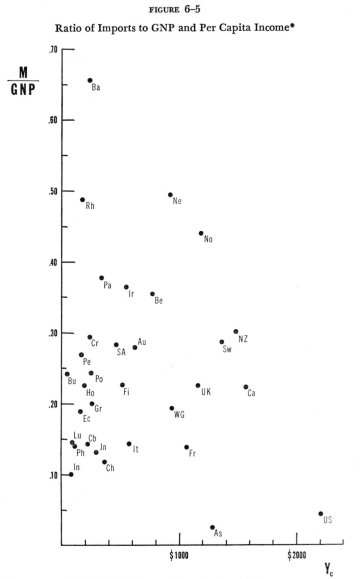

* See Appendix Table 6 for key to abbreviated notation.

two distinct clusters of observations, with little systematic relationship within either the high or low income group taken by itself. Whereas the CD/T ratio varies widely within the low income group over a range of 2 per cent (Japan) to nearly 50 per cent (Honduras), the ratio for high income countries is generally low, and the relation to per capita income is, if anything, positive. The absence of a systematic relationship reflects the fact, as shown in Figure 6–5 and previously noted in equation 12, that per capita income is not a significant explanatory variable for the import share in GNP.

CORPORATION TAX

Turning now to income and profit taxes, no significant relationship prevails for the sample as a whole (equation 42) between the corporation tax share T_{cp}/T and per capita income. This is shown also in Figure 6–6. However, per capita income becomes a significant explanatory variable (equation 43) if the higher income countries alone are considered. This is as may be expected. In low income countries, the profits tax share depends heavily on the existence of a few large firms (usually foreign) and extractive industries from which royalties can be drawn, and the existence of such industries does not dominate the level of per capita income. In higher income countries, the share of income that accrues in the form of corporation profits may be expected to rise with per capita income, and so will the T_{cp}/T ratio.

PERSONAL TAXES

The share of personal taxes T_p, defined to include income taxes as well as total (employer and employee) social security contributions, is shown in Figure 6–7. It is related positively to per capita income (equation 44). If the overall level of taxation (T/GNP) is added as a second variable (equation 45), the value of R^2 is greatly increased, but the

152

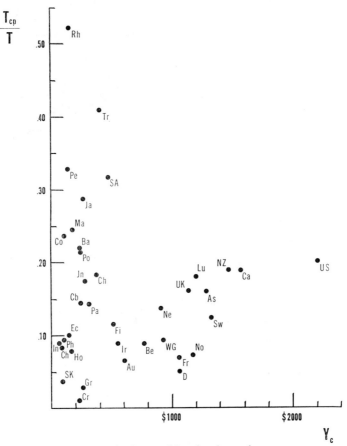

FIGURE 6–6

Corporation Tax Share and Per Capita Income*

* See Appendix Table 6 for key to abbreviated notation.

significance of the Y_o coefficient is reduced. This is not surprising, given the high correlation between Y_o and T/GNP shown in Table 4–6. As distinct from equation 38 where a similar approach was taken to the T_{id} ratio, the sign of the

FIGURE 6–7

Personal Tax Share and Per Capita Income*

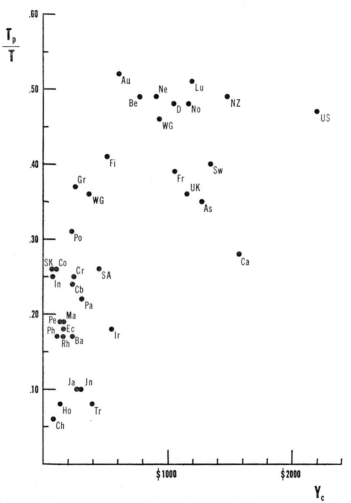

* See Appendix Table 6 for key to abbreviated notation.

154

T/GNP coefficient is now positive. This is in line with the evidence previously obtained for indirect taxes. For the sample covered, indirect rather than direct taxes appear to have been the initially "preferred" type of tax.

Less satisfactory results are obtained if social security contributions are excluded, and the share of personal income taxes T_y only is considered. The results (see Figure 6–8 and equation 46) show per capita income to be a barely significant explanatory variable.

SOCIAL SECURITY TAXES

Turning finally to social security taxes, the dependent variable is defined as the ratio of social security taxes T_s to national income YN, rather than as the payroll share in total tax receipts.[8] This is preferable since payroll taxes are typically earmarked for specific transfer functions and thus are not generally available as a flexible component of the revenue structure. Per capita income (equation 47) is a significant explanatory variable for T_s/YN.

As may be seen from Figure 6–9, the relation again differs for the lower and higher income groups. Taken by itself the lower group shows a distinctly positive relationship, whereas that for the upper group is negative. This is in line with the hypothesis that, with rising per capita income, a country becomes more able to afford transfer systems; but that as a high level of per capita income is reached, the need for transfers declines, relative to total income. The necessary "income minimum" is seen in absolute rather than relative terms. Over our lower income range, the former tendency dominates the situation, while thereafter the latter becomes decisive.

The empirical evidence on tax structure development, on both the historical and cross-section basis, is well in line

8. The use of national income in lieu of GNP reflects the easier availability of data for this particular sample.

FIGURE 6–8

Personal Income Tax Share and Per Capita Income*

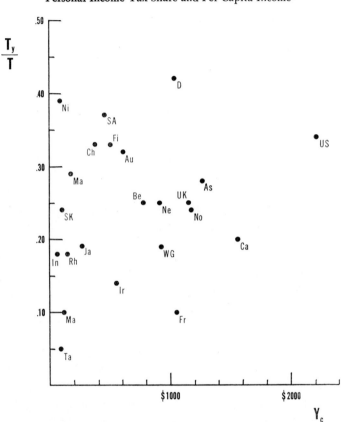

* See Appendix Table 6 for key to abbreviated notation.

with expectations. Both approaches support our hypothesis regarding the role of indirect taxation in the revenue structure. In the historical approach, both sociopolitical and economic forces work in support of a falling T_{id}/T ratio and cannot be separated; but as shown in the cross-section ap-

FIGURE 6–9

Social Security Tax to National Income Ratio and Per Capita Income*

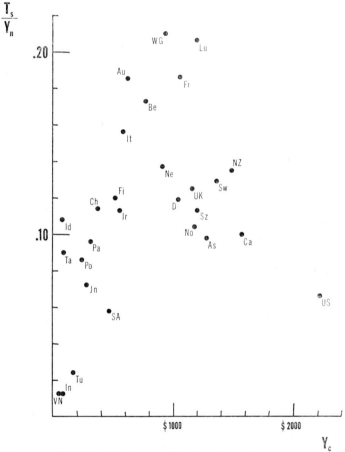

* See Appendix Table 6 for key to abbreviated notation.

proach, the hypothesis remains valid even if the time dimension of historical change is excluded. Use of agriculture as a share in total output improves the fit, as may be expected on the basis of our tax-handle hypothesis. The relation holds

157

for the sample as a whole, as well as for countries with low per capita income. But as in the analysis of overall tax or expenditure levels, the relationship breaks down within the subgroup of high income countries. Our earlier hypothesis, suggesting a rising T_{id}/T ratio with rising T/GNP, is not borne out on either the historical or the cross-section basis.

Turning now to other taxes, we find that the ratio of customs duties to total tax revenue is related inversely to per capita income. This reflects only the fact that the average ratio is lower for high income countries than for low income countries, without there being significant relationship within either group taken by itself. The hypothesis (derived from the tax-handle theory) of a strong positive relationship between high tax to GNP ratios and the openness of the economy is not borne out by our data, even for the under $600 income group taken by itself. However, such relationship has been shown to apply to a larger sample of countries with per capita incomes below $300.

The share of corporation profits to total tax revenue is not related significantly to per capita income if the sample as a whole is considered, but, as may be expected, there is a positive relation for the high income countries. The share of personal taxes is related positively to per capita income, but the fit is not as close as our hypothesis might suggest. The result is improved considerably if payroll taxes are included as well.

POLICY GUIDES

Having considered the prevailing levels and structure of taxation in a variety of countries, the evidence may be related briefly to the problem of tax policy planning. If such planning is to proceed on a firm basis, it is necessary to establish criteria by which to evaluate the prevailing tax structure of a country. Such criteria are needed by the finance minister who wishes to size up past accomplishments and to set appropriate targets, as well as by the outside agency that desires to assess a country's own-effort in determining eligibility for foreign aid. Both the overall tax effort and the quality of the tax structure are involved.

OVERALL REVENUE RATIO

The overall tax effort may be looked upon in several ways.

Ability to "Give Up." A first approach is in terms of a country's ability to give up resources for public use. If per capita income is higher in country A than in B, should A be expected to give up a larger share while making an equal effort? The underlying reasoning is analogous to that of the ability to pay, or "sacrifice," theory, which has been applied traditionally to interindividual tax burden distribution. Two countries (rather than two individuals) would now be taken to make the same effort if they incurred the same sacrifice. But how is equal sacrifice to be defined? As in the traditional doctrine, two questions have to be answered: (a) Are income utility schedules for various countries comparable and what is their shape? and (b) What concept of equal sacrifice—absolute, proportional, or marginal—should be applied? As has emerged from the traditional discussion, where these concepts were applied to comparisons between individual taxpayers, neither question can be answered on scientific grounds, but has to be handled by postulating a social value judgment.[9]

If such is the case for determining equal sacrifice among the individuals of any one country, matters are made worse when the comparison is between sacrifices incurred by groups of people living under different environments and circumstances. Since the sacrifice for each group is to be de-

9. See A. C. Pigou, *A Study in Public Finance* (3d ed. London, Macmillan, 1951), and my *Theory of Public Finance,* Chap. 5.

rived from that incurred by its individual constituents, no conclusions can be drawn without further allowance for difference in income distribution and in the distribution of tax burdens within each group. Given these insurmountable obstacles, it is better to collapse both questions into one and to *postulate* a relationship between per capita income and the revenue to GNP ratio at which "equal effort" is assumed to apply. Presumably, the equal effort ratio will be set to rise with per capita income, but at which rate is an open question.[10]

Efficient Resource Use. More important, it is hardly permissible to measure tax effort without regard for the expenditure side of the budget. Rather than thinking of ability to give up the private use of resources, one should inquire into the appropriate division of resource use between public and private goods. If the revenue is used to finance public consumption, the basic problem is one of efficient mix of consumption (private and public) at various levels of per capita income. This mix may rise with per capita income, but the underlying considerations are not

10. R. M. Bird in "A Note on Tax-Sacrifice Comparisons," *National Tax Journal, 17*, no. 3 (September 1964), suggests that equal burden or effort applies if $[T/(Y - T)]/(Y/N)$ is constant where T is yield, Y is income, and N is population. This means that the tax rate $t = T/Y$ rises with per capita income Y/N such that the ratio of revenue to residual income rises at the same percentage rate as per capita income. If $t = .10$ for $Y/N = \$500$, the value of t rises to .18 for $Y/N = \$1,000$ and falls to .04 for $Y/N = \$200$. This is one possible formulation among many others. Thus the numerator might be defined as Y/T instead of $T/Y - T$, and various weight patterns might be attached to per capita income.

Indeed there is no particular advantage in choosing any single formula. To be meaningful, the formula must be derived by postulating a utility function and a particular equal sacrifice definition, but if this is done, it is just as well to plot the desired norm (effective rate schedule) directly. See also Henry Aaron, "Some Criticism of Tax Burden Indices," and comment by R. M. Bird, *National Tax Journal, 18*, no. 3 (September 1965).

those involved in the traditional sacrifice discussion. The problem, as discussed earlier, is one of income and price elasticity for public goods. In other words, the analogy should be to the interindividual aspects of benefit taxation and the underlying issues of resource allocation, rather than to the distributional implications of the ability to pay approach.

If the revenue is to be used for the finance of capital formation, taxation becomes a form of saving and involves postponement of consumption. The problem then becomes one of ability to postpone current consumption. Since such postponement is involved in private as well as public saving, capacity to postpone must be related to total saving. Effort criteria, in this case, relate to the overall domestic savings rate (i.e. tax rate minus government consumption rate plus private saving rate) rather than to the tax rate as such. But given the savings rate of the private sector, the savings rate in the public sector (discussed in the next chapter) is set by the target rate of growth and the overall development plan of the economy.

Looking at the matter this way, tax effort may be measured as the difference between the appropriate revenue to GNP ratio (i.e. the ratio that reflects efficient resource use under a given growth target) and the ratio that is actually applied. As under the ability to give up approach, target ratios corresponding to various levels of GNP may be defined, but the underlying set of considerations differs.

Ability to Collect. It would be thoroughly unrealistic, however, to determine the optimal tax revenue to GNP ratio by these normative considerations only. Allowance must also be made for a country's ability to collect taxes, and hence to meet a desired revenue target. This ability differs greatly among developing countries. A second aspect of performance, therefore, relates to the country's ability to overcome the more or less objective difficulties of securing a certain revenue to GNP ratio. To measure performance in this

161

respect, one must decide on the major factors that should be allowed for in determining the availability of tax handles and collection ease. Among the items to be considered are the following, all of which relate positively to collection ease:

1. import involvement;
2. manufacturing share in value added, and per cent thereof originating in establishments above a certain size limit;
3. ratio of wage earners to self-employed;
4. percentage of wage earners working in establishments employing more than, say, 10 workers;
5. percentage of total consumption involving purchase from retail establishments with sales above, say, 50 times per capita income;
6. literacy level.

In addition, the quality of the tax service (including administration and enforcement) is of major importance, but it is part of the effort and hence should be treated as a dependent variable. Since there will be varying degrees of correlation among these items, the task is to select factors that will have important bearing on ability to collect but are not highly correlated. By assigning weights to these factors, one may construct an index of ability to collect, which may then be used to modify the measure of performance. In other words, our two sets of considerations—appropriate resource use and ability to collect—may be combined in a target function, defining the appropriate and feasible revenue ratio for a country.

Comparison with Average Performance. Instead of measuring a country's performance against absolute standards, it may be more feasible to evaluate a country's fiscal performance by comparing it with the average record of a group of countries.

Evidence of Tax Structure Development

One approach would be to devise a standard tax structure and to define the target revenue of a country as that yielded by application of the standard rates. This resembles the methodology which is frequently used in comparing taxable capacities or tax efforts among municipalities within one country. There are, however, important differences between the two situations. To begin with, it is not enough to specify statutory tax rates and hence the yield that results as these rates are applied to a given base. It is equally important, though more difficult, to specify the ratio of reported (actually assessed) tax base to the presumptive base.[11] Moreover, the approach is deficient because the same tax structure should not be applied to all countries. A country with large imports but few other tax handles might be expected to assess imports more heavily than another country with few imports but high retail sales. If the overall revenue target is to be assessed in this fashion, the norm of a uniform tax structure has to be dropped, and different standard tax structures must be applied to various types of countries. At this point, the evaluation of overall revenue ratios becomes intertwined with the evaluation of tax structures or revenue composition.

Pointing toward a more effective approach, a multiple regression analysis of a cross section of countries might be undertaken of the form

$$t = a + bY_{pc} + cX_1 + dX_2 + eX_3 + \cdots + hX_n$$

where t is the revenue to GNP ratio, Y_{pc} is per capita income and the variables X_1 to X_n are the tax "handle" factors of the type just listed. One may then compute the standard revenue to GNP ratio $t_s{}^j$ for any particular country j by

11. Suppose total retail sales are $100 million, sales in "substantial" establishments which *can* be reached by taxation are $40 million, while sales in small and nonpermanent locations are $60 million. Sales actually assessed are $30 million. The presumptive base is $40 million and underassessment is $10 million, not $70 million.

plugging in its values for the Y_{pc} and X variables, and measure its performance by $t_a{}^j/t_s{}^j$ where $t_a{}^j$ is the actual and $t_s{}^j$ the estimated ratio.[12] A ratio of 1 would be standard, above 1 would be superior, and below 1 would be deficient. Under this approach, the ability of various countries to draw on particular tax handles would be allowed for by inserting its own values for the respective variables. There would still be the disadvantage, however, of applying the average coefficients that result from the group pattern, while in fact the coefficients should differ depending on the very availability of tax bases. One is thus returned to a more absolute approach to the construction of model tax structures.

COMPOSITION OF TAX STRUCTURE

While it is difficult to generalize about the appropriate overall level of tax revenue, it is even more difficult to set criteria for the composition of revenues as it should be at a particular time, or for the proper path of tax structure change as the economy develops. Economic structures vary, not to speak of differences in administrative capabilities,

12. For an approach along these lines see Lotz and Morss, "Measuring Tax Effort in Developing Countries," International Monetary Fund, *Staff Papers, 14* (1967). The authors compare rankings in terms of three effort measures. The first measure is simply the tax to GNP ratio. The second measure is the ratio of this actual ratio to an estimated ratio, devised by substituting the country's value of Y_p into the estimating equation

$$T/Y = a_1 + b_1 Y_p$$

where Y_p is per capita income. The third measure uses an estimating equation which allows for openness, so that

$$T/Y = a_2 + b_2 Y_p + c_2 F/Y$$

where F is exports plus imports. The rankings under the three approaches differ substantially for particular countries, but on the whole the countries showing low effort under the first measure also do so under the other measures. In a later (unpublished) paper, additional factors relating to ease of collection and degree of compliance are considered.

164

enforcement, and cultural traditions. Yet it would be most helpful to tax policy planning if certain general principles were established.

One approach is again to compare the tax structure composition of any one country with the average picture provided by countries in similar positions. Thus the relationships established in the preceding cross-section analysis might be used, by plugging in the country's values for the dependent variables, to determine their standard value for the various tax shares. These standard values might then be taken as targets for adaptation of the actual shares. This, however, is not too satisfactory a procedure, especially at low levels of income, as it overlooks wide variations in the composition of available tax handles. An alternative approach is called for.

Beginning with the economic structure of a country or group of countries, an inventory of available tax bases may be derived. These include production bases, especially agricultural output sold at the market and manufacturing conducted in establishments above a minimum scale; and income bases, especially wage or salary income derived from employment in establishments above a certain scale. Also it includes consumption bases, especially retail sales by establishments above a certain size. Other components of output or income (such as cottage industry, food consumed at home, or retail sales in small shops) are excluded, as they do not provide feasible tax bases. To these bases are added assessable property holdings including land and/or real estate. Also additional tax bases are provided by trade on the import and/or export side.

Proceeding in this fashion, it will be evident that the total available tax base will be smallest, relative to GNP, in low income countries with little foreign trade. It will increase as the foreign trade share expands and the economy develops, so as to render a larger share of production and income accessible to taxation. Thus the range of choice among tax bases is large in the developed economy, but not at earlier stages. The determination of "proper" tax structure composition gains in degrees of freedom as the economy advances. In particular, considerations of equity can become more controlling as the technical means of securing revenue (e.g. availability of tax bases) become more abundant.

Considering the complexity of the problem, there is no simple formula by which to provide criteria for tax structure development. The only feasible approach is to develop "model tax structures" applicable to groups of countries with more or less similar characteristics regarding availability of tax bases and levels of per capita income.[13] Given such a set of target structures, the position of individual countries may then be judged in relation to the absolute standards and by comparison, and the needs of tax structure changes over time may be derived from expected changes in economic structure. Also effort in terms of overall revenue may be assessed with reference to the yield of such target structures.

In addition, tax planning must look ahead and allow for prospective changes in tax bases and revenue needs. Obviously the two objectives are not independent. If tax reform takes five years, the reform should allow for changes in the economic structure that occur during that period, rather than adapt the tax structure to a pattern of tax bases that has become outmoded when the new system is effective. Moreover, changes in the tax structure at any one time provide stepping stones for further changes in the future, requiring continuity in tax structure planning. If economic changes are slow and reform is speedy, catching up with present needs is most important. If the expected changes in economic structure are rapid and the planning period for tax structure changes is long, tax reform must be aimed

13. To the extent that they are derived from average performance, the approach would be essentially similar to that of the above regression equation.

primarily at meeting the changing needs of the future. A schedule of reforms providing for a sequence of reform plans will be needed. This points to the design of model tax reform schedules for countries undergoing similar patterns of economic change. Moreover, advance planning must be applied to the internal problems of particular taxes, as well as to the broader problems of tax structure composition.

7 COMPARISON OF TAX STRUCTURES IN DEVELOPED COUNTRIES

We now turn to a comparison of tax structures in a number of developed countries, including the United States, Canada, the United Kingdom, Germany, the Netherlands, France, Sweden, and Italy.[1] Japan is also included, as it presents an interesting middle case. Similarities and differences in the tax structures of these countries will be sketched, and certain methodological problems of tax structure comparison will be noted.

OVERALL LEVEL AND COMPOSITION

We begin with the overall level of taxation and the shares contributed by the various revenue sources.

1. For a similar comparison and literature references, see J. A. Stockfisch, *Excise Tax Compendium*, U.S. Congress, House Committee on Ways and Means, 88th Congress, Part 1 (Washington, D.C., G.P.O., June 15, 1964), pp. 109–81; see also Otto Eckstein and Vito Tanzi, "Comparison of European and United States Tax Structures and Growth Implications," in *The Role of Direct and Indirect Taxes in the Federal Revenue System*, The Brookings Institution (Princeton, Princeton University Press, 1964).

For descriptions of the fiscal systems of various countries, see Gerloff and Neumark, *Handbuch der Finanzwissenschaft*, 2d ed., *3*. For descriptions of current tax laws in various countries, see the *World Tax Series*, Harvard Law School International Program in Taxation (Boston, Little, Brown).

Comparison of Tax Structures

In assessing the overall tax burden, revenues at all levels of government must be included. Otherwise the tax burden in fiscally centralized countries such as the Netherlands and the United Kingdom is exaggerated compared to that of decentralized countries such as the United States and Canada. In principle, profits of public enterprises should be included along with taxes, since they are equivalent to excise taxes on publicly sold products; and fee proceeds levied on a cost basis should be excluded since they are equivalent to price payments for purchases. Also there is some question as to whether payroll taxes should be included along with general tax revenue, a matter that is of major importance for comparative results.

Column 1 of Table 7–1 gives tax to GNP ratios for 1961, with payroll taxes included. The ratios for our Western countries range from 26 per cent (Canada) to 35 per cent (Germany), with an average of 31 per cent. The European ratios are closely clustered together, ranging from 30 per cent in Italy to 34 per cent in Sweden. Those for the United States and Canada lie somewhat lower at 27 and 26 per cent, while Japan is substantially lower at 21 per cent. For a more recent year (1968) the United States ratio stood somewhat higher at 30 per cent.

If social security taxes are excluded, the ratings (col. 4) are changed substantially, with Germany dropping from first to third place, and Sweden rising from second to first. The United Kingdom which was in fifth place is now second, while the United States remains in seventh place. Japan remains lowest, but the gap is narrowed considerably. While the inclusive ratio is perhaps the more significant one, the second is not without merit. Where payroll taxes reflect the financing of social security on a quid pro quo basis, it might be argued that they do not impose a tax burden in the usual sense and that if the tax burden distribution is regressive, it

169

TABLE 7-1

Taxes as Per Cent of GNP, 1961*

	Including Social Security Contributions			Excluding Social Security Contributions			Including Social Security Contributions	
	Total	Direct	Indirect	Total	Direct	Indirect	Central	Local
	(1)	(2)	(3)	(4)	(5)	(6)	(7)	(8)
United States	26.7	15.3	11.4	23.0	13.6	9.4	17.8	9.0
Canada	25.7	11.1	14.6	23.5	9.9	13.6	17.0	8.8
United Kingdom	31.1	15.6	15.5	27.0	13.3	13.7	28.1	3.0
Federal Republic of Germany	34.9	17.5	17.4	25.4	12.8	12.6	23.7	11.2
Netherlands	32.4	19.2	13.2	23.6	13.9	9.7	32.0	0.4
France	32.6	9.7	22.9	24.1	7.5	16.6	28.9	0.7
Sweden	33.8	20.7	13.1	29.6	18.2	11.4	26.2	7.6
Italy	30.3	7.6	22.7	20.2	5.7	14.5	27.3	3.0
Japan	20.8	11.2	9.6	18.2	9.9	8.3	15.6	5.2

* Source: *Excise Tax Compendium*, Part 1 (1964). Data for 1961.

will be marked by a progressive distribution of transfer benefits. A regressive burden element remains only in that the transaction is compulsory.[2] However, most social security systems involve substantial redistributional elements; and even where there is a case for excluding the employee contribution, that for excluding the employer contribution is more dubious.

COMPOSITION OF REVENUE SOURCES

The composition of tax revenues is shown in Table 7–2. The contribution of the individual income tax ranges widely from a low of 11 per cent in Italy and 15 per cent in France, over a middle range of 32 to 35 per cent in the United States and the United Kingdom, to a high of 53 per cent in Sweden. The average ratio is 26 per cent, with a fairly wide dispersion around it. The corporation tax share ranges from 2 per cent in Italy to 16 per cent in the United States. The much higher ratio of 27 per cent in Japan is noteworthy, Japan being the only country in our sample where the share of the corporation tax exceeds that of the individual income tax. This reflects the broader coverage of this particular tax and its extension into the noncorporate sector.

The contribution of excises and customs ranges from 29 per cent in the Netherlands to 47 per cent in Italy, with a fairly close cluster around the average of 35 per cent. The property tax share is highest in the United States and Canada with 13 and 14 per cent, and in the United Kingdom with 10 per cent. The other countries show much lower ratios as land taxation is handled under the income tax or in other forms. Social security contributions, finally, range from 9 per cent in Canada and 12 per cent in Sweden to 33 per cent in Italy. The average ratio is 19 per cent with a wide dispersion around it, reflecting in considerable part differ-

2. See my "The Role of Social Insurance in a System of Social Welfare," in *The U.S. Social Security System*, ed. F. Harbeson (Princeton, Princeton University Press, 1968).

TABLE 7-2

Composition of Tax Revenue*
(per cent of total)

	United States	Canada	United Kingdom	Federal Republic of Germany	Netherlands	France	Sweden	Italy	Japan
Direct									
Individual income tax	32.3	19.5	35.5	19.7	27.4	14.7	52.8	11.3	20.3
Corporation income tax	16.3	16.1	4.0	6.9	10.4	6.0	—	2.1	26.8
Employees' social security contributions	6.7	4.9	7.3	13.5	16.2	6.9	7.4	6.3	6.4
Other	2.0	2.7	3.2	10.0	5.3	2.2	1.0	5.5	0.5
Total	57.3	43.2	50.0	50.1	59.3	29.8	61.2	25.2	54.0
Indirect									
Excises, sales, customs	21.4	38.3	34.6	32.7	29.3	44.8	33.8	46.6	33.1
Property tax	13.2	14.2	9.5	1.6	0.5	1.0	—	—	5.7
Employers' social security contributions	7.5	4.1	5.9	13.7	10.9	19.3	4.9	27.1	6.0
Other	0.6	0.3	—	1.9	—	5.1	0.2	1.2	1.2
Total	42.7	56.9	50.0	49.9	40.7	70.2	38.8	74.4	46.0
Employee contributions excluded									
Direct	54.2	40.3	46.1	42.3	51.4	24.6	58.0	20.2	50.9
Indirect	45.8	59.7	52.9	57.7	48.6	75.4	42.0	79.8	49.1
Social security contributions excluded									
Direct	59.0	42.1	49.2	50.3	59.1	31.0	61.4	28.4	54.3
Indirect	41.0	57.9	50.8	49.7	40.9	69.0	38.6	71.6	45.7
Social security contributions included									
Direct, including property tax	70.5	57.4	59.5	51.7	59.8	30.8	61.2	25.2	59.7
Indirect, excluding property tax	29.5	42.6	40.5	48.3	40.2	69.2	38.8	74.8	40.3

* Source: Same as Table 7-1.

ences in the pattern of social security financing. Most countries show about an equal division of payroll tax revenue between employers and employees, with the exception of France and Italy which rely more heavily on the employer contribution.

DIRECT VERSUS INDIRECT TAXES

A comparison of tax structures is made frequently in more summary terms, arranging the various taxes under the general headings of "direct" and "indirect." This may be considered significant because tax structures that rely on direct taxes are held to be more progressive, less favorable to growth, or disadvantageous on trade grounds. The first point is generally valid, although much depends on the pattern of income taxation. The second is an interesting hypothesis but, as noted below, empirical evidence does not seem to support it. The third proposition, as noted below, is largely mistaken.[3]

However this may be, such comparisons suffer from ambiguity in the very distinction between direct and indirect taxes. This distinction may be drawn in various ways. Some have suggested that (1) indirect taxes are taxes which are shifted, and others that (2) they are taxes which are meant to be shifted. Still others hold that (3) they are taxes which are assessed on *objects* rather than on individuals and therefore not adaptable to the individual's special position and his taxable capacity; or finally (4) that they are simply taxes which are not on income. While (3) is probably the most useful criterion, this is not the place to resolve this terminological matter. It is evident, however, that under most criteria, the classification of certain taxes is far from clear-cut.

The individual income tax, under all the criteria, is most clearly direct. An expenditure tax of the Kaldor type, imposed on individuals, does not fit (4) but meets the other

3. See p. 286.

requirements for direct taxation. The corporation tax, if not shifted, meets all the criteria except (3), and if shifted, it is indirect. Excise and retail sales taxes on consumer goods are indirect under all criteria, and the same goes for a value-added tax of the consumption type. A value-added tax of the income type might be considered direct by all criteria but (3) which, however, is the most essential. Property taxes are usually (e.g. for purposes of national income statistics) treated as indirect, but a good case can be made for considering them direct under most of the criteria. Provided that capital value is a function (capitalized value) of imputed income, capital taxes do not differ greatly from taxes on capital income. The classification of property taxes as direct is especially appealing with regard to owner-occupied residential property.

The payroll tax is usually classified as indirect. This seems dubious, especially for the employee contribution, which on most grounds, with the possible exception of (3), should be grouped as direct. In a competitive labor market, the same might be said for the employer contribution, but under more realistic assumptions this part of the payroll tax might be considered as indirect. It remains to be seen how much difference the alternative classifications of the payroll tax make in the comparative picture.

The split treatment of the payroll tax is used in the following classification system,[4] which underlies Table 7–2:

Direct Taxes:
  Individual income tax
  Corporation income tax
  Death and gift taxes

4. This classification system was used in the U.S. Treasury's presentation (see Stockfisch) of "International Comparisons on Direct and Indirect Taxes," in *Excise Tax Compendium,* Part 1 (1964). With the exception of the liquor monopolies, the Treasury data exclude profits of government-operated enterprises from the revenue figures. As noted before, they should be included in a more complete comparison.

> Net wealth tax
> Taxes on investment income
> Income taxes with property base
> Municipal trade tax
> Social security contributions by employees

> Indirect Taxes:
> Excise, sales, and production taxes
> Customs taxes
> Property taxes
> Social security contributions by employers

The percentage composition of total tax yield for the various countries falls into four groups. The United States, the Netherlands, and Sweden rely most heavily on direct taxation with 57 to 61 per cent of total revenue from this source; the United Kingdom, Germany, and Japan rank next with 50 to 54 per cent; and France and Italy have the lowest ratio of direct taxes with 25 and 30 per cent. Canada falls midway with direct taxes somewhat over 40 per cent of the total. The three countries that rank highest clearly owe their position to the preeminence of the individual and corporate income taxes.

Exclusion of the employee contribution generally lowers the direct share, but the overall pattern is not greatly affected since the share of the employee contribution in total tax revenue is fairly uniform. Only in the case of Germany and the Netherlands, where it is somewhat higher, does the direct share fall off more sharply. Exclusion of all social security contributions has a more significant effect on the overall pattern since the employer contribution provides more widely differing shares. The direct tax share is increased especially for Italy and France, but the same overall pattern continues to prevail. In all, it turns out that the treatment of social security taxes does not greatly affect the direct tax proportions.

In all three English-speaking countries (the United Kingdom, the United States, and Canada), property taxes account for a relatively high proportion of tax revenue. Transferring property tax revenues from the indirect to the direct tax category, therefore, raises their direct tax share sharply.[5] The United States, with a direct tax share of over 70 per cent, now far outstrips all other countries. Italy and France stay in the same low position (25 and 31 per cent); Germany occupies an intermediate position (52 per cent), while the remaining countries (Canada, the United Kingdom, Japan, the Netherlands, and Sweden) show marked similarity with direct taxes as a proportion of the total clustered around 60 per cent.

CENTRAL VERSUS LOCAL TAXES

There is considerably more variation in the division of revenue between the central and lower levels of government. This is shown in Table 7–3. In the Netherlands almost the entire revenue is central. In France, Italy, and the United Kingdom roughly 90 per cent of total revenue (including social security contributions) accrues to the central government, while in the United States and Canada only two-thirds of such revenue belongs to the central government. Sweden falls between these two groups with 78 per cent of central government revenue. This general picture is not greatly changed if social security contributions are omitted. However, the central share is now somewhat lower since, with the single exception of the United States, social security receipts all accrue to the central government.

Note that the shares shown in the table give the central government's share in tax revenue. This is a significant index of fiscal centralization, but not the only one. An index

5. The property tax comparison is somewhat misleading since some countries (e.g. Italy) tax land under the schedular income tax, while others (e.g. the Netherlands) tax property under a net wealth tax. These items are here included under the heading of income or other direct taxes.

Comparison of Tax Structures

TABLE 7–3

Percentage Composition of Tax Revenue by
Level of Government, 1961*

	Central Government		Local and State Government	
	Including Social Security Taxes	Excluding Social Security Taxes	Including Social Security Taxes	Excluding Social Security Taxes
United States	66.6	65.8	33.4	34.2
Canada	65.9	62.6	34.1	37.4
United Kingdom	90.5	89.1	9.5	10.9
Federal Republic of Germany	68.0	56.0	32.0	44.0
Netherlands	98.7	98.3	1.3	1.7
France	88.8	84.8	11.2	15.2
Sweden	77.6	74.4	22.4	25.6
Italy	90.2	85.3	9.8	14.7
Japan	74.9	71.4	25.1	28.6

* Source: Same as Table 7–1.

of expenditure centralization is of equal interest and may differ from tax centralization because of transfers. In all, expenditure systems are less centralized than tax systems.[6] Thus Japan, which ranks midway in tax centralization, has extensive transfers and a much more decentralized expenditure system. Also, the index of tax revenue centralization is not the same as that of tax administration centralization. In Germany, for instance, revenue from the income tax accrues largely to the Laender governments, but the tax is administered as a central tax. If income tax revenue is included centrally, the German ratio rises to over 80 per cent.

INTERRELATIONS

It remains to be seen how the different tax structure characteristics are interrelated. For this purpose, the respec-

6. Reference is to the distribution of expenditures made to the public, rather than to expenditures plus grants to lower levels. See p. 341.

TABLE 7-4
Ranking by Tax Structure Characteristics*

	Including Social Security Taxes			Excluding Social Security Taxes		
	Tax Revenue as % of GNP	Direct Taxes as % of Total Taxes	Central Taxes as % of Total Taxes	Tax Revenue as % of GNP	Direct Taxes as % of Total Taxes	Central Taxes as % of Total Taxes
Canada	8	7	9	6	7	8
Federal Republic of Germany	1	5	7	4	5	9
France	3	8	4	5	8	4
Italy	6	9	3	8	9	3
Japan	9	4	6	9	4	6
Netherlands	4	2	1	6	2	1
Sweden	2	1	5	1	1	5
United Kingdom	5	6	2	2	6	2
United States	7	3	8	7	3	7

* Based on Tables 7-1 to 7-3.

tive rankings of the various countries are assembled in Table 7–4.

There is surprisingly little relationship between the various characteristics; this is true whether or not social security taxes are included. For some countries, such as Germany and France, a relatively high tax to GNP ratio ranking is combined with a relatively low direct tax share ranking, while for others such as Sweden and the Netherlands, a relatively high tax to GNP ratio goes with a high direct tax share. Similarly, for some countries such as the United States, a low tax to GNP ratio ranking is matched by a high direct tax share ranking, while Italy combines a low overall ratio with a very low direct share. There is no support here for the hypothesis that income taxes are "preferred" taxes which are administered first so that the indirect share rises with the tax to GNP ratio.[7]

Nor is there much relationship to be found between the overall tax to GNP ratio and the share of central taxes. Canada and the United States combine a low overall ratio ranking with a low central share ranking, while Germany (subject to the previously noted qualification) combines a high overall ratio with a low central share. Indeed, for the small sample here included, rank correlation is positive for countries with low tax to GNP ratios and negative for countries with high ratios. In all, there is no support for the hypothesis that fiscal centralization makes for a more aggressive fiscal policy and more rapid expansion of the public sector.

Nor do we find much relation between direct and central shares in total revenue. The plausible hypothesis that a high direct share should be associated with a high central share is borne out at the extreme ends by Canada and the Netherlands, but most other countries do not fit the pattern. Thus, the United States combines a high ranking for direct share with a low ranking for central share, while Italy combines a

7. See p. 149.

low direct share ranking with a high central share ranking. Evidently fiscal structures, traditions, and the setting of fiscal policies among the developed countries are too varied to permit simple generalizations of this sort.

Individual Income Tax

We now turn to a comparison of specific taxes, beginning with the individual income tax. Such a comparison may involve many aspects—including rates, income concept, treatment of family unit, and so forth—not all of which can be considered here.

Rates on Wage and Salary Income

Comparison of rate levels is always a matter of interest, and results will differ depending on how the comparison is made, i.e. what type of tax payments are included under the heading of income tax, what type of income the taxpayer is assumed to receive, what his family status is; and, most important, what levels of income are to be compared.

To illustrate the latter problem, we begin with a broadly defined concept of income tax. Basic and supplementary rates are included, as are global and schedular rates, as well as certain supplements to be found in some of the countries here compared. Moreover, we assume that the taxpayer's income is entirely from employment (i.e. in the form of wages and salaries), and consider a taxpayer with a wife and two dependents.

Income tax liabilities are then compared as follows. Having chosen certain levels of dollar income to compute the United States tax liability, we convert these dollar incomes into foreign incomes in three different ways. One is by applying the official exchange rate. Another is to apply a purchasing power parity rate. Finally, we obtain foreign income equivalents by expressing dollar incomes as a per cent of per capita income in the United States, and then compute the corresponding percentages of foreign per capita incomes.

A comparison of "effective" or average rates (liability as a per cent of earnings before deductions and exemptions) is given in Table 7–5 and Figure 7–1. Beginning with case I, we find the rates of Sweden and the United Kingdom much the highest, followed by Japan, Italy, and Germany, with the United States and France in the lowest group. This first procedure is clearly unsatisfactory. If one wishes to compare the tax burden borne by people with similar real incomes, the corresponding levels of income should be computed by a purchasing power parity rate. Since the dollar may be somewhat overvalued by the official exchange, this adjustment results in a reduction in effective rates for the other countries; but as shown in the table, the difference between cases I and II is minor.

In case III (see Figure 7–2) a basically different view is taken. Comparison now is not between people in equal absolute income positions but between people in equal relative positions. Ideally this would be done by comparing tax rates at, say, the midpoints of income deciles or quartiles. Since distributions of family incomes are not available for all the countries, the same picture is approximated by comparing equal multiples of per capita income. We now find three distinct groups of effective rate patterns. Sweden and the United Kingdom are still ahead, with Sweden being much higher than the rest. Canada, the United States, Germany, Italy, and Japan form a very similar middle group. France lies somewhat lower. As one may expect, the pattern has become much more uniform than in cases I and II.

Of the three comparisons, case III is the most significant and useful. Consider two countries with similar distributions of income but different levels of per capita income. Similar effective rates in the case III sense now indicate the

181

TABLE 7–5

Effective Income Tax Rates*

(wage and salary income, married taxpayer with two dependents)

Case I: Comparison based on official exchange rates.
Case II: Comparison based on purchasing power parity rates.
Case III: Comparison based on multiple of per capita income.

U.S. $	3,000	4,000	6,000	10,000	20,000	50,000	100,000	500,000
Case I								
United States	—	4	8	11	16	27	38	57
Canada	—	2	6	11	22	38	49	69
United Kingdom	6	12	19	24	32	57	74	88
Federal Republic of Germany	6	9	13	18	29	41	47	51
Sweden	19	21	26	35	47	60	65	70
France	1	4	6	10	18	28	36	42
Italy	9	11	14	19	32	43	50	71
Japan	11	14	19	27	36	43	54	70
Case II								
United States	—	4	8	11	16	27	38	57
Canada	—	2	6	11	22	38	49	69
United Kingdom	2	18	16	22	29	50	70	87
Federal Republic of Germany	3	7	11	15	25	38	45	49

Sweden	18	20	24	33	46	58	65	70
France	—	2	5	8	15	29	36	42
Italy	6	8	11	16	26	40	47	62
Japan	6	8	13	20	29	41	49	67
Case III								
United States	—	4	8	11	16	27	38	57
Canada	—	—	2	7	15	32	43	65
United Kingdom	—	—	6	16	24	37	57	84
Federal Republic of Germany	—	—	6	12	19	32	41	51
Sweden	15	18	21	27	40	54	63	70
France	—	—	2	5	10	20	29	39
Italy	3	4	5	8	13	26	38	54
Japan	—	—	3	7	15	28	37	54

* See notes following Table 7–6.

TABLE 7-6

Marginal Income Tax Rates
(wage and salary income, married taxpayer with two dependents)

Case I: Comparison based on official exchange rates.
Case II: Comparison based on purchasing power parity rates.
Case III: Comparison based on multiple of per capita income.

U.S. $	3,000	4,000	6,000	10,000	20,000	50,000	100,000	500,000
Case I								
United States	14	15	17	19	25	48	58	70
Canada	—	11	17	26	45	55	65	80
United Kingdom	23	32	32	32	54	89	91	91
Federal Republic of Germany	20	20	23	33	43	52	53	53
Sweden	26	26	40	52	62	71	71	71
France	4	11	14	22	29	36	40	42
Italy	15	16	29	29	46	52	58	93
Japan	26	25	35	40	50	55	65	75
Case II								
United States	14	15	17	19	25	48	58	70
Canada	—	11	17	26	45	55	65	80
United Kingdom	16	32	32	32	37	84	91	91
Federal Republic of Germany	20	20	20	27	40	50	53	53
Sweden	26	26	40	52	62	71	71	71
France	—	4	11	14	29	36	40	42
Italy	12	13	17	25	42	48	55	68
Japan	15	20	25	35	45	55	60	75
Case III								
United States	14	15	17	19	25	48	58	70
Canada	—	—	11	19	35	50	60	75

	—	—	23	32	32	64	89	91
United Kingdom	—	—	—	—	—	—	—	—
Federal Republic of Germany	26	—	20	20	33	47	52	53
Sweden	20	26	36	52	62	71	71	71
France	—	—	4	11	22	29	36	40
Italy	—	6	8	14	20	45	51	63
Japan	—	—	10	15	30	40	50	65

Notes to Tables 7–5 and 7–6.

The official exchange rates (1965) used for conversion in case I are from International Monetary Fund, *International Finance Statistics* (March 1966). The parity ratios used in case II are from Bela Balassa, "The Purchasing Power Parity Doctrine; A Reappraisal," *Journal of Political Economy*, 72, no. 6 (December 1964), p. 588. The ratios are for 1960, so that the difference between cases I and II would be even less with more recent ratios. The per capita income figures underlying case III are obtained as the ratio of national income to population data (for 1964) from *International Finance Statistics*. The eight income levels as per cent of per capita income are 112, 149, 224, 374, 747, 1,868, 3,736, and 18,675 per cent. Effective rates are the ratios of liability to basic income before exemptions and deductions. Marginal rates are the ratios of increase in liability to increase in basic income at the level of income.

In computing tax rates for the particular countries, the general procedure was to include exemptions for husband, wife, and children, with one child under eleven and one over thirteen years old. Family allowances and child subsidies other than deductions from taxable income are excluded. All earned income credits and deductions are excluded. All earned income credits and deductions are allowed for. Family allowances in the nature of exemptions (deductions from taxable income) are taken into account, but child subsidies are excluded. Where possible, tax laws applicable to the latest year (mostly 1965) are used.

For the United States the minimum deduction is allowed for and above this a deduction of 10 per cent is applied. For Canada the special tax credit of 10 per cent applicable to 1965 is allowed for. For the United Kingdom liabilities provided for in the May 1966 budget are shown. For France, the 10 per cent occupational expense deduction is allowed for, as is the earned income allowance of 20 per cent, the 5 per cent earned income tax credit, the special tax credit for low incomes, and the surcharge of 5 per cent on incomes above Fr. 62,500. For Italy, the movable wealth tax, schedule C2, is allowed for, which includes local surcharges. Also included is the progressive complementary tax, with 20 per cent deduction and basic allowances. The family tax is included as well. The rates for Sweden include the proportional local tax of 8 per cent. For the Federal Republic of Germany, a deduction of 10 per cent is assumed.

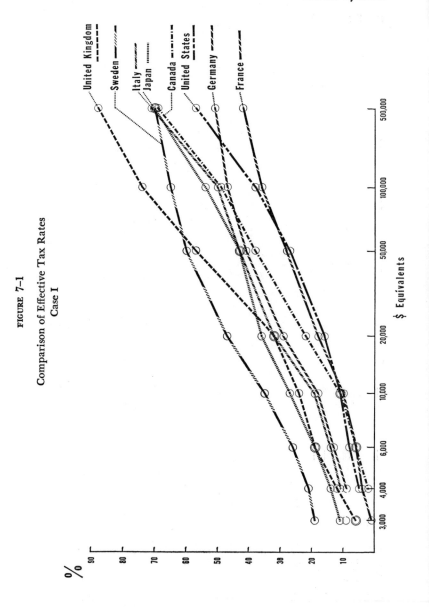

FIGURE 7-1

Comparison of Effective Tax Rates

Case I

Comparison of Tax Structures

FIGURE 7-2

Comparison of Effective Tax Rates
Case III

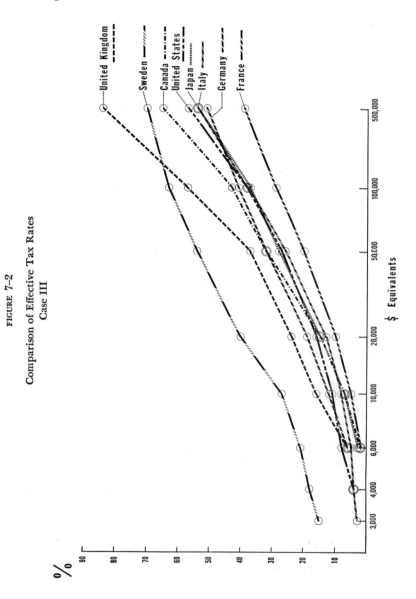

same revenue to GNP ratio, as well as the same degree of effective progression.[8] A higher effective rate schedule reflects a higher tax to GNP ratio, and if effective rates are the same throughout, the higher schedule also reflects a correspondingly higher degree of effective progression.

In Table 7–6, the same comparison is repeated for marginal rates (the increase in tax as per cent of increase in income) at the various income levels. The general picture is rather similar. The difference in marginal rates is substantially greater at the lower end of our illustrative income scale than at the top end. While the United Kingdom is highest with a rate of 91 per cent, the United States, Canada, Sweden, and Japan are all at or near 70 per cent. Germany and France, however, are substantially lower.

GLOBAL VERSUS SCHEDULAR APPROACH

So far we have dealt with the statutory tax treatment of wage or salary income only. Allowance for other types of income renders the comparison more complex. A distinction must be drawn between two basic philosophies of income tax, i.e. the schedular and the global view. According to the latter, incomes from various sources, once determined, are combined into a global amount, and the rate schedule is applied to this global or total income, independent of source. According to the former, net income from different sources may be subject to different rates. As a result, the ratio of total tax to total income is a function of income composition, whereas it is not under the global tax.

Looking at the income tax as a personal tax, the essence of which is adaptation of tax liability to the individual's

8. Effective progression is defined as the ratio of Lorenz coefficients of equality of disposable income to similar coefficients applied to income before tax. Other concepts of progression may also be applied to the Case III comparison. For a discussion of various concepts of progression, see Richard A. Musgrave and Tun Thin, "Income Tax Progression, 1929–48," *Journal of Political Economy, 56,* no. 6 (December 1948), 498–514.

ability to pay, the global concept is vastly superior. Indeed, a nonglobal approach which involves progressive rates is an incongruity. While there has been a distinct tendency for income taxes to move toward a global pattern, the schedular tradition still lingers on in a considerable number of countries, including, among our sample, the United Kingdom, France, and Italy. Other countries, such as Germany, the United States, and Canada have followed a more or less global approach from the beginning. Survival of the schedular approach in some measure reflects a historical confusion between factor shares in national income as an economic phenomenon and the household's personal income as an index of taxable capacity. The early contributions of Schanz and Haig,[9] and the later contribution of Henry Simons[10] did much to disentangle this confusion. The recent report of the Carter Commission in Canada is a landmark in implementing a truly global approach.[11] As such it differs sharply from the pragmatic view of the income concept, taken ten years earlier in the Report of the Royal Commission on the Taxation of Profits and Income.[12]

We may note, however, a basic consideration that continues to be advanced in support of the schedular view. This

9. See Georg Schanz, "Der Einkommensbegriff und die Einkommenssteuergesetze," *Finanzarchiv, 13* (1896), 1–87; and Robert Murray Haig, "The Concept of Income—Economic and Legal Aspects," in *The Federal Income Tax,* ed. Haig (New York, Columbia University Press, 1921).

10. See H. C. Simons, *Personal Income Taxation* (Chicago, University of Chicago Press, 1938). Also see Goode, *Individual Income Tax.*

11. See *Report of the Royal Commission on Taxation* (Ottawa, 1966).

12. See United Kingdom, *Royal Commission on the Taxation of Profits and Income, Final Report,* Cmd. 9474 (London, H.M. Stationery Office, 1955), p. 7. The memorandum of dissent by G. Woodstock, H. L. Bullock, and N. Kaldor constitutes a notable exception. For a first appearance of a more systematic approach in the United Kingdom, see also Prest, *Public Finance in Theory and Practice,* Chap. 14. For recent illustrations of the pragmatic view, see B. I. Bittker, "A Comprehensive Tax Base as a Goal of Income Tax Reform," *Harvard Law Review, 80* (1967), 1032–45, and my response in vol. *81* (1967), 44–62.

is the view, of long standing in the literature on public finance, that capital income should be taxed more heavily than work income. Capital income should be subject to a higher rate, or special credits or deductions should be allowed for wage income. Reflected semantically in referring to one as "unearned" and the other as "earned," this view may be rationalized by Pigou's concept of "equal sacrifice" as including the disutility of work effort as well as of forgoing income.[13] If the index of equality is thus redefined, the case for schedular taxation follows, but the case is dubious at best. Moreover, it would call for discrimination between types of work income (some occupations being more pleasant than others) as well as between work and capital income. A further argument for higher taxation of capital income has been that the very holding of property bestows a taxable capacity that is not reflected in the human capital underlying labor income. Those (including myself) who subscribe to a pure accretion concept of income will find this argument of dubious value, simply because the option to accumulate is open to every income recipient.[14]

But though there is little basis for the schedular approach on conceptual grounds, other arguments may speak in its favor. Thus schedular taxation may be used as a politically feasible means of increasing progression. Also, and this is a widely held view in South American tax thinking, higher rates on capital income may be used to offset a higher degree of evasion on such income.[15] Moreover, even where a global approach applies, distinction between income sources remains relevant in designing tax returns. Different patterns of adjustment apply in going from gross income to taxable

13. See Pigou, *A Study in Public Finance*, p. 42.

14. If the accretion concept is followed consistently, the acquisition of property from sources other than current income (e.g. from gifts or bequests) will be subject to income tax at the outset and hence need not be taxed separately thereafter.

15. See Francesco Forte, "Comment on Schedular and Global Income Taxes," in *Readings on Taxation in Developing Countries*, pp. 185–86.

income, and different provisions for defining deductible costs are needed in each case. Such distinction is wholly compatible with a global approach, provided that the various components of net income are then combined, that general deductions (e.g. for medical expenses) are made from the combined income, and that uniform rates are then applied to the total amount of taxable net income.

DIFFERENTIATION BY TYPE OF INCOME

The earlier comparison of Table 7–5 was rather unrealistic, since it assumed all income to be in the form of wages and salaries. This assumption is more or less permissible for low income groups but becomes increasingly unrealistic as we move up the income scale where other income sources gain in importance. Source of income would make no difference if all countries followed a truly global approach, applying uniform rates of tax on total income. But, in fact, there is considerable differentiation, patterns of differentiation differ, and the sources of income matter greatly. For this reason, the earlier comparison is repeated in Table 7–7, allowing now for different sources of income. Effective rates are shown for three income levels, drawn from case III of Table 7–5. The following types of income are distinguished:

1. wage and salary income;
2. independent and professional worker;
3. dividend income;
4. mixed salary and dividend income;
5. dividend income, with both corporation tax and individual income tax allowed for.

As shown in Table 7–7, the United States, Canada, the United Kingdom, and Sweden do not differentiate between wage and salary income and the earned income of the self-employed or professional person. Germany in effect discriminates in favor of the latter by granting more liberal deductions. France and Italy discriminate against the latter group.

191

TABLE 7-7

Average Tax Rates by Type of Income[a]

Income level as per cent of average income	Wage and Salary			Independent and Professional Worker			All Dividend Income			Mixed Salary and Dividend Income[b]			Combined Corporate and Personal Income Tax on All Dividend Income		
	374	1868	3736	374	1868	3736	374	1868	3736	374	1868	3736	374	1868	3736
United States[e]	.11	.27	.38	.11	.27	.38	.10	.26	.38	.11	.27	.38	.54	.62	.68
Canada	.07	.32	.43	.07	.32	.43	—	.12	.23	—	.18	.27	.50	.59	.64
United Kingdom	.16	.37	.57	.16	.37	.57	.25	.56	.72	.20	.49	.67	.55	.74	.83
Sweden	.27	.54	.63	.27	.54	.63	.26	.54	.63	.26	.54	.63	.64	.77	.82
Federal Republic of Germany	.12	.32	.41	.06[c]	.26[c]	.35[c]	.13	.33	.41	.11	.32	.41	.26	.43	.50
France	.05	.20	.29	.15	.39	.50	—	.21	.35	—	.30	.39	.39	.60	.68
Italy[d]	.08	.26	.38	.14	.31	.41	.06	.23	.31	.06	.21	.30	.15	.30	.38

a. For married man with two children.
b. Dividends as 40 per cent, 70 per cent, and 80 per cent of three income levels respectively.
c. Allowing maximum deductions.
d. Except for the last column, the movable wealth tax is not important to dividend income, since it is paid by the corporation.
e. For the United States, the corresponding absolute levels of income are $10,000, $50,000, and $100,000 respectively.

In France, various deductions and credits applicable to dependent workers are not permitted the self-employed, while in Italy a higher rate schedule applies.

Turning now to the treatment of capital income, Germany applies the same treatment as to earned income. The United States and Sweden provide for a small dividend exclusion from taxable income, which reduces the rate at the lower end of the scale but becomes insignificant at higher levels. Canada goes further and allows a credit against tax of 20 per cent of dividends received, but without refunds. The result is a substantially lower rate of tax and elimination of "double taxation" of dividends in a way that favors the high income shareholder. The French pattern is more complex. On one side, the dividend recipient receives a credit against his tax of one-half the corporation tax imputed to his profit share, and where needed the credit is given in refund form. On the other, the earned income credit granted to wage and salary income is disallowed for capital income. The net result, as shown in the table, is an effective rate below that on dependent work income at the lower end of the scale and a rate above that at the upper end. Among our group of countries, only the United Kingdom goes in the opposite direction and applies a higher tax on dividend income. This results not from a different rate schedule, but from disallowing the credits applicable to earned income under both the income and the surtax schedules. In all, the United Kingdom rates are the highest, followed closely by Sweden and, after some distance, by the other countries. The rates for the United States and Canada are at the lower end of the scale.

Given the previously noted reasons for discriminating against unearned income, it may seem surprising that most of our countries do the opposite. The explanation, of course, lies in the ambiguous nature of the corporation tax. The deductions granted by the United States and Sweden, as well as the credits given by Canada and France, may be interpreted as partway measures (not very well conceived ones at that) to "integrate" the corporate with the individual income tax. That is to say, the corporation income tax may be looked upon not as an absolute and separate tax but as a device to withhold at the source individual income tax on dividend income, and to substitute for individual income tax on retained earnings. Under this view, "equal" treatment of dividend income requires individual income tax rates thereon that are below those on earned income, so that the latter are matched by the combined individual and corporate rates.[16]

This calls for a comparison of the combined individual and corporate rates. As shown in the last three columns of Table 7–7, these rates are much above those applicable to earned income.[17] Sweden's combined rates are highest, followed closely by the United Kingdom. In all, the pattern is more uniform than for the individual income tax on dividend income only. Whether or not the higher combined rates are taken to discriminate against capital income or the lower dividend rates are taken to discriminate in its favor thus depends on whether one views the corporation tax as an absolute tax or as a part of the individual income tax. But however this may be, it is the combined rate that matters from the point of view of investment decisions by the individual investor and resulting effects on capital allocation.

16. For equal treatment to result, the individual income tax rate $t_i{}^d$ on dividend income should relate to the individual income tax rate $t_i{}^e$ on an equal amount of earned income such that

$$t_i{}^d = \frac{t_i{}^e - t_c}{1 - t_c}$$

where all rates are average rates and t_c stands for the corporation tax rate.

17. The combined tax equals $t_c D/(1 - t_c) + t_i D$ where $D/(1 - t_c)$ is grossed up dividend income. The tax is divided by $D/(1 - t_c)$ to obtain the average rate shown in the table.

Finally, Table 7–7 shows a comparison of rates for mixed incomes, using typical combinations of earned and unearned income of various income levels. The result reflects a mixture of the previously observed results for the component cases.

CAPITAL GAINS

Dividends, of course, are not the only type of capital income. Other types, including interest, rent, and capital gains, also deserve notice. Among these, the latter is much the most important for our purposes. Capital gains receive highly preferential treatment in all the countries here considered. In no case is there a tax on unrealized gains, and realized gains are taxed at lower rates, if at all.

Consider first the taxation of gains from the sale of assets other than real estate. Most countries tax realized gains at the full rate (applicable to earned income) if the asset was held for a short period only. This is defined as six months in the United States and Germany, one year in the United Kingdom, and two years in Sweden. Assets held for a longer period are taxed at rates of 25 per cent in the United States, 30 per cent in the United Kingdom, and not at all in Germany. Sweden includes a declining fraction of gains in taxable income as the holding period lengthens. France applies a tax only under special circumstances (sale of shares where the taxpayer has a controlling interest), and there is no tax at all in Japan and Italy, even for short holdings.

Gains from the sale of real estate are treated similarly to other assets in the United States and in the United Kingdom, except that the latter exempts owner-occupied real estate. In Sweden they are fully taxable unless held for seven years, and for longer holdings a declining fraction is included in taxable income. In Japan such gains are taxed if held under three years but not thereafter. In Germany the tax applies up to four years and not thereafter. Italy taxes land gains.

195

In France a tax of 15 per cent applies if held less than five years, and there is a further small tax on the sale of unimproved land. The general picture may be summarized as follows:

France: Individuals are not taxed, except for a tax of 8 per cent where the seller's interest in a corporation is controlling. Sale of a capital asset by a business is taxed with roll-over provision. Losses are fully deductible against gains. Speculative gains from the sale of real estate are taxed at 15 per cent if the asset was held for less than five years. There is also a special tax on gains from the sale of unimproved land.

Germany: Gains are fully taxed if held for under six months, not if held longer. Losses are deducted against gains from the same year only. Gains from the sale of real estate are taxed fully if held for under two years, not if held longer.

Italy: Individuals are not taxed, except for gains of professional speculators and gains from residential lots.

Japan: Gains made by individuals are not taxed, unless accruing to professional speculators. Gains from the sale of real estate are subject to tax if held for under three years.

Sweden: If held under two years, 100 per cent of gains is subject to tax; 75 per cent if held three years; 50 per cent if held four years; 25 per cent if held five years; 0 per cent if held longer. Losses are set off against gains from the same year only. Gains from the sale of real estate are 100 per cent taxable if held for less than eight years, taxable at a declining per cent if held eight, nine, and ten years, and tax-free if held longer.

United States: Gains are fully taxable if the asset is held under six months; inclusion of 50 per cent of gain, with maximum rate of 25 per cent, if held longer. Losses are offset against gains with limited offset against other income.

United Kingdom: Individuals are fully taxed if the asset is held under six months; if the asset is held longer, two·

thirds of the gain is included, with maximum rate of 30 per cent. Coporations are fully taxed under the corporation income tax. Gains from the sale of owner-occupied real estate are exempt; otherwise, gains from the sale of real estate are treated similarly to gains from other assets.

As this brief survey shows, income taxation has failed universally to come to grips with income accruing in the form of capital gains. With the single exception of Sweden, realized gains are only lightly taxed by the countries covered in our sample, while unrealized gains escape taxation altogether. As has been pointed out in connection with United States data, preferential tax treatment of capital gains stops progression far short of the supposed level suggested by the nominal rate structure. In the United States it, in fact, results in regressive taxation over the higher income ranges.[18] The reason, of course, is that capital gains rise sharply as a share of income when moving up the income scale, and that capital income frequently may be converted into capital gains.

While this is not the place at which to discuss possible remedies to this situation, it should be noted that prevailing undertaxation of capital gains constitutes the most important inequality in the treatment of various income sources. Income taxes, such as those of the United States and Germany, which appear highly global in character, are in fact far from global once the capital gains problem is considered. Preferential treatment of capital gains, typically, more than outweighs the discriminatory treatment of dividends or, for that matter, the earned income credit at the lower end of the income scale.

The preceding reasoning, it should be pointed out, is

18. See, for instance, *Tax Reform Studies and Proposals*, U.S. Treasury Department, Part 1, p. 81, U.S. Congress, House Committee on Ways and Means (Washington, D.C., G.P.O., Feb. 5, 1969). See also J. Pechman, "Individual Income Tax Provisions of the Revenue Act of 1964," *Journal of Finance*, 20 (May 1965).

based on the proposition that capital gains—whether realized or not—constitute an increment to wealth and, conceptually, should be included as taxable income. While it is a matter of judgment whether the basic personal tax should be on income or on consumption, capital gains are part of income once the base is chosen. It cannot be argued convincingly that income derived from the sale of capital assets adds less to taxable capacity than income derived from dividends. Nor can it be argued that the addition to taxable capacity occurs only at realization. The decision *not* to realize simply reflects the taxpayer's desire to reinvest in the same asset.

While there is an overwhelming case, conceptually, for treating capital gains like other income, some practical difficulties must be noted. First, taxation of realized gains at ordinary rates results in inequities under progressive rates, since sales tend to fluctuate. This may be met by averaging provisions. Second, taxation of realized gains at ordinary rates results in a locked-in effect unless unrealized gains are taxed as well. This distorting effect on capital transactions can be avoided only if unrealized gains are taxed as well. Third, annual taxation of unrealized gains is administratively unfeasible. However, the problem may be solved by "constructive realization at death," i.e. taxation of gains at death *as if* assets have been realized. Combined with interest for delayed payment, this is the key to proper capital gains taxation under a global income tax.

If, then, the problem is technically solvable, why has it been disregarded so generally? The answer, in part, may lie in confusion regarding the nature of the taxable income concept. But more important, it will be found in the realm of fiscal politics, i.e. a compromise between the desire to give the appearance of steeply progressive rates and the further desire to cushion their impact on capital income. Whatever the merit or demerit of steeply progressive rates, the result is a severe distortion in the treatment of various income sources. Tax structures would be improved greatly if the highly progressive set of nominal rates could be exchanged for a lower but more fully applicable rate structure.

TAXPAYING UNIT

All our comparisons have referred to a married taxpayer with two dependents as the most representative tax-paying unit. Since the relative treatment of single and married taxpayers and the allowance for dependents differs between countries, different results are obtained for other units.

In the United Kingdom, Sweden, Canada, and Japan, husband and wife must file joint returns so that the progressive rate schedule applies to the family income. In the United States and Germany, they may exercise income splitting, i.e. divide the combined income by two and pay twice the tax on this amount. As a result, the tax is determined at a lower point in the progressive rate schedule, and the tax on married taxpayers is reduced compared to that on single taxpayers. In France the principle of income splitting is carried to an extreme, the number of permitted splits rising with the number of children. Thus discrimination against the single taxpayer and in favor of the large family is greatest in France, especially over income ranges where the split is of major importance. In Italy earned incomes of husbands and wives are taxed separately under the schedular tax, but mandatory joint returns are required under the progressive complementary tax.

All of our countries, with the exception of France, permit personal exemptions for husband and wife, and additional exemptions for children, which, in some cases, depend on age. France, instead, exempts a minimum amount of income and offers other forms of income tax relief for small incomes. Depending on the level of first bracket rates, which also differ considerably among our countries, the level of personal exemptions is the major determinant of progressivity over the lower end of the income scale.

The preceding sketch of income tax comparisons should suffice to show the variety of forms this tax may take, as well as a considerable degree of common practice. Many interesting aspects of the problem, including savings incentives, the treatment of imputed income, and deductions of items such as interest, might have been added. Above all, the reader will keep in mind that the liabilities shown in our tables reflect an assumption of complete compliance. Actually there is no country in which compliance is perfect, and though comparative data are not available, the degrees of compliance differ by countries and by taxes. Thus actual liabilities may compare rather differently from the statutory amounts shown in these tables.

OTHER TAXES

We now turn to a brief consideration of taxes on business units, including those on profits and on sales.

PROFIT TAXES

All the countries here considered impose taxes on corporation income. As shown in Table 7–8, the tax is generally imposed on profits, except for the case of Italy, which also has a tax imposed on excess profits. Rates are usually lower on small companies, and range to about 50 per cent for most of our countries, with a somewhat higher rate in Sweden.

Of the countries here compared, Germany is now the only one that employs a split rate, with profits paid out subject to only about half the rate as applies to profits retained. This policy, which has been in effect since 1956, reverses the earlier practice, which had placed a heavier tax on distribution. The United Kingdom, which had traditionally imposed a lower rate on distribution, recently moved in the opposite direction and now imposes a uniform rate. The recent change in the United Kingdom toward the United States

TABLE 7–8

Profit Taxes in Selected Countries

Country	Tax	Base	Global Rate	Split Rate Distribution	Split Rate Retention	Shareholder Deduction or Credit	Type of Investment Incentive
United States	Corporation tax	Profits	22–48[a]	—	—	Deduction of $200	Investment credit
United Kingdom	Company tax	Profits	40	—	—	—	Investment allowance
Federal Republic of Germany	Corporation tax	Profits	—	23[b]	51	—	Accelerated depreciation tax-free reserves
Sweden	Business tax	Profits	13[c]	—	—	—	—
	Corporation tax	Profits	50[d]	—	—	—	Investment reserves
France	Company tax	Profits	50	—	—	50% dividend credit[e]	Accelerated depreciation
Netherlands	Corporation tax	Profits	42–57	—	—	—	—
Italy	Company tax	Excess profits	0–13[f]	—	—	—	—
	Income tax	Profits	23–29[g]	—	—	100% dividend credit	—
Canada	Corporation tax	Profits	50	—	—	20% dividend credit	Accelerated depreciation

a. State taxes varying between 0 and 5 per cent not included.
b. The rate on distribution is 15 per cent, but tax on distribution is counted as retention and subject to 51 per cent rate.
c. The business tax is based on three indices, payroll, profits, and capital. The profit-based rate amounts to some 13 per cent, including 5 per cent basic rate plus 300 per cent local multiplier.
d. Includes local income tax averaging 17 per cent and national corporation income tax on net profits of 40 per cent.
e. 50 per cent of dividends credited against personal income tax, imposed on dividends grossed up by credit. Refunds granted where due.
f. The tax equals 15 per cent on profits in excess of 6 per cent, applied to income net of movable wealth tax paid in prior year. There is also a 0.75 per cent tax on capital, which is not included here since it does not enter into the marginal rate.
g. Tax on movable wealth, category B, at rates from 18 to 24 per cent, plus 2 per cent flat rate for chamber of commerce and a 15 per cent provincial surcharge. The marginal rate for large and profitable companies thus equals $.24 + .15(.24) + .02 + .15(.704) + .15(.1056) = 42$.

system runs counter to the tendency of the Common Market countries to apply a lower tax on distributed earnings.[19]

Use of a split rate may be looked at from the point of view of economic policy or equity. From the former point of view, lighter taxation of retention will encourage capital formation but make for expansion of already profitable firms and increase concentration; lighter taxation of distribution, on the contrary, leads to higher consumption and makes for a wider distribution of funds to be invested through the capital market. On equity grounds, lighter taxation of distributed earnings is in line with an integrated view of the individual income and corporation tax, and with the latter's role as an income tax substitute on retained earnings.

The other side of the picture is given by the treatment of dividends under the individual income tax. As shown in the table, three of our countries permit crediting of corporation tax against individual income tax on dividend income. While Italy grants a 100 per cent credit of income tax paid by companies, France credits 50 per cent, and Canada, 20 per cent. The United States recently dropped the crediting approach and now permits a deduction of the first $200 of dividend income. Only the French method offers a satisfactory approach to integration, and in most cases it is difficult to know whether the dividend adjustment is more for equity (integration) or incentive reasons.[20]

The deduction method, followed by the United States, is not a basis for achieving integration, but may be rationalized in a different equity context. If investment incentive re-

19. This was recommended by the Neumark Committee report. See "Report of the Fiscal and Financial Committee," *The EEC Reports on Tax Harmonization* (Amsterdam, International Bureau of Fiscal Documentation, 1963).

20. On equity grounds, proper use of the credit requires inclusion into taxable income of dividends grossed up to include corporation tax, determination of personal tax liability on this basis, and then crediting against it of corporation tax paid. In Canada there is no grossing up, nor is there in Italy.

quires relief for profit income, and given the fact that the share of such income in the total rises when moving up the income scale, incentive policy may have regressive implications. If this is held to be undesirable, it might be offset by the progressive nature of a fixed deduction.

Finally, all the corporation taxes here considered make special provision in one or another form for investment incentives. In most cases these relate to accelerated depreciation (Germany, France, Canada), while in others special investment credits, allowances, or reserves are given (the United States, the United Kingdom, Sweden). The Swedish provision for investment reserves is of particular interest, as it is the only measure that is explicitly designed for use in a countercyclical setting.[21] The variety of provisions regarding the definition of income, combined with the widespread application of investment incentives, means that there is a substantial difference between the overall rates shown in Tables 7–5 to 7–7, and the actual effective rates that result after these provisions are allowed for.[22] And again, it must be noted that there are substantial differences in compliance which further affect the comparative picture.

SALES AND EXCISE TAXES

Sales and excise taxes remain to be considered. As noted in Table 7–2, such taxes provide an especially large share of the total revenue in Italy and France, and a much lower one in the United States. On the average, somewhat over one-third of the total is derived from this source.

The pattern of such taxes for 1964 is shown in Table 7–9. Most of the countries place substantial reliance on a general

21. See Gunnar Eliasson, *Investment Funds in Operation* (Stockholm, National Institute of Economic Research, 1965).

22. See Peggy B. Musgrave, "Direct Business Tax Harmonization," in Carl S. Shoup, ed., *Fiscal Harmonization in Common Markets, 2* (New York, Columbia University Press, 1967), p. 253, where a comparison of effective rates adjusted for differences in depreciation practices is given.

TABLE 7-9

Composition of Sales and Excise Taxes[a]

(all levels of government; as per cent of Total Sales and Excise Taxes)

	General			Selective			
	Value Added	Turnover	General Sales	Tobacco, Alcohol, Beer	Automotive	Other	Customs
United States	—	—	19	28	20	30	3
Canada	—	—	38	14	12	22	14
United Kingdom	—	—	18[b]	46	4	27[a]	5[c]
Germany	—	52	—	13	14	11	10
Netherlands	—	—	45	17	4	9	25
France	56[d]	—	—	9[e]	—	16	19
Sweden	—	26	—	30	13	19	12
Italy	—	29	7	3	15	38	4
Japan	—	—	9	42	16	21	12

a. Based on *Excise Tax Compendium*, Part 1 (1964), pp. 125 ff.

b. Purchase tax.

c. Includes "protective tariffs" only.

d. Includes tax on services and retail sales.

e. Includes profits from liquor and match monopoly.

tax, including a value-added tax in France, a turnover tax in Germany, Sweden, and Italy, and general sales taxes in the remaining countries. For the United Kingdom the purchase tax may also be included in this general category. The weight of this single revenue source in the total sales and excise structure is especially great in France, Germany, and the Netherlands, and less so in Japan, Italy, and the United States.

Other domestic sales and excise taxes include throughout a heavy contribution by tobacco and alcoholic beverages, reflecting a widespread acceptance of the proposition that the consumption of such items should be discouraged. The weight of these taxes is especially significant in Japan and the United Kingdom. Automotive taxes also provide substantial contributions. Customs duties remain of major importance in France and Italy, and are least significant in the United States.

The widespread use of turnover taxes (until recently) should be noted. These taxes applied to the wholesale and manufacturing stage, and in some cases (Italy and Sweden) retail sales were included as well. In some cases rates were lower at the wholesale stage. Thus the German tax was 1 per cent at the wholesale and 4 per cent at the manufacturing stage.

Turnover taxes have the political advantage of yielding large amounts of revenue at what appear to be low rates, and (compared with a single-stage tax) of increasing the likelihood that the tax bite will be effective at least somewhere along the line of production. At the same time the implicit ad valorem rate on various products differs arbitrarily with the number of turnovers involved, and vertical integration of firms is encouraged. For this reason there has been much interest in recent years in the replacement of turnover taxes by a value-added tax. The French enactment of such a tax has been of particular interest. Imposed at the rate of 20 per cent at the manufacturing and wholesaling stage (with the retailing stage exempted), the tax is levied at each transaction on the buyer, who may credit the tax paid previously by the seller. Thus a degree of self-enforcement in administration is introduced. This tax is supplemented by a tax on services and a tax on retail sales. Following the French example of 1954, replacement of the turnover tax by a value-added tax has recently been effected by Germany and the Netherlands. It has also been recommended by the Neumark Report, which looks toward a uniform rate value-added tax in the Common Market.[23] While the revenue shares drawn from various types of tax continue to differ sharply, there is a tendency for the structure of particular taxes to become more similar.

23. See p. 280.

8 THE CHANGING FUNCTION OF FISCAL POLICY

Having considered the specific problems of expenditure and tax structure, I now turn to the changing macro role of fiscal policy.[1] Throughout the course of development, fiscal policy has important bearing on the level of employment and prices and on the rate of growth; but the modus operandi of fiscal policy and the requirements placed upon it vary as the economy advances. To simplify our task, we distinguish between three stages of development and, at the risk of overdrawing the picture somewhat, examine the role of fiscal policy at each stage.

EARLY STAGE

At an early stage of economic development, there is the greatest need for fiscal action to initiate growth, yet the

1. For general discussions of fiscal policy and growth in less developed countries, see B. Higgins, *Economic Development;* Higgins, "Financing Accelerated Growth," in Peacock and Hauser, eds., *Government Finance and Economic Development;* Lewis, *Theory of Economic Growth;* W. Heller, "Fiscal Policies for Underdeveloped Countries," in *Readings on Taxation in Developing Countries;* N. Kaldor, "The Role of Taxation in Economic Development," in *Fiscal Policy for Economic Growth in Latin America;* K. S. Krishnaswamy, "The Evolution of Tax Structure in a Development Policy," and B. Hansen, "Tax Policy and Mobilization of Earnings," both in *Government Finance and Economic Development.*

means of fiscal policy are more limited than in developed economies. This is but another aspect of the vicious circle of poverty and stagnation in the subsistence economy.

THE BASIC PROBLEM

The economy is characterized by a low level of income with large parts of the population living at subsistence wages. There is a high degree of unemployment, or "underemployment" of labor. In some cases, there is also substantial underutilization of land and of other natural resources. Now it is evident that income can be raised only by raising productivity and/or the level of employment and resource utilization.[2] Raising productivity requires increased capital formation, including investment in human skills; and to finance such investment there is need for increased saving and reduced consumption.

With exceedingly low consumption levels, this is extremely burdensome and politically difficult to accomplish. Increased employment would be much more attractive as the first step. Output could be raised, and economic growth could be launched without reducing consumption. Why then should it be so difficult to secure this increase in employment, especially if the unemployment problem in developed economies has been largely mastered?

In the developed economy the Keynesian problem of unemployment arises when the level of aggregate demand is too low to purchase the full employment output. This will be the case if the rate of investment falls short of that rate of savings that income recipients wish to undertake at a full employment level of income. Such a deficiency may arise because interest rates are too high or investment prospects are too poor. In either case, the remedy lies in policy measures that raise demand, be it private (via monetary expan-

2. For the time being, we avoid the distinction between raising total and per capita output by assuming a constant population, leaving the population problem for later consideration. See p. 217.

sion or tax reduction) or public (via increased public outlays).[3]

Certain difficulties remain in the application of this policy—short-run cyclical swings are difficult to predict, the effectiveness lag of policy measures is troublesome, and structural maladjustments in the labor market may set a temporary barrier to full employment—but there is no question that sustained periods of severe unemployment can be avoided. In all, the basic mechanism of high employment policy in the developed economy is relatively simple and effective.

But unfortunately this mechanism cannot be transferred to low income countries. Here the causes of unemployment (or underemployment) are different, as are the policies needed to resolve it.[4] Underemployment (as distinct from Keynesian unemployment) may exist simply because it does not pay to work. The capital stock being very small, labor productivity and hence the wage rate are very low. This does not mean that labor productivity need be zero. Wages may be at the subsistence level, or they may be higher but,

3. If money wages are downward rigid, the increase in demand must involve rising expenditures in money terms. If prices can fall, unemployment may lead to declining wages and prices, but this will not raise employment, as demand in money terms will fall as well, leaving demand in real terms unchanged. A decline in money wages will help only to the extent that the resulting increase in the real value of money balances leads to an upward shift in the consumption function, a possible relationship that, however, has little operational significance. See my *Theory of Public Finance,* Chap. 17.

4. For a discussion of the limitations of Keynesian theory as applied to underdeveloped economies, see V. K. R. V. Rao, "Investment, Income and the Multiplier in an Underdeveloped Economy," *Indian Economic Review* (February 1952); W. Arthur Lewis, "Economic Development with Unlimited Supplies of Labor," *The Manchester School, 23* (May 1955); both reprinted in D. N. Agarwala and S. P. Singh, *The Economics of Underdevelopment* (London, Oxford University Press, 1958). A review of disguised unemployment concepts is given in P. Wonnacott, "Disguised and Overt Unemployment in Underdeveloped Economies," *Quarterly Journal of Economics, 76* (May 1962), 279.

combined with a low aspiration level, remain such that the gain in income to be derived from work is not worth the leisure that must be surrendered. In the classical sense of the term, there is full employment, as people work as much as they wish at the prevailing real wage. In such a case raising expenditures will not increase employment but only prices. In order to raise employment (increase the work input that people wish to undertake) there must be an increase in aspiration levels and/or an increase in productivity and hence in wage rates. To accomplish this, increased employment must be preceded by increased saving and transfer of resources from the production of consumer goods into capital formation.

A further cause of underemployment may be found in rigidities in the proportions in which labor and capital can be combined.[5] In the absence of more capital, more labor cannot be employed, even though people would be willing to work at a lower wage rate than prevails. But for technical reasons, involving fixed proportions or discontinuities in factor combinations, this is not possible. Now unemployment in the classical sense exists, but increasing aggregate demand is again not the proper remedy. Employment, as before, can be increased only by increasing the capital stock, and fiscal policy will be helpful only to the extent that it can accomplish this. Merely raising the level of consumer demand will not do.

Finally, the situation may be such that increased output could be achieved with little additional capital, provided the necessary organizational effort and know-how were forthcoming. Agricultural labor surplus, for instance, could be

5. See R. S. Eckaus, "The Factor-Proportions Problem in Underdeveloped Areas," *American Economic Review, 45* (September 1955), reprinted in Agarwala and Singh. Eckaus, in addition to dealing with technological restraints on factor variability, also deals with the case where factor proportions (though variable) are distorted by market imperfections, e.g. a wage floor imposed by unions. This leads to more capital intensive production and, if capital is scarce, lower employment.

put to work in community projects if so organized. But again a shift in the structure of resources is needed to raise employment, and expansion of aggregate demand is called for only to the extent that the economy can respond to increased output.

What is worse, the difference between fiscal policies in high and low income economies is an asymmetrical one. While the low income economy may not share the advanced economy's favorable employment response to demand expansion, it will share the penalty of excess demand. Inflation results in the underdeveloped as well as the developed economy, and it is harmful in both cases. While this does not make a case for deflation—a high and rising level of demand (high relative to feasible outputs) is essential to economic growth—the basic problem of economic growth in the low income economy is one of supply and does not lend itself to simple solution by demand expansion.

DOMESTIC FISCAL POLICY

The first step for fiscal policy, then, is to raise productivity. By the nature of the problem, this is largely a precondition to increased employment. It may be approached in a number of ways.

Shifting Resources from Consumption to Capital Formation. The most direct, if most painful, way is by shifting employed resources from production for consumption to production for capital formation.[6] Since the average level of consumption is extremely low, this may be a difficult task. Luxury consumption such as that which exists in highly developed countries may absorb but a small part of total income, and a large part of the population be close to subsistence. Yet income distribution is skewed, and typically

6. To the extent that labor productivity is raised by increased consumption, production for such consumption is "human investment" and equivalent to capital formation. See Carl S. Shoup, "Production from Consumption," *Public Finance, 20,* nos. 1–2 (1965), 173.

more so than in developed countries.[7] Thus even low income countries may have substantial luxury consumption, especially if defined in relative rather than in absolute terms. The fiscal task then is to cut back such dispensable consumption and to make it available for saving and capital formation.[8]

Luxury consumption may be reduced through progressive income taxation. But as noted before, an effective system of progressive income taxation may be difficult to enforce. Moreover, it has the disadvantage of reducing private saving as well as luxury consumption, and it may hit precisely those savings that will give rise to the most productive investment, i.e. entrepreneurial savings in the capitalist sector as distinct

7. Kuznets finds that the share of the top 10 per cent of the population is considerably higher in underdeveloped countries than in developed ones. While the situation differs by countries, the ratios range around 45 and 30 per cent respectively. He also finds the ratios for the lowest 60 per cent to be about similar for both groups, ranging around 30 per cent. The share of the middle 35 per cent is considerably higher in the developed group, with ratios of 25 and 40 per cent. The difference is explained by wider intersector differences in product per worker, as well as by wider inequality within the urban sector. See Simon Kuznets, *Modern Economic Growth* (New Haven, Yale University Press, 1966), p. 420, and "Quantitative Aspects of the Economic Growth of Nations: VIII. Distribution of Income by Size," *Economic Development and Cultural Change, 11,* no. 2 (January 1963), Part II, pp. 1–80.

For a contrary view, especially of distribution in India, see P. D. Djha and V. V. Bhatt, "Income Distribution: A Case Study of India," *American Economic Review, 54* (September 1964), 711, which shows a surprising degree of similarity in decile distributions between low and high income countries. Income received by the top 20 per cent in developed countries ranges from 45 to 50 per cent, whereas the corresponding figures for low income countries range from 40 to 60 per cent. See also the subsequent comments by Eva Mueller, I. R. K. Sarma, and S. Swamy in *American Economic Review, 55* (December 1965).

8. Lewis, *Theory of Economic Growth,* p. 236, holds that "no nation is so poor that it could not save 12 per cent of its national income if it wanted to." He attributes failure to do so to the absence of an entrepreneurial class and of a larger profit share.

from those of wealthy landowners which are put to less productive use.[9]

A more flexible and effective approach is through consumption taxes. A personal expenditure tax not being feasible at this stage, various commodity taxes must be used. Since luxury consumption typically involves imported goods, customs duties play a strategic role. Regarding domestic output, a selective system of manufacturers' excises is called for. If such a system rarely exists in low income countries, the reason is not to be found in administrative difficulties but in the policy maker's reluctance to cut back such amenities as exist. Being well acquainted with Western standards of consumption, he understandably succumbs to the demonstration effect. Yet severe taxes on luxury consumption are one of the preconditions for capital formation and growth.

As will be noted presently, public investment is of decisive importance at the early stage of economic development, but the need for public saving (excess of receipts over consumption expenditure) is equally basic. Since the rise of private saving is a slow process, apt to follow the course of economic development rather than to lead it, initial emphasis must be on public saving. At the same time, such saving need not all go into public investment, as it may be transferred into private investment via lending or credit expansion. This is indeed the primary function of central banking at the early stage of development.

Increasing the Efficiency of Investment. We have argued so far that an increased level of capital formation is needed to increase labor productivity. But productivity may be raised also by increasing the efficiency of the investment mix.

With regard to *public* investment, the need is for careful evaluation of the returns to be derived from alternative

9. Ibid.

investments, allowing for immediate monetary returns as well as social gains generated by the externalities of the projects. If such evaluation is difficult in the setting of developed countries, it is more so in low income countries where capital markets are imperfect, externalities tend to be more important, and the dynamics of the development process are more difficult to predict. Yet it is a counsel of despair to hold that the problem is beyond assessment and to rely entirely on the market to provide the solution. Certain types of investment will not be made privately, and even with regard to others, the organization of a market may not exist. Government must do as well as it can with available information.[10] The process of evaluation, moreover, needs to include human investment as well as plant and infra structure.

Capital allocation in the *private* market, similarly, may be far from optimal with regard to growth. Private savings, generated by the high income groups, typically tend to be diverted into luxury housing and commercial structures. The result is luxury consumption rather than growth-inducing investment, and the remedy is again through consumption taxes, including progressive real estate taxation. Next, such savings frequently flow into foregin investment—to escape the risks of political instability at home, to circumvent exchange controls, or for other reasons. As a result, domestic economic development is retarded and measures to control capital outflow may be needed. The remedy here is in policies for social reform and political stability that

10. See H. B. Chenery, "The Application of Investment Criteria," *Quarterly Journal of Economics, 67* (February 1953), 67; and Chenery, "Comparative Advantage and Development Policy," *American Economic Review, 51* (March 1961), 18; W. Galenson and H. Liebenstein, "Investment Criteria, Productivity and Economic Development," *Quarterly Journal of Economics, 69* (August 1955). For a general survey of the literature see Otto Eckstein, "Investment Criteria for Economic Development and the Theory of Intertemporal Welfare Economics," *Quarterly Journal of Economics, 71* (February 1957).

render domestic investment more attractive; but where this will not do, constraints on foreign investment may be needed as well.

Beyond this, other inefficiencies of private investment may arise. Pockets of savings in the agricultural sector may be locked into conventional and inefficient investment practices, and thus not become available for more efficient use in industrial investment. Both tax and capital market devices may be helpful in accomplishing this, together with borrowing and redisbursement of funds through a public development bank. Indeed, there are many instances in the low income economy where the social return on investment differs from the private return, due to the dynamics of the development process to which the investment gives rise.[11] The needed adjustment may call for redirecting private rather than public investment, but fiscal instruments are needed in both cases.

Surplus Land. Failure to utilize land intensively, or in the most efficient lines of production, is a widespread malaise in South American countries, as well as in parts of the Near East. It reflects absentee ownership and the attractiveness of landholding as an inflation hedge. While the basic solution may require land reform, tax measures can be helpful. More intensive use may be induced by heavier taxes on acreage, as this renders the holding of unused land less profitable. Going further, the tax may be placed on potential as distinct from actual output, and the profitability of intensive cultivation may be raised by relating tax and utilization rates.[12] Collection of taxes in cash may force farmers into cash crops and encourage the integration of isolated sectors of the economy with the market. Capital gains taxation may prevent misdirected land speculation, and classified or even progressive real estate taxes may be

11. See p. 126.

12. See the proposal for "A Graduated Land Tax" in *Readings on Taxation in Developing Countries,* p. 442.

used to discourage the squandering of resources in luxury construction.

At early stages of economic development there is a strong case for encouraging capital inflow. The rate of return on investment is high, but the sacrifice in releasing resources from already low levels of consumption is even higher. By importing capital now and repaying it later, investment may be financed by savings drawn from a higher (future) level of income, thus reducing the sacrifice involved. Moreover, capital inflow may be crucial because investment involves import of capital goods, which imports cannot be financed merely by the release of domestic saving, even if that were feasible. Finally, foreign capital inflow is helpful because it will bring with it the needed resource of technical and managerial know-how.

It is thus desirable for fiscal policy to lend encouragement to capital inflow, either in public loans or aid to government, or in the finance of private investment. Which is preferable from the point of view of the low income country will not be examined here, but tax policy enters in the latter connection only. As we shall see later, unilateral tax measures by the low income country do not suffice, cooperation by the developed (capital-exporting) countries being needed as well.[13] Also it is important to note that tax relief to foreign capital is not a costless matter and must thus be handled with great care. The increase in output or income from capital import may be divided into (1) profits to foreign capital after domestic tax, (2) domestic tax, and (3) income gains accruing to other factors. Gains (2) and (3) accrue to the capital importing country, but (1) does not. Tax reduction for foreign capital reduces (2) and raises (1). It must thus be measured against the gains in (3) as new capital inflow is induced by the reduction. The

13. See p. 255.

greater the volume of foreign capital that has been imported already, the more responsive the inflow will have to be to justify a rate reduction.[14]

POPULATION CONTROL

Population control falls outside the jurisdiction of fiscal policy as an instrument of macro policy, but it is too crucial an aspect of development policy to go unmentioned. The purpose of economic development is to raise per capita income. Thus economic development, leading to growth in output, is to no avail if population growth operates to cancel output gains, maintaining per capita income at starvation levels.

Accentuated by a falling death rate and declining infant mortality, the population growth in many low income countries bids to swamp such gains as are now being made through budgetary and other development measures. Budget policy, therefore, cannot overlook this aspect. Public financing of birth control may well be the most important contribution that budget policy can make to economic development. Beyond this, tax policy may be used to influence family size. If birth control is not accepted because people consider large families as profitable, tax measures to penalize large families may be a helpful, if inequitable, device to neutralize this error in aggregation.

MIDDLE STAGE

Important though these functions are, the use of fiscal policy as an instrument of macro policy remains limited so

14. See Peggy B. Richman (Musgrave), *Taxation of Foreign Investment: An Economic Analysis* (Baltimore, Johns Hopkins Press, 1963), Chap. 5. Assuming that tax revenue is invested in public capital formation and that all private investment is from foreign capital, the author inquires what rate of capital inflow is needed so that total capital formation is increased by granting tax exemption.

long as the basic problem is one of structural adjustment and of overcoming rigidities that prevent the play of market adjustments. Fiscal policy does not come into its own until a substantial excess of income above subsistence has been created. Population control may thus have to pave the way for fiscal action. As a larger potential surplus becomes available, fiscal measures may be directed at realizing this surplus and at channeling it into growth-intensive use. This objective is more suited to the capabilities of fiscal devices, and its role accordingly gains in importance.

In order to point up the essential contribution of fiscal policy in this setting, let us assume that the economy corresponds to the system visualized by the classical economists: Available savings at high levels of employment are readily invested, there is no Keynesian problem of unemployment, and the policy issue centers around internal balance and the rate of growth. For growth to be speeded, a larger share of resources must be diverted into capital formation, and the central task of fiscal policy is to create savings by restraining private consumption. For capital formation to be profitable, there must, to be sure, be a concurrent expansion in consumer markets, and this requires that the *level* of consumption rise, as well as that of saving. Yet the *rate* of saving must be increased relative to that of consumption if growth is to proceed at a more rapid rate. The need for creating an expanding market for consumer goods, which arises especially in the less open economy, is very real, but this does not mean that it is not necessary also to raise the savings rate; the conflict between these objectives is precisely one of the difficulties that need to be overcome to move into more rapid growth.[15]

15. If the ratio between consumption and capital formation is fixed —as seems to be implied by Krishnaswamy—the chances for takeoff into higher growth are slim indeed, unless foreign capital can be secured.

Let it be noted once more that the fiscal task of creating saving, especially in this stage of development, must be distinguished from that of public investment. Public saving, defined as the excess of tax receipts over public consumption, involves restraining public as well as private consumption; and public savings, once created, may be channeled into either public or private investment. The latter may take the form of public lending of surplus tax receipts through development banks and credit agencies, or the surplus may be withheld and be offset by extension of capital loans through the private banking system. While public investment remains important, the primary issue is that of public saving.

TAX VERSUS LOAN FINANCE

Restraining *public* consumption is a matter of expenditure policy and budgetary control. The key factor in revenue policy, whether it is in the choice between alternative taxes or between taxation and borrowing, relates to the effectiveness of various revenue sources in restraining *private* consumption.

How are the various revenue sources related to this fiscal policy objective? Three sources may be distinguished, including (1) taxation and profits from government enterprise, (2) borrowing of existing funds,[16] and (3) finance by creation of new funds. Regarding effects on aggregate demand, the essential line of demarcation is not between (1) on one side and (2) and (3) on the other, as is the case in the Keynesian setting where taxes reduce aggregate demand

16. This includes borrowing from the non-bank public and borrowing from commercial banks, provided such banks are loaned up, so that acquisition of public debt is substituted for acquisition of private debt. It excludes borrowing (whether from the central bank or from commercial banks) which is financed by credit expansion.

and borrowing does not. Here the essential difference is between (1) and (2) versus (3), as the loan dollar tends to be as effective in reducing private spending as the tax dollar. Income received will be fully respent, be it on consumption or investment, and there are no substantial income-leakages into hoards or liquid funds. Thus both revenue sources (taxes and loans drawn from existing funds) tend to reduce demand equally.[17] The balanced budget multiplier is inoperative. Since the marginal propensity to spend (consume or invest) in the private sector is unity, redistribution toward the public sector does not raise aggregate demand.

But this does not mean that the choice between tax and loan finance has become irrelevant. Far from it. The crucial difference now is that the tax dollar falls less heavily on private saving, and hence investment, than the loan dollar. If saving is a function of income only, but not of the interest rate, the loan dollar will fall entirely on private investment, whereas the tax dollar does so only to the extent that it reduces private saving. If saving depends on interest only but not on income, tax finance leaves private investment unchanged, while it is reduced by loan finance. In the general case, where saving is related positively to both income and interest, the investment displacing effect of loan finance remains greater—and more so the lower the propensity to

17. But what of the famous demand for jewelry, gold, and other treasure as a savings medium in India and some other countries? To the extent that A invests his savings by purchasing jewels from B, we are left with the question of what B does with the funds. If, as our argument postulates, he will consume or invest them, we simply have a transfer from A to B and the basic proposition is unchanged. The situation differs, however, if saving takes the form of an imported asset (e.g. gold) and thus results in import leakage. To the extent that this is the case, loan finance reduces import demand and is less deflationary (as far as the demand for domestic output is concerned) than tax finance.

save. Thus tax finance is more favorable to a high growth rate than loan finance is.[18]

REQUIREMENT FOR DOMESTIC REVENUE

The needed level of taxation (or, defined more broadly, of domestic revenue) may be determined as a function of certain basic requirements of price level stability and economic growth. To finance the desired rate of growth in a noninflationary fashion, income that is not spent on consumption but is saved must be sufficient to pay for the needed level of investment. Otherwise inflation results. Sav-

18. This may be demonstrated very simply as follows. With income $\overline{Y}$ given at full employment, the composition of output is given by the system

$$S = a + s(\overline{Y} - T) + bi$$
$$I = d - ei$$
$$I + G = S + T$$

where S is private saving, T is tax revenue, I is private investment, G is government purchases, and i is the interest rate.

For the case of *tax finance*, $dG = dT$ and

$$\frac{dI}{dT} = -\frac{es}{b + e}$$

The investment depressing effect of taxation varies directly with s and indirectly with b and e. If S is interest inelastic so that $b = 0$, we have

$$\frac{dI}{dT} = s$$

For the case of *loan finance*, we have $dG = dL$, where $L = G - T$,

$$\frac{dI}{dL} = \frac{-e}{b + e}$$

Investment depressing effects will again vary indirectly with e and b, but s now does not enter. If $b = 0$, the entire loan finance is reflected in reduced private investment.

Also, we may conclude that the investment reducing effect of tax finance equals s times that of loan finance.

ings that are not derived from the private sector or from abroad through capital inflow must be provided by government. Since government saving equals domestic revenue minus government consumption, the required ratio of domestic revenue (tax and nontax) to GNP will have to be larger,

1. the higher the needed rate of investment, i.e. the higher the growth rate and the marginal capital output ratio;
2. the higher the rate of government consumption;
3. the lower the savings rate in the private sector;
4. the higher the degree to which revenues draw on private saving rather than consumption;
5. the lower the contribution of foreign savings, or rate of public and private capital inflow; and
6. the higher income velocity, or the lower the desired ratio of cash balances to income.

Given the desired growth rate, the marginal capital output ratio, the propensity to save in the private sector, and the ratios of government consumption, net imports, and balances to national income, the required ratio of tax revenue to income follows. Given a marginal capital output ratio of 3, a government consumption rate of 15 per cent, a marginal savings rate in the private sector of 5 per cent, a net import rate of 5 per cent, and an income velocity of 3, it follows from equation (8) below that a country desiring a growth rate of 6 per cent would require a tax rate of about 22 per cent.

Since the mechanism of income determination in the low income economy is closer to the classical than to the Keynesian model, the primary concern of fiscal policy is to secure a proper division of resource use between consumption and capital formation. Concern with aggregate demand is primarily with excess demand and inflation rather than with deficient demand and unemployment. Monetary expansion at the proper rate is needed to prevent a decline in price level which would result if output growth were not matched by a rise in money expenditures, but monetary expansion in excess of this rate will exceed output growth and be inflationary.

These relationships may be brought into focus with the help of a simple model, as follows:

(1) $\quad e = t + b + m$

(2) $\quad m = \dfrac{r}{v}$

(3) $\quad i_p = s(1 - t) - b + n$

(4) $\quad i_t = kr$

(5) $\quad e = c_g + i_g$

(6) $\quad i_t = i_g + i_p$

(7) $\quad i_g = j i_t$

Small letters are used to express absolute values as a percentage of national income. Equation 1 is an identity, saying that government expenditure equals taxation t plus borrowing from existing funds b, plus increase in money supply m.[19] Equation 2 shows the appropriate increase in money supply which is required to match income growth. This equals the reciprocal of v, the income velocity times the growth of income r.[20] Equation 3 shows private investment i_p matching private savings out of disposable income or

19. To simplify, we assume the budget deficit to be the only source of increased money supply. To allow for an expansion of private credit, equation 2 may be written as $(m + z)v = r$, where z is private credit expansion, and equation 3 becomes $i_p = s(1 - t) - b + n + z$. To simplify further, we also assume a 100 per cent reserve system, but multiple credit expansion can be readily incorporated into the system.

20. The assumption of constant income velocity is an oversimplification, and structural changes of increasing monetization, making for a falling v, can be incorporated. Further, a real balance equation may be added to obtain a more realistic framework of analysis.

$s(1-t)$, minus lending to government b plus net imports n. To simplify, a constant average propensity to save is assumed and n is treated as given for the time being.[21] Since we are dealing with a classical system, equation 3 is not an identity but shows how private investment is determined.[22] Equation 4 defines the required level of total (private plus government) investment i_t as the product of the growth in output r and the capital-output ratio k.[23] Equations 5 and 6 are identities, showing total government expenditures e to be the sum of government consumption c_g and government investment i_g; and total investment i_t to be the sum of private investment i_p and government investment i_g. Equation 7 finally shows the division of total investment i_t between public and private, where j gives the "efficient" share of public investment. Given r, v, n, s, k, c_g, and j, the system permits us to determine e, t, m, b, i_p, i_t, and i_g.

Solving the system for the required tax to national income ratio t, we obtain

$$(8) \quad t = \frac{c_g - s + r\left(k - \dfrac{1}{v}\right) - n}{1 - s}$$

As noted before, the tax rate t is related positively to c_g, r, k, and v, and negatively to n. Since $t < 1$, it is also related negatively to s. But t is independent of j and the level of government investment i_g. This is the case because with a given rate of private saving, its short fall below the required level of private investment must be provided by public savings. An impression of the required range of tax rates may be obtained from Table 8–1, where plausible values of s, c_g, n, r, and k are combined. It will be seen that the required

21. By disregarding differences in the propensity to save of various taxpayers, qualitative aspects of tax structure policy are overlooked at this point. See p. 227.

22. Since private saving is assumed to be interest inelastic, borrowing reduces private investment on a 1:1 basis.

23. This follows from $k = I/\Delta Y$, with $\Delta Y/Y = r$, and $I/Y = i$.

TABLE 8-1
Levels of Required Tax to GNP Ratio*

s	c_g	n	r = .04 k = 2	r = .04 k = 3	r = .06 k = 2	r = .06 k = 3	r = .08 k = 2	r = .08 k = 3
0.00	0.05	0.05	.08	.12	.12	.18	.16	.24
		0.10	.03	.07	.07	.13	.11	.19
	0.10	0.05	.13	.17	.17	.23	.21	.29
		0.10	.08	.12	.12	.18	.16	.24
	0.15	0.05	.18	.22	.22	.28	.26	.34
		0.10	.13	.17	.17	.23	.21	.29
0.02	0.05	0.05	.03	.10	.10	.16	.08	.26
		0.10	.01	.05	.05	.11	.09	.17
	0.10	0.05	.11	.15	.15	.23	.21	.29
		0.10	.03	.10	.10	.16	.08	.26
	0.15	0.05	.16	.20	.20	.26	.24	.32
		0.10	.11	.15	.15	.21	.19	.27
0.05	0.05	0.05	.03	.07	.07	.13	.11	.19
		0.10	−.02	.02	.02	.08	.06	.14
	0.10	0.05	.08	.12	.12	.18	.16	.24
		0.10	.03	.07	.07	.13	.11	.19
	0.15	0.05	.13	.17	.17	.23	.21	.29
		0.10	.08	.12	.07	.13	.16	.25

* Computed from text equation, v term omitted.

levels of tax rate vary widely, and respond sharply to variation in the various parameters.

The same system may be used to derive b, the government's rate of borrowing from the public, as well as i_g and e. With c_g given, all budget variables are thus determined. The tax rate appropriate for a given growth rate may thus be derived from the values of c_g, s, k, and n. But this should not be taken to imply that t is always the dependent variable in the system. Equation 7 may be solved as well for r, taking t as given. The availability of tax handles may be limited and may circumscribe the feasible levels of t. Given these restrictions on t and the permissible n, the growth rate r may have to be adjusted accordingly.

COMPLICATIONS

It goes without saying that this model takes a very simplified view of the problem, and some complications may be noted.

External Balance.   While I have made allowance for net imports as a factor that reduces the required tax rate, net imports have been taken as given, the foreign sector being treated as exogenous to the system. Since this sector is a vital aspect of most developing economies, a more extended analysis must introduce trade as an endogenous part of the system. This will be done later on, by making imports a dependent variable.[24]

Moreover, the requirement of foreign balance must be introduced. The value of net imports n must be equated with the available capital inflow, and the feasible growth must be determined so as to meet this requirement as well as that of internal balance.

A further tie between foreign balance and growth may arise from technological rigidities in factor combinations, rendering capital formation contingent on the import of

24. See p. 321.

capital equipment that cannot be purchased at home. In the absence of foreign loans, the release of resources from consumption must then be distributed in an appropriate way between home consumption and consumption of imports, as growth will be limited by the excess of exports over consumption imports.

Tax Structure Policy. So far, we have proceeded on the assumption that all taxes are uniform in their impact on consumption and savings. This, of course, is not the case. The propensity to save out of disposable income s is a function of the tax structure, and maintaining a higher level of s is itself an objective of tax structure policy. How well this can be done depends, as we have seen, on how far the economy has advanced toward a reasonably efficient operation of sales and income taxes. Ruling out an expenditure tax approach as excessively difficult at this stage, a set of taxes on luxury consumption, including imports as well as domestic products, is called for. But even this may prove too demanding. Thus reliance will have to be placed on import duties and selective excises on domestic products imposed at the manufacturing level, including sales by public enterprise. As effective income taxation becomes possible, consumption taxes may be supplemented by moderately progressive income taxes. From the point of view of growth policy, maintaining a high s is helpful, but it is not the only way of raising the overall savings rate. As noted before, this may be done also by raising the level of t and hence public saving.

Transferability of Savings. The required level of taxation in our model is thus independent of government investment but depends on total investment only. Putting it differently, the distribution of savings between private and government is independent of the distribution of investment. That is to say, private savings can be borrowed by government to finance public investment, and public saving

227

can be loaned to the private sector for the finance of private investment. The former requires a market for government bonds, while the latter calls for the appropriate government lending institutions. If such transferability does not exist, further constraints are imposed on the system.

Capital-Output Ratio. Our model oversimplifies matters by postulating constant coefficients, and especially a constant value of k. More realistically, the level of k at any one time will depend on the composition of investment, including its division between public and private and various types of investment in either category.[25] Moreover, k will vary as factor combinations change and the capital stock increases relative to other factors. This may mean that one fixed coefficient, applicable over a certain range of income growth, is replaced by another, or it may call for a production function with variable factor proportions over the relevant scale.

As shown by recent growth theory, this may greatly change the role of fiscal variables, especially of their longer run effects on growth. Much depends upon the nature of the postulated production function, and the rate at which adjustments are taken to occur. With a Cobb-Douglas function, for instance, the equilibrium growth rate becomes independent of the savings rate.[26] A fiscal policy that raises the savings rate will affect the growth *rate* only in the short run. However, the short run may be rather long, and the

25. In particular, it is desirable to attribute a different capital-output ratio to durable consumer goods such as housing and to production equipment.

26. See Robert Solow, "A Contribution to the Theory of Economic Growth," *Quarterly Journal of Economics, 70* (February 1956); R. Sato, "Fiscal Policy in a Neo-classical Growth Model: An Analysis of Time Required for Equilibrating Adjustment," *Review of Economic Studies, 30,* no. 1 (February 1963), 16–23; Marian Krzyzaniak, "Effects of Profits Taxes: Deduced from Neoclassical Growth Models," in *Effects of Corporation Income Tax,* ed. M. Krzyzaniak (Detroit, Wayne State University Press, 1966).

future *level* of income will be raised, even in the longer run, if the current savings rate is higher. Given the drastic structural changes that must come about as an economy moves from a stationary low-income level into accelerated growth, the relevance of equilibrium growth-path models to low income countries is limited in its usefulness. The fiscal policy implications derived from a temporarily constant k assumption may offer a more useful guide to policy.

CONCEPTS OF BUDGET BALANCE

The state of budgetary balance is a strategic factor in the determination of fiscal policy, but it is important that the relevant concept of balance be chosen. How it should be defined depends on the objectives of budget policy and on the nature of the economy to which it applies. Using our preceding symbols, consider these three concepts of budgetary balance, as defined in terms of rates of surplus:

(1) $(1 - s)t - e$

(2) $t + b - e$

(3) $(1 - s)t - c_g$

Both concepts 1 and 2 reflect the state of balance as related to budget effects on aggregate demand. Concept 1 is relevant for a system where consumption is a function of disposable income while planned investment does not adjust itself to the level of saving. Adapted to such a system, concept 1 measures the withdrawal from the income stream, which results from the impact of the budget, and is thus a fair index of the budget's aggregate demand effect.[27] It is

27. The reader may wish to restate the concepts in absolute terms:

(1) $(1 - s)T - E$

(2) $T + B - E$

(3) $(1 - s)T - C_g$

where the large letters are absolute levels. Note also that (1) measures the multiplicand, not the total multiplier.

229

similar to the United States concept of deficit on national income account, except that the latter includes total tax receipts.

But the state of balance thus defined is not relevant to a system such as that depicted in the preceding model.[28] Here private investment is taken to adjust itself to savings that are available for private use. Both b and t reduce private expenditure on a 1:1 basis and are hence equivalent in their restrictive effect. Demand balance is thus defined according to concept 2 as the excess of receipts (tax and loan) over expenditure. The deficit, or $e - t - b$, equals the increase in money supply m, with the proper rate of deficit being defined by equation 2 in the preceding model.

The income determination systems to which concepts 1 and 2 are tailored are both extreme models, one reflecting a simplified Keynesian and the other a simplified classical system. While it can be said that concept 1 is more relevant for the highly developed economy and concept 2 for the low income economy, features of both appear in either situation. This is to say, a more complex view—combining both aspects—must be taken.[29]

Concept 3 does not relate to aggregate demand effects but to the budget contribution to capital formation. In the classical system it measures its contribution to actual capital formation, as the withdrawal of resources from consumption (the excess of withdrawal from private consumption over government consumption) will in fact shift these resources into capital formation. In the mixed system, the contribution is to potential rather than actual capital formation, but the concept remains relevant, if only as a per-

28. While concept 1 is of little analytical interest in such a system, it may of course be computed from the income accounts, and the familiar ex post identities hold in either case.

29. See the recent U.S. budget reform according to which both concepts 1 and 2 are to be shown. See United States, *Report of the President's Commission on Budget Concepts* (Washington, D.C., G.P.O., October 1967).

missive factor. The concept of balance now measures the government's contribution to saving, not in the Keynesian sense of a surplus of receipts which must be offset (at the pain of unemployment) by investment in the private sector, but in the classical sense of net resource withdrawal from total (public plus private) consumption and release for capital formation. Government saving in this classical sense equals the surplus in the so-called current budget. It must suffice to finance the excess of required investment (private plus public) over private plus foreign saving. Whereas the demand balance involves total budget expenditures e and hence the public investment share j, the growth balance involves government consumption c_g only, and is independent of j.[30]

Other concepts of balance, relating to the balance of payments and other factors, might be added. But what has been said will suffice to show that the concept of budgetary balance has to be interpreted carefully, and that different types of economies call for different formulations. In view of this, the introduction of worldwide uniformity into budget statements, while helpful to the comparative statistician, is of dubious merit for economic policy formulation.

ADVANCED ECONOMY

It remains to take a brief look at the setting of fiscal policy in the advanced economy. This setting typically differs from that of the "classical" environment of the low income country, and the nature of fiscal tools is changed accordingly. Since this aspect is covered extensively in the fiscal literature, a brief consideration will suffice in this connection.

The crucial difference lies in the pattern of investment

30. As noted before (see p. 227) this implies that savings funds may be transferred between the public and the private sector via the necessary lending arrangements.

behavior. With the growing financial complexity and importance of liquid assets in the advanced economy, it is no longer correct to assume that all income will be spent, be it on consumption or investment, or (which is the same) that investment will always suffice to absorb the flow of planned savings out of a full employment income. Savers have the option to hold balances rather than to invest in the purchase of currently produced capital goods, and investors may draw on existing balances rather than finance their purchases out of current income. Thus the system is characterized by changing degrees of financial slack and stringency. The rate of investment may fall short of planned saving at a full employment level of income, resulting in a deficient rate of expenditures in money terms. Since prices tend to be rigid in the downward direction, this results in a declining level of demand in real terms and hence in underutilization of resources. At other times, investment may exceed the rate of saving, tending to call forth an excessive increase in the rate of money expenditure and eventual inflation.

Because of this, fiscal policy assumes a dual function. In the preceding system, its main task was to bring about that level of consumption and saving, and hence capital formation, that will secure the desired growth of output. Potential output was always realized, and the control of aggregate demand was one of price level stability only. Now emphasis must be placed on the distinction between actual and potential output. Not only must potential output be made to grow at the desired rate, but the actual rate of expenditure growth must be made to proceed at the same rate.

The task of securing the growth of potential output remains essentially the same, but the determination of the actual rate of expenditure growth becomes a quite different matter. Fiscal variables again play an important role but they enter in a different fashion. While the precise formulation depends on the particular pattern of investment be-

232

havior, the direction of fiscal effects may be readily seen.[31] For the level of total expenditures to rise in money terms, there must be an excess of private investment over total saving, defined as the sum of private, foreign, and public saving. As noted before, the latter is now defined as $(1 - s)t - e$, or the excess of tax receipts from consumption over government expenditures. Borrowing does not enter, since it does not affect the rate of private spending, and the choice between taxing and borrowing becomes a means of controlling aggregate demand. The rate of expenditure increase will thus be larger if t is low and e is high. Thus, whereas t was related positively to the rate of capacity growth, it is related negatively to the rate of expenditure growth; and whereas c_g was related negatively to capacity growth with i_g indifferent, both c_g and i_g are related positively to expenditure growth. The task of fiscal policy, then, is to devise a combination of t, c_g, and i_g that balances the capacity and expenditure rates of growth at the desired level.

The role of monetary policy is changed as well. In the previous system, monetary policy was essentially a matter of maintaining price level stability. Now, monetary policy may affect the level of private investment i_p, provided that investment is interest elastic while the demand for balances is inelastic, and there are no other (e.g. balance of payments) reasons that preclude free use of monetary policy. Monetary expansion thus offers an alternative to raising e or lowering t in securing an increase in the rate of expenditure growth. To the extent that this alternative is available and

31. While it is thus useful to distinguish between the two (demand and growth) concepts of budgetary balance, the double balance approach is not without its danger. In the low income setting, the choice among types of capital formation may be disturbed by the arbitrary allocation of some outlays (e.g. school buildings) to the capital budget while holding others (e.g. human investment) in the current budget. In the high income setting, the double budget tends to distort expenditure decisions as government attempts to carry out stabilizing measures while maintaining balance in the current budget.

effective, the division of i_t between i_p and i_g can again be determined according to equation 7 of the preceding model. Under conditions when monetary policy is ineffective, i_g will be given by $i_g = rk - i_p$, which may not furnish the most efficient mix of public and private capital formation. This dilemma might be avoided, however, by devising alternative policy tools such as profits taxes and subsidies to maintain i_p at desired levels. With some ingenuity in policy making, sufficient tools should be available to permit reaching the desired policy goals.

Fiscal policy, together with monetary policy, thus plays a key role in maintaining a proper balance between the broad aggregates of income and expenditure components upon which balanced growth depends. Beyond this, public capital formation continues to play a vital part. Given the high capital to labor ratios characteristic for a developed economy, the ratio of gross capital formation to GNP will be high as well. Thus there will be a large base of capital formation (gross, if not net) into which new techniques may be embedded. The return on investment in technological progress will be high, even if that on net investment is not. Since the social return on such investment tends to exceed the private return, especially where "basic" research is concerned, public capital formation has a new and important role to play.

PART III

PUBLIC SECTOR IN
THE OPEN ECONOMY

9 TAX COORDINATION UNDER THE BENEFIT RULE

I now leave the problems of economic development and turn to the operation of the public sector in the open economy. While the economics of public finance has been dealt with traditionally in a closed economy setting, its international aspects have recently come to the fore. The coordination of tax policy has demanded increasing attention with the development of common markets; the creation of international organizations such as the U.N. or NATO has posed the problem of financing international budgets; and the relation of domestic stabilization to external balance has placed the theory of compensatory finance in a broader context. At the same time population shifts and the development of metropolitan areas have brought problems of regional finance within nations or states to the fore.

THE ISSUES

We begin with the coordination of national tax structures. In the closed economy, tax policy is concerned with allocating the tax burden among individuals in an equitable fashion, with avoiding interference with (or indeed promoting) the efficiency of private resource use, and with serving the needs of economic stabilization. In the open economy, these issues remain but become more complex, and additional concerns arise.

The traditional problem of tax equity is complicated in two respects. Equitable tax treatment of individuals must be redefined because individuals are subject to more than one jurisdiction. In addition, there now arises a problem of internation equity, i.e. of dividing shares in the international tax base among taxing jurisdictions or nations. The traditional considerations of efficiency similarly must be extended to include effects upon resource use in international transactions, including commodity and factor movements. Regarding the former, emphasis shifts from inefficiencies in consumption choice (caused in the closed economy by discriminatory taxes on the production or consumption of particular products) to inefficiencies in production location caused in the open economy by differential taxation of the production of similar products in different regions. Similarly, factor flows are affected by differential income taxes in various regions. Resulting effects on efficiency, moreover, may now be appraised from both a national and a worldwide point of view, with possible conflicts between the two. In addition, there is the previously noted extension of stabilization to include external balance.

Given this interdependence, it becomes necessary to coordinate tax policies between nations or other governmental units. This may be approached in various ways.[1] At one extreme, coordination may be interpreted as equalization, leading all coordinating countries to adopt a uniform tax structure. Thereby most conflicts are eliminated, but the

1. On the distinction between tax harmonization and equalization see Douglas Dosser: "Theoretical Considerations for Tax Harmonization," in *Comparison and Harmonization of Public Revenue Systems*, Luxembourg, Congress of the International Institute of Public Finance, 19th Session, September 1963, and "Economic Analysis of Tax Harmonization," in *Fiscal Harmonization in Common Markets, 1*, ed. Carl S. Shoup (New York, Columbia University Press, 1967). Also, for an earlier discussion of the problem, see Shoup, "Taxation Aspects of International Economic Integration," *Papers of the International Institute of Public Finance*, 9th Session, Frankfurt, 1953 (The Hague, W. P. Stockum, n.d.).

baby is lost with the bath water. A more challenging view is to define the task of tax coordination as providing a framework within which individual countries are permitted maximum freedom in arranging their own tax structures without, however, interfering with efficiency and equity in the international setting. This is the view here adopted.

A Model Solution

Tax coordination involves a host of technical issues, as tax practices and legal institutions vary widely. These points of detail cannot be bypassed in designing concrete solutions, but lest the forest be lost for the trees, let us see first what principles can be set forth to define an equitable and efficient system.

As a standard, consider a setting where general use is made of benefit taxation. Under such a system, a distinction would be drawn between the financing of "intermediate" and "final" expenditures of government. Intermediate expenditures provide for the supply of public services that reduce the cost of private output. This cost, under the benefit rule, is to be charged to the producer of that output. These charges enter into his cost of production and are reflected in the price paid by the consumer. If the products happen to be exported, such taxes are paid for by the foreign consumer who, in fact, becomes the beneficiary of the service. Products would thus be taxed on an origin rather than a destination basis. This, it will be noted, runs counter to the usual principle (applicable in a nonbenefit taxation regime) that product taxes should be on a destination basis.[2]

The cost of public outlays that render final services to the

2. The difference is one in underlying assumptions. Product taxes imposed on a destination basis meet efficiency requirements (regarding the flow of traded goods) *if* we assume that such taxes bear no relation to intermediate goods inputs. Product taxation by origin meets the requirement under benefit taxation.

consumer would be defrayed from charges levied directly upon him. Such charges would be imposed on the consumer at the place where he lives and thus enjoys the consumption benefits.[3] The general term "where he lives" is used to avoid the legal concept of residency, which may or may not coincide therewith. Indeed, if charges for public consumer goods were levied on a fee basis—i.e. in process of consumption—the question would be answered by the simple prescription that a person will pay where he consumes. If benefits accrue through particular types of consumption, associated in varying degrees with physical presence, taxes would be paid according to where such consumption occurs. Length of stay, or time spent in various jurisdictions, might approximate a proper solution, but in any case, tax charges would apply independent of whether the person is also a citizen of the particular country. Citizenship, indeed, is irrelevant (and residency is relevant only by proxy) in the benefit context: You pay whichever store (or government) you buy from.

In such a system, income or profit taxation would not be of major importance. It would apply only to the extent that intermediate services of government (e.g. technical education) raise the earnings of particular factors and be limited to the cost of such services, which would be charged against the earnings of the factor. If a resident of country A invests in B, B would tax his capital income to the extent that it reflects services rendered. Taxation of capital income would thus not only be of minor importance but, to the extent that it occurs, would be primarily on a "source"-of-value-added rather than on a "residency"-of-owner basis.[4] This is again contrary to the usual rule (based on efficiency considerations

3. Origin and destination of the public service being in the same place, both rules would be the same in this case.

4. Country A would tax income earned in B only to the extent that A assists the income recipient in earning such income. This might be the case through legal protection or other facilities that A provides for the foreign investment of its citizens.

under nonbenefit taxation), according to which capital income should be taxed on a residency rather than a source basis.

The system of benefit taxation just outlined would take care of both tax and expenditure coordination. On one side, there would be a fair allocation of the cost of public services among individuals residing in various countries, each paying for services rendered. On the other, there would be an equitable division of tax yield among nations.[5] Each nation or tax jurisdiction would be paid in line with the services it renders. Moreover, the efficiency requirement would be met as well. If production were taxed on an origin basis and in line with intermediate inputs, relative prices and the efficient flow of commodities between countries would not be disturbed. Similarly, if "residents" were taxed in line with consumption services received, there would be no fiscal distortion of residency choice. Nor would capital movement be distorted, since taxation of income by the country of source would apply only to the extent that such income was increased through the input of intermediate goods.

Unfortunately, matters cannot be settled along these simple lines. Benefits may spill over through forms other than exports, in which case recoupment of costs is more difficult. Moreover, even in the normative model, not all taxes are imposed on benefit grounds. Taxes and transfers are used also to secure distributional adjustments. Assuming the distributional norm to be in terms of income, income taxes now enter the picture as a major policy instrument. This raises the question of whether and to what extent income originating abroad or flowing out should be included in the redistributional pool of any one jurisdiction. Thus the legal problem of tax allegiance (defined in terms of residency or

5. Note that we refer here to division of tax *yield* rather than of tax *base*, which will be discussed later on. Under the benefit system, one cannot speak of equitable division of the base, since the appropriate levy is already given by the cost of expenditure benefits.

citizenship) has to be coped with in this context, even though it may be bypassed in the benefit model, where concern is with the tax finance of public services only.[6]

So much for the normative setting. In reality, taxes to pay for public services are not separated from taxes to secure redistribution. Moreover, even if the former could be separated, this would not distribute the cost of public services along benefit lines. In reality, production taxes are imposed largely independently of intermediate goods inputs, income is used as at best a rough index of consumption benefits received, and the tax bill is distributed in line with more or less ambiguous equity concepts of ability to pay.

This being the case, it is not feasible to derive international tax coordination from the hypothesis of benefit taxation. A workable framework is needed. Unsatisfactory though this may be to pure fiscal theory, there is a need for coordination rules that can be applied to the tax side of the problem, taken by itself. This does not deny that expenditure and benefit considerations should be added where possible, but merely recognizes that the hypothesis of benefit taxation does not offer a realistic solution.

6. The benefit taxes imposed by the "Allocation Branch" (see Musgrave, *Theory of Public Finance,* Chap. 1) are now supplemented by income taxes imposed to secure redistributional adjustments under the "Distribution Branch" of the fiscal operation. Presumably each country will concern itself with distributional adjustments among its citizens (or residents) only, and income flowing to noncitizens (or nonresidents) would be excluded from this income tax. Thus distribution branch taxes could be brought into the system without interfering with the neutrality of capital and commodity flows.

10 COORDINATION OF INCOME TAXES

I begin with taxes on income. Here the equity aspects of the problem can be seen most clearly, and the complications introduced by the legal forms of business organization are most disturbing. Efficiency considerations are related primarily to the pattern of factor movement, whereas in the case of product taxes the problem is primarily one of commodity trade.

PRINCIPLES

Certain general principles, relating to equity and efficiency are examined first.

EQUITY

As noted before, tax policy in the open economy meets with two equity problems: (1) we must define what constitutes equitable treatment among *individuals* who receive income that is exposed to several tax jurisdictions; and (2) we must determine how *countries* are to share equitably in the tax base created by international transactions between them. We use a simple two-country model, where both countries receive their entire revenue from income taxes. Individuals whose country of primary tax allegiance (c.p.t.a.) is country A may work in A or B, and they may

243

derive capital income from investments in A or B.[1] Thus they may be subject to taxation by both A and B. How are these taxes to be related?

Among Individuals. In deciding the individual's tax bill,[2] the traditional principle of horizontal equity may be drawn upon. The rule says that people in equal economic positions should be treated equally. As applied to income taxation in the closed economy, this means that the tax should be independent of income composition as between personal compensation (wages and salary) and various types of capital income. In the open setting, there is the added requirement that the tax should be independent of income composition as between domestic and foreign source income. This new requirement may be interpreted in various ways.

A first approach takes the rule of "equal tax for equal income" to mean equal total (domestic plus foreign) tax. Horizontal equity is made to apply on an *international* level, including taxes paid at home and abroad. The individual's total tax bill, as adjusted by his c.p.t.a., will then be the same as that paid by someone with the same total income and c.p.t.a. whose entire income is from domestic sources. Alternatively, and obviating the need for a c.p.t.a. concept, his tax may be prorated according to the tax laws of the countries from which his various income slices originate.[3]

1. For further discussion of c.p.t.a. and its relation to residency or citizenship, see p. 258.

2. The individual's tax bill, in the last resort, includes his personal income tax as well as the corporation income tax paid by the corporation in which he holds shares. This complicating factor of personal-corporate tax integration is bypassed here but will be considered later. See p. 268.

3. Simple assessment of different income components by the respective tax rates of the origin countries would not do because income should be treated on a global basis, i.e. rate progression should apply to total income taken as a whole. Suppose an individual receives income from countries A, B, and C. Equitable treatment would involve (1) determining the tax under the laws of each country, assuming the

Coordination of Income Taxes

This criterion, however, is rather complex if applied to the concept of a global income tax, which requires that the progressive rate schedule be applied to total income. Thus a final adjustment of total liability according to the c.p.t.a. rate schedule and the c.p.t.a. concept is needed for a global tax.

According to this international view, an individual is thus treated equitably if his combined tax liability is the same as that of others with the same c.p.t.a. and equal income, independent of whether this income is from domestic or from foreign sources. To implement this rule, taxes imposed abroad must be *credited* by the c.p.t.a. against its own tax. If the foreign tax is less, the c.p.t.a. tax must be reduced accordingly; and if it is more, a refund will be due.

A second approach interprets the rule of equal tax for equal income to mean equal domestic or c.p.t.a. tax only. Horizontal equity is now made to apply on a *national* level. The c.p.t.a. now imposes its tax on foreign income after foreign tax as if it were domestic income. Foreign income taxes are *deducted* in arriving at net income for domestic tax purposes, and there is no crediting. Foreign income taxes are considered as costs of doing business abroad, similar to indirect taxes, domestic or foreign. Under this national concept, each country may collect whatever income tax it chooses, without requiring adjustment to income taxes paid abroad.

A third approach, taking an *ultranational* view, would go even farther and disallow the taxes paid abroad. The c.p.t.a., in other words, would consider equal treatment to mean equal c.p.t.a. taxes relative to total income before domestic or foreign taxes. Deduction of foreign income taxes would be disallowed under this system, such taxes being considered irrelevant to c.p.t.a. taxes.

---

individual's entire income (from all three countries) to have originated there; and (2) taking the average of the three taxes, weighted by the share derived from each country.

Which of these three systems is most appealing as a matter of interindividual equity is not readily answered. The international approach goes farthest in securing an integrated view of tax structures and, as shown below, has distinct advantages on efficiency grounds. But equity being basically a matter of value judgments, one cannot say that the other views are inherently wrong.

Among Countries. So much for interindividual equity. Next we must consider how the revenue should be divided between countries. A country is entitled to tax income originating within its borders, even though the factors (labor or capital) to which the income accrues belong to foreigners.[4] Here a distinction must be drawn between division of (a) national gains or losses between the economies of two countries and (b) division of revenue gains or losses between their treasuries.

An investor, whose c.p.t.a. is country A, invests in country B, and B imposes a tax on his income derived in B. This tax involves two types of loss for country A. First, A suffers a *national* loss, as the total income of its nationals is reduced. This loss equals the amount by which the foreign investment income is reduced by the tax. Second, B's tax affects the revenue obtained by A's treasury. The magnitude of this revenue or *treasury* loss depends not only on B's tax but also on how foreign income is taxed in A. If A takes the national view of individual equity (deduction method), its treasury loss equals $t_A t_B \pi_B$, where t_A and t_B are A's and B's tax rates, and π_B is profits earned by A's citizen from investment in B. It is less than the national loss which equals $t_B \pi_B$. If A takes the international (crediting) view, the treasury loss equals B's tax or $t_B \pi_B$, and is the same as the national loss. If t_B exceeds t_A, the A treasury must make a refund and suffer a negative yield. This, however, is only an internal transfer, as the national loss always equals B's

4. For a discussion of what is meant by "originating," see p. 261.

revenue or $t_B\pi_B$. It is a function of the B tax only and independent of the adjustment made by A.[5]

The basic question of internation equity is thus one of national (not of treasury) loss. The issue, therefore, is how high a tax country B should be permitted to impose on income generated in B but accruing to investors whose c.p.t.a. is A. One view of the matter is that B has total jurisdiction within its borders (the principle of territoriality) and that it can tax as it pleases. As long as investors whose c.p.t.a. is A decide to invest in and to draw income from B, B may tax such income as it sees fit. Unilateral action by B, however, leads to countermoves by A, and a bargaining situation results. Mutual adherence to a reasonable principle of base sharing or acceptance of such a principle in tax treaty making is the sensible solution. The question is how to formulate it.

It seems reasonable to argue that, in analogy to equal treatment among persons and as a matter of good international manners (if not international property law), a rule of "nondiscrimination" should prevail. That is to say, a country should tax income earned within its borders by individuals with c.p.t.a. abroad as if it were earned by its own citizens.[6] Under this rule, B (the country of income source) is the primary claimant; but since it must not discriminate against foreign income, excessive national (and, under the credit system, treasury) losses to A are ruled out. The country of citizenship, or A, then determines the final liability of the individual (and its treasury loss) in line with its view of individual equity. If A follows the international view, it will impose a supplementary tax (if the B rate is lower) or pay a refund (if the B rate is higher) so as to equate the investor's total liability with that imposed on a corresponding

5. If A takes the ultranational view and disregards B's tax, A suffers no treasury loss, but the national loss remains at $t_B\pi_B$.

6. For further interpretation of this requirement, see p. 260.

income from A sources. If it takes the national view, the B tax is deducted and no need for refunds arises.

This approach appeals as a fair principle of yield sharing, but alternative rules might be considered as well. Thus, the prior claim by the source country might be limited, and B might be restricted to imposing a tax equal to, say, 50 per cent of that imposed on domestic income in B. Or the adjustment might go in the other direction, and B might be permitted to impose a discriminatory rate. While there is no absolute basis on which to judge this matter, nondiscrimination seems to offer the most appealing solution, at least for the general case. Exceptions might be made as a means of international redistribution, but in most cases such redistribution can be implemented more effectively by direct means.[7]

In concluding these considerations of equity, it may be noted again that interindividual and internation equity are different things. Various principles as to the former (i.e. the credit or deduction approach) might be combined with various principles as to the latter (i.e. nondiscrimination or discrimination). While it is true that B's discrimination against foreign capital, combined with A's credit approach, may lead to heavy treasury losses in A, this does not mean that the credit principal cannot be applied by A if considered desirable as a matter of interindividual equity, and without affecting A's national loss.

EFFICIENCY

I now leave equity aspects and turn to efficiency considerations which, in this context, relate to effects on factor flows. Emphasis will be on capital flows, but similar considerations apply to labor flows as well. Various efficiency concepts are to be distinguished.

World Basis. If there is to be an efficient allocation of capital on a worldwide basis, taxes should not interfere with

7. See p. 309.

the choice between domestic and foreign investment or with the distribution of foreign investment among various countries. Efficiency regarding capital export prevails if relative net (after tax) rates of return at home and abroad are the same as relative gross (before tax) rates of return. This is the case if income is taxed in either country provided all countries have the same rate of tax. But so drastic a solution is not needed. The same result is achieved without rate uniformity if investment income is taxed according to the rates applicable in the investor's country of p.t.a., whether of residency or of citizenship. Assuming the former, if a resident of A invests in B, the final tax liability of his foreign source income is set by A's tax. This does not exclude B from levying a tax, provided A grants a full credit, including refunds where B's tax is higher. The requirement of worldwide efficiency thus coincides with the international view of interindividual equity. Both call for a full crediting system. The deduction system, on the other hand, discriminates against foreign as compared to domestic investment in general, and against foreign investment in high rate countries in particular.

National Basis. Considerations of worldwide efficiency, however, differ from those of national efficiency. Taxes may cause a significant divergence between the flow of foreign investment that is efficient from a world point of view and the flow that is efficient from a national point of view.[8] If the before-tax rate of return in A is Y_A while that in B is Y_B, residents in A, operating under the crediting rule,

8. I disregard here other, nontax reasons, which may cause private investment to be extended beyond the nationally optimal ceiling, e.g. because new foreign investment reduces the return on old units of foreign investment, and because a potential gain to domestic labor (from increase in domestic capital stock) is transferred to foreign labor. Also, terms of trade effects, favorable or unfavorable, may result. See Ronald W. Jones, "International Capital Movements and the Theory of Tariffs and Trade," *Quarterly Journal of Economics, 81,* no. 1 (February 1967), 1.

are confronted with after-tax rates of return of $(1 - t_A)Y_A$ when investing in A and of $(1 - t_A)Y_B$ when investing in B. They will thus carry foreign investment to the point where $Y_A = Y_B$. This is in line with world efficiency. But A's national rate of return (accruing to A's investors *and* taxpayers as a group) on investment in B equals $(1 - t_B)Y_B$ only. From a national point of view it is thus in A's interest to hold foreign investment down to a level where Y_A equals $(1 - t_B)Y_B$. This happens to be accomplished by application of the deduction approach.[9] Here the net return on investment in A is $(1 - t_A)Y_A$ and that on investment in B is $(1 - t_A)(1 - t_B)Y_B$, so that the ratio of net rates (as seen by the investor) is $Y_A/(1 - t_B)Y_B$. A's investors will now invest in B until $Y_B = Y_A/(1 - t_B)$, thus pushing to the margin of national profitability and stopping at a higher gross rate of return. From a purely national point of view, the deduction approach has thus considerable merit, even though it is defective on world-efficiency grounds.

By the same token, the ultranational approach (which disallows B's taxes) is efficient on neither ground. It is more detrimental to foreign investment than the deduction approach and leads to underinvestment in B even from the national point of view.

Tax Union. Between the extremes of world and national efficiency, the efficiency concept may be applied also to a group of countries that are joined in a tax union.[10] Beginning with a situation of unequal rates of profits tax, not neutralized by crediting, total equalization of rates among all countries is likely to improve efficiency from a world point of view. Such changes in capital flow as result will increase efficiency

9. See Peggy B. Musgrave, *United States Taxation of Foreign Investment Income: Issues and Arguments*, Harvard Law School, International Tax Program, forthcoming.

10. For literature on tax and customs unions see pp. 286–87.

But this cannot be said for partial equalization among union members only.[11] Suppose again that initially countries A, B, and C have different rates of profits tax, which are not neutralized by crediting. As a result, capital flow may be diverted from its most efficient pattern. Now let A and B form a direct-tax union by equalizing their rates, but leaving out C. Any resulting changes in capital flow between A and B must be efficient, because they are in response to pretax differences in return. But this need not be the case with regard to changing flows between A or B on one side and C on the other. Depending on the particular circumstances of the case, such changes may either raise or lower world efficiency. Thus direct-tax unions may but need not improve the efficiency of capital allocation from a world point of view. Net gains are likely to result if inefficient flows among union members are removed and if the common rate in the union is set so as to move the rates of union countries toward rather than away from the outside rates.

A more positive conclusion can be drawn if neutralization between A and B is achieved through introduction of crediting rather than rate equalization. In this case, resulting changes in capital flow between A and B must again be efficient. Since A's and B's positions vis-à-vis C remain unchanged, redirection of A's previous flows to C toward B (or of B's previous flows to C toward A) must also be efficiency increasing; and since C's position vis-à-vis A and B is unchanged, no change in flows originating in C will result. The net result must therefore be a gain in world efficiency.

COMPATIBILITY OF EFFICIENCY AND EQUITY

We have seen that the international view of equity among individuals is compatible with world efficiency just as the national equity view serves the goal of national efficiency. At the same time, either pair of objectives is com-

11. See Peggy B. Musgrave, "Direct Business Tax Harmonization," in *Fiscal Harmonization in Common Markets,* ed. Carl S. Shoup, 2, 237.

patible, assuming the necessary refunds to be made under the crediting approach, with various concepts of internation equity or ways in which the revenue is to be allocated between countries. Effects on capital flow depend on the total tax finally imposed on the individual investor, as set by the country of p.t.a. (be it citizenship or residency), but not on who gets the revenue. If country A follows a full crediting policy with refunds where B's rates are higher, effects on capital flow will be neutral. This will be the case whether B follows the rule of nondiscrimination, imposes penalty rates, or offers tax inducements to capital inflow. However, in actual practice crediting by A is limited so as to exclude refunds. This being so, the system will be efficient in the world sense only as long as B's rate does not exceed that of A. By forestalling penalty rates that would require A to pay refunds, adherence to nondiscrimination is thus a helpful condition in securing world efficiency in capital flow.

SHIFTED PROFITS TAX

The preceding argument was based on the assumption that taxes on investment income do in fact reduce such income. Suppose now that such taxes, especially if imposed in the form of a corporation profits tax, are shifted in the short-run sense of administered price adjustments.[12] In considering the consequences of such shifting, let us assume that foreign capital services a small part of the market of the country in which the physical investment occurs, so that shifting is always limited to the rate of tax applicable in that country. Assuming B's profits tax to be higher than A's, how must our preceding conclusions regarding equity and efficiency be amended to allow for shifting?

Little can now be said on grounds of interpersonal equity,

12. See Marian Krzyzaniak and Richard A. Musgrave, *The Shifting of the Corporation Income Tax* (Baltimore, Johns Hopkins Press, 1963) and the discussion thereof by Richard Goode and Richard Slitor, in *Effects of Corporation Income Tax*, ed. Krzyzaniak, Chaps. 4, 5, and 7.

and such considerations as apply relate to the treatment of the consumer rather than the investor. The issue of internation equity, similarly, is solved automatically, since each country's tax will be paid by its own consumers.[13] The imposition by B of a tax on profits will not burden foreign investment in B, and will impose no national burden on the foreign investor's c.p.t.a. unless the tax discriminates against foreign investors. It is only this excess part of the tax that cannot be shifted and hence falls on the foreign investor.

Turning to efficiency, the crediting rule, which secured world efficiency by neutralizing tax effects in the no-shifting case, now discriminates against foreign investment if the investor's home rate is higher. If the tax in A is higher than that in B, A's investor investing in B will be able to shift B's tax, but not the additional tax imposed by A. Since home investment permits shifting of the entire A tax, foreign investment is deterred. The opposite holds and foreign investment is encouraged if the B rate is higher, so that A's investor receives a partial refund on B's tax which he has been able to shift. The neutralizing procedure is now to exempt foreign investment income from corporation tax. The profits tax has become a cost tax and, as explained in the next chapter, should be treated accordingly.[14]

The same conclusion holds if efficiency is considered from the national point of view. Since B's tax now does not reduce the profits obtained by A's investor, no national loss to

13. For equity considerations applicable to traded products, see p. 271.

14. The situation becomes more complex if asymmetries are introduced. Suppose the tax is shifted in A but not in B. Under the usual crediting procedure, foreign investment by A investors is discriminated against. To obtain neutrality, A should not tax foreign investment income and should, in fact, refund the corporation tax paid to B. For B, crediting discriminates against domestic investment, and income from foreign investment should be taxed without crediting the tax paid in A. Similar complications result if there is shifting in both countries, but to different degrees.

A results. It is thus in the interest of A to encourage its investors to invest in B until the rate of return after B's tax equals that of investment in A after A's tax. The policy prescriptions for world and national efficiency, which differ in the no-shifting case, now coincide.

FURTHER CONSIDERATIONS

The preceding considerations set the basic framework in which the issues of direct tax coordination (neutrality and equity) are to be resolved. But certain other considerations enter which may call for the use of tax policy to direct capital flows away from their "efficient" channels.

Import Neutrality. We have seen that taxation of capital income at the rates of the investor's c.p.t.a. (as implemented by the crediting method) is neutral. It does not interfere with the investor's choice among countries. At the same time, neither does it provide for equal tax treatment among investors competing in any one country. Investors who are citizens of country A but invest in B may be subject to a higher tax than competitors who are nationals of B or C. This may impede their ability to compete, either by reducing available funds for reinvestment or by making it more difficult to attract outside capital. Accordingly A's investors may argue that neutrality requires equal taxation of all investors in B. This may be referred to as neutrality of capital import, as distinct from the neutrality of capital export which is secured by crediting.[15]

To achieve import neutrality, the rates of country B would have to be controlling, but this would be non-neutral for capital export. The only way in which both import and export neutrality could be achieved is through uniformity of tax rates in all countries. Short of this, one or the other type of neutrality must be sacrificed. But the two requirements are not of equal importance. From the point of view of effi-

15. See Richard A. Musgrave, "Criteria for Foreign Tax Credit," *Taxation and Operations Abroad,* Tax Institute Symposium, 1959.

cient allocation under competitive conditions, export neutrality is clearly the relevant concept and import neutrality is not. The state of import neutrality, however, may affect capital flows if preference for internal funds and various market imperfections are taken into consideration.

At the same time, it is possible that differential rates of profits tax may affect the share of various countries in total foreign investment. Different countries may take different views on how capital income should be taxed and how output should be divided between consumption and capital formation. If a country desires to increase its relative growth rate, a lower profits tax may be helpful, but, given adequate allowance for crediting, there is no particular reason why that of other countries should be matched.

Aid to Developing Countries. As in other matters of public policy, efficiency considerations may be qualified by distributional concerns. Thus it may be desirable to direct capital to low income countries in order to raise their relative income position. Or such direction may be called for, even on efficiency grounds, if private rates of return in low income countries fall short (with adjustment for risk) of social returns.

The low income country L, acting alone, is limited in what it can do to attract capital from the high income country H. Suppose L reduces its tax rate applicable to foreign investment in L. The results will depend on (1) H's tax policy, and (2) whether the H investors plan to leave their funds in L or to repatriate. Provided H grants tax deferral (taxes profits from foreign investment only when repatriated), tax reduction in L will render investment in L more attractive, but only to investors who are planning to *re*invest there. Assuming H to be on a crediting system, the net return to investors who wish to repatriate their earnings will not be affected by a rate reduction in L. In this case, rate reduction by L merely transfers revenue from L to H, causing a treasury and national loss to L. If there is to be an effective incentive, H must permit its investors to benefit from the lower rates offered by L.

Turning now to policy in H, appropriate action again depends on the intentions of the investor. Consider first the inducement for *new* capital to flow out. If the investor plans later on to reinvest in L, and assuming tax rates in H to be higher, outflow is induced by deferral, and by a general rate increase in H. If the investor plans later on to repatriate profits, deferral will not help much; H must offer a preferential rate. As inducement to reinvestment of capital already in L, deferral by H will again be helpful. But preferential treatment at repatriation will now be harmful. Thus deferral is generally inducive to foreign investment, while the effect of preferential treatment at repatriation depends upon the balance of the annual flows of new and old investment.

A type of preferential treatment by H, subject to cooperation, is offered by "tax sparing." Here H permits a credit equal to the normal rate of tax in L, even though L gives tax relief to foreign investment and in fact charges a lower rate. This permits L to take the initiative, knowing that its rate reduction will be passed on, and, in fact, enables L to initiate preferential rate reduction in H.[16] This will induce new capital to flow from H to L, but it also reduces the tax payable to H upon repatriation. The net result again depends on the balance of outflows and inflows. Moreover, sparing may interfere with the creation of a strong revenue base in developing countries, especially if the tax incentives are extended to both domestic and foreign investment.

In all, there is considerable doubt as to whether differential tax rates offer an appropriate means of granting economic aid to developing countries. Devices such as risk

16. Sparing also differs from unilateral preferential rate reduction in H (without reduction in L) in its internation equity implications. Substitution of sparing for unilateral action by H causes L to suffer a national loss and gives a gain to H.

insurance, outright grants, and public as well as private loans are to be preferred.

Balance of Payments Effects. Another occasion for non-neutral policy is to combat balance of payments deficit. Tax treatment that discourages capital outflow and encourages repatriation of earnings will be helpful, at least from a relatively short-run point of view.[17] As a minimum, this calls for avoidance of preferential treatment of foreign investment income from new capital outflow, as well as disallowance of deferral where foreign rates are lower. Or the law may go farther and impose penalty rates on foreign capital income to discourage outflow. The effectiveness of such policies, however, requires some degree of international cooperation, just as is the case with monetary adjustments. If country A has a deficit while B has a surplus, outflow-restricting measures in A could be combined with inflow-restricting (penalties on foreign capital) measures in B; or, at the least, absence of retaliation by B must be assured.

As with the staking out of revenue shares, international tax coordination must be based on more than the temporary policy needs of one particular country. Thus a good case can be made against permitting balance of payments objectives to enter tax treaty arrangements, especially since payments needs will change. At the same time, tax measures to influence capital flow may be needed (in addition to monetary and general fiscal policy) to achieve the triple objectives of stability, growth, and foreign balance.[18] For

17. In the longer run, current capital outflow adds to the stock of foreign investment, profits from which may be repatriated in the future. Current restrictions on outflow thus reduce the level of future repatriation; and the higher the repatriation rate, the shorter will be the period over which restriction on capital outflow results in a net gain in the balance of payments. This is the case especially if deterrents to repatriation, such as deferral, are removed. See Peggy B. Musgrave, *United States Taxation of Foreign Investment Income,* Chap. 2.

18. See p. 331.

this reason a compromise between stability of international tax arrangements and domestic stabilization must be found. This may be done by gearing basic tax treaties to considerations of neutrality and equity, while permitting temporary penalty rates on capital outflow (as exemplified by the United States interest equalization tax) as an instrument for securing payments balance.

Beyond this there is the basic policy question of whether balance of payments policy should operate on product or capital account. Essentially the same economic principles that (from the point of view of world efficiency) favor free commodity flow also favor free capital flow. If it is necessary on balance of payments grounds to restrict one or the other, is there a presumption that it will be better to operate on capital than on trade account? Some points may be arrayed on either side of the argument. Capital flows may be more adjustable over time, and thus more amenable to control without causing distortions over the longer run; but per dollar of flow prevented, the world efficiency effects may be more potent.[19] Moreover, capital flows carry political implications which differ from those of commodity flows.

INDIVIDUAL INCOME TAX

The development of general principles for tax coordination is only a first step. These principles must then be applied to particular types of income recipients and to the interplay of individual and corporation taxes. We begin with the individual income tax.

PLACE OF TAX ALLEGIANCE

According to the preceding discussion, a taxpayer who owes tax allegiance to A but earns wage income in B will be taxed on such income by B. In line with nondiscrimination

19. See Jones, "International Capital Movements."

this tax will be imposed at B rates; but if his basic tax allegiance is to A, his final liability will be determined by A's law. Assuming A to take the international view, the tax paid to B will be credited against his tax obligation in A, computed on his pretax income in B. If the B tax is higher, a refund from A is due. The matter now to be considered is where his basic tax allegiance should be.

The primary contenders are residency and citizenship. Some countries, including the United States, hold to the principle that they may tax the entire income of their citizens whether or not resident, but that residents who are noncitizens should be taxed on income earned in the United States only. Other countries proceed on the residency basis, and further differences arise as to how residency is defined. Even if the citizenship base is used, a country may choose not to tax in case of extended absence, and such absence may also be taken to interfere with residency. Thus frequently a mixture of principles (citizenship, residency, place of stay) is involved. From the point of view of efficiency (noninterference of tax considerations with factor movements), tax liability on earned income should be determined on citizenship basis, since residency tends to coincide with place of work. Tax liability on capital income, on the other hand, may be determined on either basis without interfering with capital movement, since location of owner and of investment need not coincide.[20] Since income should be taxed globally, the citizenship principle wins out.[21]

Such at least is the case if the expenditure side of the fiscal process is disregarded. But this is hardly tenable, especially for labor income. Differential levels of public services, such as social security benefits, welfare and educational facilities,

20. Similar considerations apply to the corporation tax. See p. 249.
21. To be sure, even citizenship can be changed for tax purposes. While this does not directly affect location of work choice (unless citizenship is linked to residency), it still opens an avenue for tax avoidance. In this respect, nationality would be the ideal base.

enter into the choice of residency. Taxation according to residency (in the place of living, not necessarily legal residence, sense) may thus give a more neutral result, while taxation by country of citizenship diverts labor to areas in which public service levels are high. This returns us to the principle of benefit taxation; but taxes, as noted before, also serve redistributional objectives. Since one and the same rate structure combines both benefit and redistribution taxes, separate treatment, such as residency for service charges and citizenship for distribution taxes, is not feasible. Moreover, the pattern of rate progression differs among countries, so that the extent and direction of non-neutrality in net benefits depends on the taxpayer's particular level of earnings.[22] For the high income worker, at least, taxation by country of citizenship may prove to be the more neutral solution.

NONDISCRIMINATION

The progressive nature of the income tax structure calls for more specific interpretation of what constitutes nondiscriminatory treatment. Suppose that a citizen of A derives $20,000 of income from B and an additional $80,000 from sources in A. Now it is evident that B should tax the $20,000 only. If B's income tax was proportional, this rate would be applied. But given progressive rates under B's law, should it tax at the average rate that applies to a B income of $20,000 only or at that applicable to the total income of $100,000? While the matter is of indifference to the individual investor, provided his ultimate liability depends on A's law only, the rate used by B will determine B's national gain, and A's loss.

On principle, the average rate applicable to the full income more nearly reflects the spirit of global income tax, but B cannot determine it readily. This is the case especially for

22. The international problem of tax integration here differs from that of regional integration, where rate differentials (e.g. between U.S. states, or municipalities) are less pronounced, but mobility in response to fiscal differences is higher. See also p. 306.

capital income, in particular capital gains, where the recipient is not a resident of B. In practice, a presumptive withholding rate is thus applied by B. Under the nondiscrimination principle, this rate should be independent of tax rates in A and be set to correspond to the rate applicable on the average to income from such source when received in B.

CORPORATION PROFITS TAX

Coordination of corporation profits taxes, and its relation to the coordination of income taxes, raises complex problems, of both a legal and an economic nature.[23] All I can do here is to pose the major issues.

ORIGIN OF INCOME

I have argued that as a matter of internation equity, a country will tax income that originates within its borders. But how is the term "originate" to be defined?

Single Unit Operation. Consider an enterprise that is incorporated and has headquarters in A but produces in B and sells in C. Evidently, its profits originate in various countries and must be divided up among them.[24] Various rules may be used for the division.

23. For a discussion of the technical aspects, especially of the tax credit, see Elisabeth A. Owens, *The Foreign Tax Credit,* International Tax Program (Cambridge, Mass., Harvard Law School, 1961).

24. Application of these problems also arises in the context of fiscal federalism within a country. Thus the states in the United States must apportion corporation profits for purposes of state corporation taxes. This has been done traditionally with a three-factor formula, involving with equal weights location of plant, employment, and sales. Recent recommendations for revision advise that the sales component (which is least relevant on benefit grounds) be dropped. See *State Taxation of Interstate Commerce,* U.S. Congress, Report of the Special Subcommittee on State Taxation of the Committee on the Judiciary, 88th Congress, 2d Sess., House Report No. 1480 (Washington, D.C., G.P.O., 1964).

Under the benefit approach, there is a clear-cut rationale for base allocation, but the appropriate tax is not a profit tax. If we assume that intermediate goods furnished by public services reduce all costs equally, the appropriate division of the tax base is in terms of the costs the firm undergoes in various countries. Thus, suppose that a firm drills oil in A at an operating cost of $40, refines in B at a cost of $25, sells in C with a merchandising cost of $10, and has a headquarters cost of $5 in D. In each case, all costs, including depreciation of plants located in the particular country, are included. Gross receipts in C are $120, costs are $80, and profits equal $40. Under the above assumption, the appropriate bases are $40, $25, $10, and $5 respectively.[25] As each country applies its cost charge or rate against its base, government inputs are paid for and an equitable and efficient revenue distribution results. If the level of intermediate goods contributed by government is higher to some cost payments than to others, a correspondingly differentiated set of changes is in order.

Taking a more realistic view, the benefit approach does not meet the problem of base allocation for a profits tax. Here the problem is not to charge for services rendered, but for the government to appropriate a share in profits. It is thus necessary to determine where profits originate so that they may be allocated among the governments. If we proceed on the assumption that the profit margin is the same for each dollar of cost payment, profits will be prorated in line with a country's share in cost payments. Thus, the countries' shares in total profits would be $20, $12.5, $5, and $2.5 respectively.

It might be argued, however, that this shortchanges country A, where the oil well is located. Suppose that the eco-

25. It will be noted that allocation by cost shares is not the same as allocation by value added, which, in the above illustration, would be $40, $25, $50, and $5 respectively. If differential costs are not reduced equally, the allocation of profits would be adjusted accordingly.

nomic rent derived from this well accounts for one-half the profits. This $20 might then be allocated to A, leaving only $20 for distribution by cost payments, and resulting in total shares of $30, $6.25, $2.5, and $1.25. Presumably this is the line of reasoning that underlies the practice of transferring a substantial share of oil profits in royalty form.

Leaving aside the special problem of extractive industries, it is evident that the largest share of the profits base should go to the country in which most of the cost is incurred. Country C would benefit to the extent of sales cost only. While it may be true that profits could not have been earned without the market in C, this does not mean that the profits originate in C. Factor returns always depend on the market for the product that a factor contributes, but the return nevertheless is imputed to the factor that produces the product.

The issue, it should be noted, is one of internation equity and should be decided as such. From an efficiency point of view the allocation formula should not matter; it should determine how the revenue is to be divided, not what the investor's final liability is to be. This, under proper crediting arrangements, is to be determined according to the law of the country of tax allegiance.[26] But allocation does matter if there is no such crediting and the final tax is the sum of the taxes imposed by A, B, or C, or $(t_a s_a + t_b s_b + t_c s_c)\pi$, where t and s indicate the respective tax rates and base shares. Rate differentials are then equivalent to tariffs and distort commodity flows to the extent that shares are based on the sales factor, and they are equivalent to origin-type-product taxes and distort the location of production to the extent that shares are based on location of production. To the extent that location effects on tax liability are neutralized by benefits received, the latter distortion does not arise and allocation by production site is efficient.

26. Given an absolute corporation tax, there arises the further question of where the corporation's tax allegiance should be.

Intra-Firm Allocation. Further allocation problems arise from multiple-unit operations, i.e. where a corporation operating in A also operates a branch or a subsidiary in B. As the parent purchases from or sells to its branch or subsidiary, the prices charged will affect the distribution of total profits between the units. This affects the distribution of national gains and losses, as well as the firm's tax liabilities, provided crediting is imperfect or deferral applies. While the basic principle embodied in the "arm's-length" rule is reasonably clear—the units are to charge each other as they would if they were independent firms without concern for the trading partner's profits—its application is difficult in practice and further complicates determination of the profits base.

TYPES OF INVESTORS

Let us suppose now that these problems have been solved. Country B is to tax profits originating in B, whether the capital is owned by citizens of A or B; and it is to do so in line with the nondiscrimination rule. We assume to begin with that both A and B impose an "absolute" corporation tax, i.e. a corporation tax that applies independent of and in addition to the individual income tax on dividend income. It remains to consider some of the specific problems that arise for various types of investors. In this connection, we will be concerned primarily with United States practice.

Individual Investor. A citizen of A who invests in a B corporation finds his profits reduced by B's corporation tax. If B's corporation rate equals A's no adjustment is needed. If it exceeds A's, efficiency (noninterference with investment choice) requires that he be given credit (against individual income tax) for the difference; and an additional tax should be imposed if A's corporation tax exceeds B's.[27] Yet such a

27. In both cases, appropriate grossing up is called for, and is assumed to apply throughout this discussion wherever crediting occurs.

credit or penalty is not given in practice. The corporation tax is taken to fall on the corporation as such rather than on the individual and is not allowed for in interpersonal equity considerations. Thus B's tax is only subject to deduction (in determining dividends taxable under A's personal income tax) and some discrimination against or for foreign investment remains.

But this is not all. B also imposes a withholding tax. This tax may be interpreted as intended discrimination; or B may hold that nondiscrimination entitles it not only to impose corporation tax, but also to follow through to the taxation of dividend income in A at the individual level. This is approximated by imposing a withholding tax on dividend payments to shareholders in A. Where B's withholding is allowed for as a credit against personal income tax by A, as is the case in the United States, it does not interfere with capital flows, although it poses a problem in internation equity, as it causes a national and treasury gain to B and loss to A. The question is whether internation equity should be interpreted to permit B's participation in A's personal tax. There is no categorical answer, especially if the two countries adopt different views regarding the integration of personal and corporation tax. Where the credit is not given, discrimination against foreign investment results.

Corporate Investor: Foreign Branch. The branch operated by an A corporation in B will be subject to B's corporation tax. Yet the branch's country of tax allegiance is that of the parent. Given the international view of equity, A will grant a "direct" credit for the corporation tax paid in B. With full crediting, capital flow is not affected. But again B may impose an additional withholding tax on branch profits, perhaps to grant it participation in A's individual income taxes payable at the time of distribution. The withholding tax, similar to the corporation tax, may be credited (as in the United States) against A's corporation tax, although the proper response would be to pass the credit

265

through (with proper grossing up at both corporate and personal level) and apply it against the personal income tax of the dividend recipient. This is difficult to administer, however, and under certain assumptions (proper grossing up and full distribution) both crediting procedures give the same result.

Corporate Investor: Foreign Corporation. The situation is more complex if the foreign investment of the A corporation is not in branch form but in a business that is incorporated in B. Under United States practice (and practices in this respect differ widely among countries) this changes the situation in two respects.

First, and most important, imposition of the United States corporation tax is now deferred until foreign profits are repatriated.[28] At the time of dividend payment, the treatment is the same as for the branch. Subject to the presently noted exception, the parent in A is given a credit against A's corporation tax for the corporation and withholding tax paid to B. In other words, dividends received from the foreign corporation are treated as if they were ordinary income earned abroad by the parent's branch. And as for the branch, a case can be made that the crediting of the withholding tax should be passed through to the individual shareholder in the A corporation.

Deferral is profitable to the A corporation and discriminates in favor of foreign investment if the tax rate in A exceeds that in B. Whether the practice of deferral is appropriate in the equity sense depends on the nature of the relationship of the A to the B corporation. If the B corporation is in fact controlled by the parent, as is the case with many subsidiaries, the "separate entity" doctrine is artificial

28. Deferral is denied on certain so-called "sub-part F"-type income if the U.S. corporation owns at least 10 per cent and total ownership by U.S. corporations exceeds 50 per cent. The object in excluding such income is to prevent foreign incorporation for purposes of tax avoidance, and thus the worst abuses of deferral.

and treatment similar to that of the branch is called for. Where control is loose and the investment is more in the nature of portfolio investment, deferral is appropriate on equity grounds. As in the case of domestic intercorporate investment, profits are not taxed to the shareholder until distribution occurs.[29] On efficiency grounds deferral is undesirable in either case since it diverts capital to low rate countries and suspends the neutralizing effect of crediting. Allowing for both efficiency and equity aspects, a compromise eliminating deferral for narrowly controlled corporations seems the best solution.

Second, there are certain situations in which dividends received from investment in foreign corporations are not eligible for crediting of the foreign corporation tax. Where the ownership share in the foreign corporation is very small (below 10 per cent under United States rules), the administrative difficulties of crediting and provision of the necessary information may become excessive. These difficulties are much less severe for the crediting of foreign withholding tax which, therefore, continues to apply.

COMPLICATIONS

As is evident from this brief discussion, the technical difficulties of working out an equitable and efficient arrangement are substantial. This was so even though a simple two-country case was considered, and the wide variety of special situations resulting from the existence of different legal forms and tax devices were overlooked. These will not be followed up here, but brief notice must be taken of certain major complications. One of these, the implication of corporate tax shifting, has been considered already.[30] Two others remain to be noted.

29. If domestic intercorporate dividends are subject to a supplementary tax, foreign dividends of the portfolio type should be similarly taxed.
30. See p. 252.

Integrated Corporation Tax. So far I have dealt with an absolute corporation tax only. Now consider a corporation tax that in both countries is partially integrated with the individual income tax. That is to say, profits distributed as dividends pay individual income tax only. This may be accomplished via a dividend paid or a dividend received credit.[31]

In the case of the former, a citizen of A who invests in a corporation in B will now be subject to B's withholding tax only, which is credited against his individual income tax in A. A corporation of A operating a branch in B is subject to withholding tax by B. This tax will be credited against its withholding tax in A and, at the time of ultimate dividend distribution, be passed through to the individual shareholder in A as a credit against his individual income tax. Precisely the same holds for investment in a subsidiary, or for portfolio investment. There is little basis, in this case, for deferral of A's corporation tax on the profits of a subsidiary in B. The very purpose of the tax is to anticipate the shareholder's individual income tax on retained earnings; the corporation is a conduit only and the legal relationship between parent and subsidiary does not matter.

Matters are complicated considerably if the role of the corporation tax in the two countries is not symmetrical, with one country using an absolute and the other an integrated tax, or one country operating with partial and another with complete integration. Proceeding under the nondiscrimination rule, the country of income origin should now impose whatever taxes are appropriate under its structure, while the country of income receipt will determine the final liability and grant credits in line with its own approach.

31. Under the former, taxable profits equal total profits minus dividends paid. Under the latter, the corporation tax applies to total profits, while the dividend recipient (after computing individual income tax on grossed-up dividends) may credit the corporation tax as source withholding.

Given adherence to the principle of nondiscrimination, a capital importing country would thus find it costly (in terms of reduced national gain) to proceed from an absolute to an integrated corporation tax, as this would not permit retention of both corporation and withholding tax on dividends paid to shareholders in other countries.[32]

Equivalent Rates. Finally, attention must be drawn to the difficulties of measuring equivalent rates of tax. Nonneutralities result because rates differ, but the relevant difference is that in effective rates of tax, not in statutory rates. Effective rates may be defined as the percentage reduction due to tax in the present value of the income stream.[33] This effective rate depends upon the statutory rate, but also on many features of income definition, such as depreciation rules, the treatment of debt as distinct from equity capital, and so forth. This being the case, the degree of non-neutrality that arises in the absence of crediting or during tax deferral cannot be measured simply by comparison of statutory rates.

Moreover, differences in income concept may interfere with the neutralizing effect of the crediting approach. This would not be the case if A, in assessing final tax liability on the income derived by its citizen from investment in B, were to proceed on the basis of income determination as prescribed by A's law. But if the underlying income determination is according to B's law, foreign investment income may be treated differentially even though A's statutory rate applies.

32. In proposing retention of both taxes, the recent *Report of the Royal Commission on Taxation* (Ottawa, 1966) departs from the nondiscrimination rule.

33. See Peggy B. Musgrave, "Direct Business Tax Harmonization," in *Fiscal Harmonization in Common Markets,* p. 219. The same essay contains estimates of effective rates. The use of the term "effective rate" here differs from that on p. 181.

11 COORDINATION OF PRODUCT TAXES

We now turn to product taxes, imposed on producers' sales as manufacturers' excises, or on traders' sales in the form of wholesale or retail sales taxes. As distinct from income taxes dealt with in the preceding section, these taxes enter into cost and are likely to be reflected in the relative price of products.[1] They may thus have important effects upon commodity flows, as distinct from the income tax case, where our primary concern was with effects upon factor flows.[2]

As has been shown earlier, coordination for both product and income taxes would be solved by a system of benefit taxation. The cost of public services entering into the production of private goods would be charged against them in the form of product excises. Imposed on an origin basis, such taxes would be passed on to the consumer, domestic or foreign, who thereby would pay for services rendered. The result would be an equitable distribution of the tax burden among individuals as well as an equitable sharing of revenues and costs between countries. Moreover, this would be

1. Other taxes entering into cost, such as taxes on factor inputs (e.g., employer's contributions to social security or property taxes on plant), pose similar problems.

2. To simplify matters, we now exclude the possibility of factor flows and focus exclusively on the product side. In a fuller and more complex analysis, effects on both product and factor flows must be allowed for at the same time.

270

an efficient solution since neither consumer or producer choice among products nor the location of production would be disturbed by fiscal factors.

But as in the case of income taxes, this is an unrealistic view of the matter. Product taxes (with the possible exception of user charges and automotive taxes) are typically not imposed on a benefit basis. And, unlike the income tax case, there is little to be said about such taxes under the ability-to-pay approach to interpersonal equity. If equity criteria are developed in terms of income position, product taxes are inherently inferior to income taxes. They are likely to be objectionable in their vertical equity implications (regressivity) and are deficient in horizontal terms (equal treatment of people in equal positions). If the criterion is based on consumption levels, what is called for is a personal tax on total consumption, with personal exemptions and progressive rates, rather than product taxes.[3]

But though little can be said about interpersonal equity, the issue of internation equity remains. The exporting of tax burdens now operates via taxing not the income of foreign residents but their consumption or sales. Imposed by an exporting country, the tax enters into the prices charged to the foreign consumers of its exports; or, imposed by an importing country, the tax may lower the price paid to the foreign producers of its imports.

EFFECTS ON WORLD EFFICIENCY

Free trade is efficient because it permits products to be produced by those countries that possess a comparative cost advantage. Interference through tariffs with the free flow of trade distorts relative production costs and consumer choice, and thus reduces world efficiency. Will product taxes have similar effects, and how?

3. See N. Kaldor, *An Expenditure Tax.*

CLOSED VERSUS OPEN SETTING

We begin with the case of the closed economy, defined first to exclude regional tax differentiation. Product taxes of the following types[4] may be distinguished according to their base of application:

	On All Products	*On Some Products*
On all producers	1	5
On some producers	2	6
On all consumers	3	7
On some consumers	4	8

In the *closed* economy, taxes of types 1 and 3 are equivalent, and so are taxes of types 5 and 7 imposed on the same product.[5] Taxes of types 1 and 3 are both general and affect neither consumption nor production choices.[6] Taxes of types 5 and 7 impose an excess burden because they lead to inefficiencies in consumption choice. The tax—whether imposed at the consumption level (type 7) or the producers' level (type 5)—enters as a wedge between cost and price, thus destroying the equality between the marginal rate of substitution in consumption and the marginal rate of transformation in production. In the domestic setting, the usual forms of product tax are the general retail sales tax (type 3), selective consumer taxes (type 7), and selective producers' excises (type 5). Discrimination between consumers (types 4 and 8) is not usually applied, but discrimination between producers (types 2 and 6) may occur. Sales taxes, for instance, may be limited to firms with certain characteristics, such as chain stores.

In the open setting, matters are more complex and no

---

4. We assume these taxes to be of the ad valorem type. The further distinction between unit and ad valorem taxes is disregarded here.

5. See my *Theory of Public Finance,* p. 140.

6. Effects on the work-leisure or consumption-saving choices are disregarded.

simple parallel to the preceding cases can be drawn. The essence is now that of regional differentials in tax rates, be they on consumption or production. Consumption taxes, applied at different rates in different countries, are analogous to cases 4 and 8 above. But provided they apply to domestic products and imports alike—i.e. follow the destination principle—international differentials do not interfere with the efficient location of production. The problem of excess burden, resulting from the interference with consumer choice, remains essentially similar to that of the closed economy case. Differentials in production taxes, imposed by various countries on output produced within their borders, are analogous to cases 2 and 6, but the discrimination is on a regional basis. Following the origin principle, such taxes affect the relative costs of production in different countries and thus may lead to inefficient production location. They are similar in this respect to tariffs or consumption taxes that discriminate against imports. Whereas in the closed economy truly general taxes have no distorting effects, it remains to be seen whether general taxes, imposed at differential rates in various countries, retain this advantage. As shown below, the answer depends on the assumptions made regarding the working of the international monetary mechanism, and the flexibility of domestic price levels.

Apart from differences in efficiency effects, taxes imposed on the production and consumption side also differ with regard to their revenue flow, as the location of the tax imposition determines to which government the revenue accrues. Finally, note that differential tax rates imposed by various jurisdictions within one country (e.g. among states in the United States) may be considered a special case of the open economy problem. It resembles the latter under the assumption of fixed exchange rates, and with allowance for greater mobility in factor and consumer movement. Much of what is said below about the open economy will thus be applicable to the multijurisdiction single country as well.

PRODUCTION DISTORTIONS IN ABSENCE OF COORDINATION

I consider first what distortions arise from the uncoordinated imposition of product taxes by various countries, and then proceed to the examination of coordination techniques. All this is from the point of view of efficiency effects on a worldwide basis.

General Taxes. Suppose first that country A imposes a general tax on production or consumption. The outcome depends on both the nature of the monetary adjustment mechanism and the pattern of absolute price change.

A general tax on production, if giving rise to an increase in prices, will reduce A's cost of imports relative to domestic goods and raise that of exports relative to foreign goods. Under a regime of flexible exchange rates, both will be cancelled by an automatic depreciation of the exchange rate and no trade effects will result. If the tax is reflected in reduced factor cost with prices unchanged, trade effects will be neutral without change in exchange rates. In the case of a general consumption tax, the opposite situation prevails. If the tax causes factor cost to fall, relative price changes will be adverse to imports and favorable to exports. Both will be corrected by an appreciation in the exchange rate. If the tax results in price rise, trade effects will be neutral without change in exchange rates. Given flexible exchange rates, general production or consumption taxes are trade neutral, whatever the direction of price change. No excess burden results, in either the domestic or the international setting.

The situation differs if exchange rates are fixed. Whether or not trade effects arise now depends on the response in terms of absolute prices. A general production tax (origin type) will be equivalent to exchange appreciation if it results in a general price rise. Export costs will rise relative to world market prices, and import costs will fall relative to domestic prices. But the same tax will have no trade effects if product prices remain unchanged while factor prices fall.

The reverse holds for a consumption tax (destination type). There will be no trade effects if product prices rise, while the tax will be equivalent to depreciation if factor prices fall. Export costs will now fall relative to world prices, while the prices of imported goods will rise relative to domestic prices. Which price adjustment comes about depends on the nature of concurrent monetary or fiscal measures, as well as on the nature of factor and product markets. As money wages tend to be downward rigid, the price response of both consumption and product taxes tends to be upward. Therefore, trade effects are more likely to be caused by the production (origin) tax.

How are these results for the fixed exchange rate case to be interpreted from an efficiency point of view? Suppose that the production tax leads to price rise and is thus equivalent to appreciation. Suppose also that, prior to the introduction of the tax, the prevailing exchange rate was the same as would prevail under flexible conditions.[7] The resulting change in trade (and associated changes in capital flow) will involve a departure from the efficient position; but the efficiency cost is difficult to define, not to speak of its measurement. As a disequilibrium is involved, reference must be made to a given point in time, and the implications of changed capital as well as product flows must be allowed for. These difficulties must be granted, but it does not follow that efficiency considerations should be applied to the flexible rate case only. The real world is essentially one of fixed exchange rates, and though there may be a long-run tendency toward equilibrium (either by rate changes or by changes in price levels) the periods of disequilibrium may be the rule rather than the exception.

Selective Taxes. Beginning with the production tax,

7. Difficulties are compounded if, as is likely to be the case, the initial rate of exchange was not the equilibrium rate. Here the problem of second best of measuring efficiency changes in an inefficient world, arises.

let country A impose such a tax on product X, which previously was exported by A. As a result, the gross cost of producing X will be increased (relative to costs in B) and production of X will shift to B, whose factor cost of producing X is higher. Country A in turn will produce more of product Y, to which it is less suited. World efficiency is reduced. The production distortions that result may be likened to those of a tariff, imposed by B against imports of X from A. Trade distortions arise under both a flexible and a fixed exchange rate regime. Since relative prices of X and Y in terms of A's currency are affected, an adjustment in the exchange rate will not remedy the situation.

This distortion in the location of production does not arise if A's tax on X is in the form of a retail sales (destination type) rather than a production tax. The tax then applies to all consumption of X in A, whether produced at home or imported, while exports to B are free of tax. Thus X will continue to be produced at the place of lowest cost. But all is not well, since consumers in A will incur an excess burden of the consumption type, such as results if a tax on X is imposed in the closed economy setting. The origin tax involves distortions in the location of production, while the destination tax involves distortions in the consumer's choice. Both effects must be considered, and it cannot be determined readily whether it would be better for world efficiency to have selective product taxes of the origin or of the destination type.[8] However, chances are that production effects cause the more serious distortion.

TAX COORDINATION

We now turn to the coordination of product taxes, designed to eliminate distorting effects on production.

Fixed Exchange Rates and GATT Rules. The postwar

8. I am indebted to Professor Mieszkowski for helpful discussion of this point. See also his article referred to in n. 15 and the reference to Douglas Dosser in n. 22.

world having been one of fixed exchange rates, policy discussion and formulas have developed in this setting. Assuming the prevailing exchange rate to be at the equilibrium level, distorting effects on the location of production may be avoided by adopting a uniform set of production (origin type) tax rates or by converting such taxes into destination type by the application of certain adjustments. The latter is the procedure currently followed under GATT rules.[9]

Suppose again that country A, following the origin principle, imposes a selective production tax on product X and that this causes the price of X to rise by the amount of the tax. If now an export rebate is given—i.e. exports of X are exempt from tax, and a compensating import duty is imposed on the import of X—the tax is in fact converted into a destination tax on X. The result is equivalent to A's imposing a consumption tax on X, and no interference with the location of production results.

Now it should be noted that this reasoning assumes A's tax to be reflected in an absolute rise in the price of X. If price remains unchanged and factor costs fall, a different set of adjustments is called for.[10] These may be summarized as

9. GATT statutes are rather vague with regard to both practice and underlying theory. Presumably the rules are designed to expedite world efficiency rather than national or balance of payment gains, but there is no clear statement of intent. Article IV:2 of GATT says that imports may be subjected to such internal taxes as are imposed on like domestic products. This provision is not tied to particular kinds of taxes, nor is it said explicitly what criterion (price increase?) should be used to decide which taxes are or are not eligible. Article VI:1, which rules out dumping, nevertheless permits allowance to be made for differences in taxation (without specifying particular taxes) and for "other differences affecting price comparability." Thus it appears that for the export credit the basic distinction is between taxes that do and taxes that do not affect prices, and presumably the same logic should carry over to the import compensating tax. See GATT (General Agreement on Tariffs and Trade), Part II, Articles III and XVI.

10. See Richard A. Musgrave and Peggy Brewer Richman, "Allocation Aspects, Domestic and International," in *The Role of Direct and In-*

follows, where *ER* stands for export rebate, *ET* for export tax, *CID* for compensating import duty, and *CIS* for compensating import subsidy, all imposed in country A. Also, *X* stands for the taxed good and *Y* for other goods.[11]

Tax imposed in A	Adjustment in A
On production of *X* only	
rising product prices	*ER* and *CID* on *X*
falling factor prices	*ET* and *CIS* on *Y*
On production of *X* and *Y*	
rising product prices	*ER* and *CID* on *X* and *Y*
falling factor prices	none
On sale of *X* only	
rising product prices	none
falling factor prices	*ET* on *X* and *Y*; *CIS* on *Y*
On sale of *X* and *Y*	
rising product prices	none
falling factor prices	*ET* and *CIS* on *X* and *Y*

The validity of the GATT rules thus depends on the underlying assumptions with regard to price behavior. For both Europe and the United States the assumption of downward rigid money wages is a realistic view of the postwar period. Nevertheless, product taxes might have had some effect on the rate of wage advance, and increases in such taxes might have been absorbed to some degree in profits. Moreover, earlier tax-induced increases in price level may have been adjusted for subsequently by depreciation. Thus the adjustment rules may not have been altogether neutralizing.

Certain difficulties arising with implementation of the GATT rules may also be noted. To begin with, determination of the proper rebate rate for exports may be difficult in the case of taxes that are collected at multiple stages. Proper

direct Taxes in the Federal Revenue Systems (Princeton, Princeton University Press, 1964); and my "International Commodity Flows" in *Effects of Corporation Income Tax*.

11. We do not specify whether *X* and *Y* are exported and imported. Depending on their status the various adjustments do or do not apply.

assessment is difficult especially under the turnover tax, and it is expected that the contemporary transition to value-added taxes in European countries will increase rebates. More important, it is not easy to decide just which taxes should be eligible for the credit. The proper test is whether the tax is reflected in prices or not. Certain taxes, such as manufacturers' excises, are obviously cost increasing, but for others the matter is less evident. For instance, property taxes on business plants should be eligible only if reflected in cost. In fact, they are not thus treated, the property tax being considered equivalent to an income tax. Employment taxes similarly are not eligible, presumably on the assumption (more realistic for the employee's than the employer's share) that they are absorbed in wages. Nor is the exclusion of the corporation tax beyond question. To the extent that the tax is shifted in the short-run sense, an export credit would become appropriate.[12] Finally, allowance should also be made for benefits received. Cost taxes that are payments for intermediate goods do not affect prices and should not be eligible for credit. This may justify to some degree the disallowance of property tax, as well as give some rationale to the exclusion of payroll taxes.

Application of export rebates and compensating import duties may prevent distorting effects on the location of production, but at the cost of maintaining "fiscal frontiers" at which adjustments are made. This is a disadvantage. In the context of European economic integration in particular, a high premium has been placed on the elimination of such frontiers, either as a first step toward political union or to simplify administration. Various solutions are available. One would be to replace origin taxes plus border adjustments by retail sales taxes, which could continue at differential rates. This, however, would impose hardship on countries (especially the less developed ones) whose economic and administrative structure does not permit effective use of such taxes.

12. See p. 253.

Also, it assumes that consumers will not cross frontiers. Another solution, adopted by the Neumark Committee, is taxation of production at origin but at a uniform rate. The Committee thus proposes a product (value-added) tax at uniform rates in all Common Market countries.[13] Thereby the need for border adjustments is avoided, but a certain restraint is imposed on the freedom of individual countries to arrange their own fiscal affairs.

In evaluating the GATT rules, it must be recalled that the exchange rate is assumed to be at the equilibrium level, so that no distortions in the location of production occur if all taxes are on a destination basis. Also, it must be noted that the rates are directed at eliminating production distortion only. If border adjustments are made, the location of production in the low-cost countries is not interfered with. At the same time, we have noted that transformation of origin into destination taxes may leave excess burdens of the consumption type. While these are domestic in nature, and arise even in the closed economy setting, this is no reason to exclude them from consideration. However, there is some basis for the view that international coordination should be concerned primarily with production efficiency. As noted before, potential losses from this side are likely to outweigh the consumption burden.[14] Moreover, consumption burdens that result from discriminatory destination taxes are largely "self-imposed," whereas production inefficiencies are shared outside the taxing country.

Flexible Exchange Rates. While the case of fixed exchange rates is of more immediate interest, brief consideration must also be given to coordination under flexible rates.

13. See European Economic Community, "Report of the Fiscal and Financial Committee on Tax Harmonization in the Common Market," reprinted in *Tax Harmonization in the Common Market* (Chicago, Commerce Clearing House, 1963).

14. See H. G. Johnson, "The Cost of Protection and the Scientific Tariff," *Journal of Political Economy, 68,* no. 4 (August 1960), 335.

This does not mean that we have to postulate a fully flexible system. Even though exchange rates are fixed in the short run, they are subject to correction from time to time, or equivalent corrections may come about via price level change.

Under flexible exchange rates, the absolute direction of the price change does not matter. As noted before, general taxes on production or consumption have no trade effect, as they are offset by compensating changes in the exchange rate. By the same token, the effect of selective taxes is again independent of the direction of absolute price change. What matters is resulting changes in relative prices. A general tax on exports is now equivalent to a general tax on imports. Taxes that discriminate against traded products, either exports or imports, divert resources to domestic products and reduce the volume of trade. Hence world efficiency is impaired. To avoid this result, taxes must be such as not to discriminate between domestic and traded goods. Since many goods are of the mixed type (with output divided between export and home consumption) it is difficult to approximate this result short of a uniform tax. Given a system of general taxes, tax neutrality is achieved more readily under flexible than fixed exchange rates; but given a set of selective taxes, it may be that compensating adjustments are achieved more effectively (from the efficiency point of view) under fixed rates.

Effects on National Efficiency

The preceding discussion was concerned with the effects of various tax arrangements on the efficiency of resource use as considered from a world point of view. As we found to be the case with income taxes, this differs from efficiency under the national point of view.

Whether a country gains or loses from the imposition of

product taxes depends upon its position in world trade. We have seen that imposition of a selective production (origin) tax by country A, if affecting trade, will reduce world efficiency by interfering with the location of production. But this does not exclude the possibility that country A itself incurs a gain. Similarly, imposition of a selective consumption (destination) tax by A, while imposing an excess burden on A's consumers, may nevertheless improve A's position.

Suppose first that A is a small country, without effect on world prices.[15] Also, let us assume now that trade is balanced. As A imposes a production tax on export product X, its exports of X will decline. While the exporter's net price falls, this does not involve a national loss, since the differential accrues to A's treasury. But a national loss to A arises because the decline in exports must be matched by a decline in imports. Resources previously employed in production for exports are diverted into production for domestic use and a more costly domestic product is substituted for imports. A similar situation results if A's tax is on the imported product Y. The gross price to the consumer rises, but this increase in price accrues to A's treasury and does not involve a national loss. But a national loss to A arises because the reduction in imports also reduces exports as resources are diverted into domestic production. Thus less efficient domestic production is substituted for imports. In either case, A will lose from less efficient production at a reduced volume of trade. Its terms of trade remain unchanged, but it cannot shift its tax to the outside world.[16]

15. For a rigorous analysis of a special case of this type see Peter M. Mieszkowski, "The Comparative Efficiency of Tariffs and Other Tax-Subsidy Schemes as a Means of Obtaining Revenue or Protecting Domestic Production," *Journal of Political Economy, 74,* no. 6 (December 1966) 587–99.

16. This does not mean that the outside world is wholly unaffected. If A's trade shrinks, so does that of the outside world. As a result, a part of the total burden is shared by the outside. At the same time if

Now consider a situation where A is large enough to affect world prices. As A imposes an origin tax on export product X, the world price of X rises. As a result, A's terms of trade will improve. This is the case even though net prices received by A's suppliers of X will fall, since it is the total price (including tax) that matters. But unless foreign demand is wholly inelastic, improvement in the terms of trade will be accompanied by a decline in volume. The net effect may leave A better or worse off depending on the circumstances of the case, including supply and demand conditions for both exports and imports in A and the outside world.

A similar argument applies if A imposes a destination tax on Y, a product it imports from country B. The domestic price of Y is increased, and its consumption declines. The world prices of Y falls, and A's terms of trade are improved. This is the case even though A's consumers pay more, since from the terms-of-trade point of view what matters is now the net price (excluding tax) which is paid to foreign suppliers. Again there may be a gain or loss for A, depending on the circumstances of the case. The situation resembles that of a tariff which reduces world efficiency but may nevertheless lead to a gain for the imposing country.[17]

While no exporting of burden occurred in the small country case where the terms of trade remained unchanged, a burden is now passed on to country B if the price B pays for X (including A's origin tax) rises, or if the price paid by A for Y (excluding A's destination tax) falls. Changes in

we assume that A is so small as not to affect world price, its share in trade will also be insignificant, so that a decline therein will not significantly burden the outside world.

17. See Charles P. Kindleberger, *International Economics* (3d ed. Homewood, Ill., R. D. Irwin, 1963), App. F. Also see T. de Scitovsky, "A Reconsideration of the Theory of Tariffs," *Review of Economic Studies,* 9, no. 2 (1942), pp. 89–110; and H. G. Johnson, "Optimum Tariffs and Retaliation," *Review of Economic Studies, 21* (2), no. 55 (1953–54), 142–53.

the terms of trade are thus *the* vehicle of burden transfer.[18] At the same time, changes in the terms of trade are not identical with tax-burden transfer since they also reflect changing costs of production. In all, it is difficult to define just what is meant by the "shifting" of A's tax burden.[19] If internation equity were interpreted as forbidding burden transfer, it would in fact rule out selective product taxes, either origin or destination, on traded goods. The GATT rules meet this requirement by excluding burden shifting through production taxes on exports (assuming that export rebates *must*, not only *may*, be given) but there is no corresponding constraint against burden export via consumption

18. Such at least is the case in the simple foreign trade model where resources are immobile. The situation differs in the interregional case where mobility is high.

19. Following Dalton's principle of dividing the tax burden between consumer and producer shares in a closed economy setting (see Hugh Dalton, *Principles of Public Finance* [9th ed. London, Routledge and Kegan Paul, 1936], p. 73), the burden of a partial production tax on product X in country A may be divided between the four shares borne by consumers and producers of X in A and B, respectively, and from this the total (consumers plus producer) shares borne in each country may be derived, such that the four burden components add up to the tax. If B's consumers' loss exceeds its producers' gain, burden export has occurred. Conditions will be favorable to burden export if B's supply and demand are inelastic. See Charles McLure, "Commodity Tax Incidence in Open Economies," *National Tax Journal, 17,* no. 2 (June 1964), 187–204.

This analysis permits a neat allocation of the tax burden, but it fails to allow for consumer or producer excess burdens. Moreover, the analysis is partial and allows for the taxed product only, disregarding further changes which result as resources move out of the taxed products into other uses. Finally, it may be noted that people in A gain from the tax revenue via expenditure benefits, whereas those in B do not.

For an attempt to measure the welfare cost of indirect taxes in one country, see A. Harberger on "Taxation, Resource Allocation and Welfare," in *The Role of Direct and Indirect Taxes in the Federal Revenue System,* The Brookings Institution (Princeton, Princeton University Press, 1964).

taxes, provided that such taxes apply to both imports and domestic production.

BALANCE OF PAYMENTS ASPECTS

As distinct from the efficiency gains and losses that have been examined in the preceding sections, tax policy may have important balance of payments effects.[20] Tax policies that make exports more attractive to the foreign buyer and imports less attractive to the domestic consumer will improve the balance of payments situation. But as the terms of trade are worsened this is achieved at a cost, so that tax policies aimed at improving the balance of payments tend to run counter to policies of exporting tax burden.

In pursuing balance of payments objectives, the direction of absolute price change is again of decisive importance. Assuming prices to rise with its imposition, a general product tax is equivalent to appreciation and tends to have a detrimental balance of trade effect. The same holds for selective taxes on traded goods. Imposition of an export rebate and compensating import duty neutralizes this effect. Neutralization of tax effects upon the balance of payments—designed to prevent tax dumping and to permit freedom of internal tax policy without balance of payments penalty—thus provides a further rationale for the GATT rules. Quite possibly, these rather than efficiency considerations have been the primary factor influencing GATT and EEC (European Economic Community) thinking on tax coordination. The proposed Common Market rule (equalized origin rates inside, with destination principle toward the rest of the world) appears to follow the same pattern. Finally, it should be noted that adjustments in the level of export rebates and import duties may be used as a technique by which to secure balance of payments adjustments as part of a co-

20. See p. 257 for a similar discussion of direct taxes.

285

ordinated policy of international finance. Thus countries with lasting and substantial deficits may be permitted to credit more fully and impose higher compensating duties, while surplus countries would apply more limited corrections. Used as a flexible device, this might permit balance of payments adjustments in a smooth fashion. Unlike adjustments in exchange rates, such measures would not run the risk of inducing perverse responses in capital flows.

As in our earlier discussion of efficiency effects, there arises again the question of which taxes do in fact raise costs and should thus be eligible for the rebate and compensating import duty. In this connection, it is frequently argued (1) that the United States has been placed at a disadvantage vis-à-vis European countries, because a larger part of their tax structure is eligible for credit; and (2) that the United States position would be improved if the corporation tax (which is not eligible for credit) were replaced by a value-added tax (which is eligible). Similarly, it has been debated in the United Kingdom whether introduction of a value-added tax would be helpful.

In appraising these arguments, one must begin with the basic fact that introducing a tax that raises costs, with subsequent rebating thereof, leaves the initial situation unchanged. Thus proposition (1) is correct only if initially European prices did not rise or if (which may be the case for old taxes) the rise was compensated in subsequent adjustments. Proposition (2) is correct only if the corporation tax was not only shifted in the first place (in which case it should have been eligible for rebate all along) but would in fact be reverse-shifted (reflected in reduced prices) if the tax were repealed.[21] Substitution of a value-added tax for a

21. A recent British report (*The Report of the Committee on Turnover Taxation,* Cmd. 2300 [London, H.M.S.O., 1964]) was unwilling to make this assumption, thus rejecting substitution of the value-added tax for the company tax on these grounds. N. Kaldor, arguing that

turnover tax as now in process in the Common Market may be export-increasing if the reform leads to a fuller allowance, but should be neutral otherwise.

TAX UNIONS

We have considered the effects of various tax arrangements from the point of view of world efficiency and have found that inefficiencies in the location of production are avoided if all countries move to a destination basis. We have also seen that policies which are inefficient from a world point of view may be beneficial to any one country. It remains to reconsider the case of groups of countries or of tax unions, such as the proposed tax coordination within the European Common Market. Will neutralizing measures within the union contribute to world efficiency or only to gains among the member countries? As for a customs union, the results will differ depending on the nature of the trade relations that prevail.[22] For the time being we shall deal with production efficiency only. Such effects will be efficient if formulation of the tax union results in production shifts

removal of the company tax would lower prices, took the opposite view. See N. Kaldor, "A Memorandum on the Value-Added Tax," *Essays in Economic Policy, 1* (London, Duckworth, 1964).

22. For a comprehensive discussion of various cases and review of the literature, see Dosser, "Economic Analysis of Tax Harmonization," in *Fiscal Harmonization in Common Markets, 1,* 45–62.

See also Hirofumi Shibata, "The Theory of Economic Unions: A Comparative Analysis of Customs Unions, Free Trade Areas, and Tax Unions," same volume, p. 145. Shibata emphasizes the implications for trade deflection and for the distribution of revenue among members of a free trade area where various members have different tariffs with the outside world. Also consideration is given to trade deflection and revenue implications of a tax union in which unequal origin taxation exists internally.

from high to low factor (opportunity) cost producers, and it is unfavorable if the opposite results.[23]

ORIGIN TAXATION PRIOR TO UNION

We begin with a situation where all countries (A, B, and R) are on an origin basis, using different rates of origin tax. Now various initial positions and policy changes may be considered.

Let the initial situation be such that $C_A > C_B > C_R$ and $t_A > t_B > t_R$ where the C's reflect the cost of producing X in A, B, and R and the t's are the respective rates of origin tax. We thus have

$$(1) \quad (1 + t_A)C_A > (1 + t_B)C_B > (1 + t_r)C_R$$

as defining total (factor plus tax) cost in the three countries. It follows that X is produced in R. Since this is where factor cost is lowest, the location of production is efficient. Now suppose that A and B form a tax union, involving (policy I) repeal of origin taxes and adaptation of a destination basis. Sales in A and B become subject to retail tax, independent of product origin. The cost comparison now becomes $C_A > C_B \gtreqless (1 + t_r) C_R$.[24] If $C_B < (1 + t_r) C_R$ pro-

23. What matters is whether production shifts from high to low cost countries or vice versa. These shifts cannot be identified with trade creation or trade diversion. Whereas in customs union theory trade creation is always efficient and trade diversion always inefficient, this is not so for the case of tax unions. The result of the tax change may be expansion of trade which is inefficient, or diversion which is efficient. Therefore, Viner's concepts of "trade creation" and "trade diversion" are not readily transferable to the tax union case. See J. Viner, *The Customs Union Issue* (New York, Carnegie Endowment for International Peace, 1950); and Peggy B. Musgrave, "Direct Business Tax Harmonization," in *Fiscal Harmonization in Common Markets, 2,* 239. Also see R. G. Lipsey, "The Theory of Customs Unions: A General Survey," *Economic Journal, 70* (September 1960).

24. Since the retail tax is independent of origin, it can be disregarded in the comparison.

duction location of X shifts to B and the result is inefficient. Next, suppose that the change (policy II) involves retention of origin rates by A and B, but that these rates are set at t^* equal to the average of t_A and t_B.[25] In this case, the initial cost ranking will not be changed and the production location of X will be unaffected. Finally, let the change (policy III) imply again adoption of t^* by A and B, but let exports from A and B to R be excluded from this tax and let there be no compensating tax on imports from R.[26] The results will be the same as for policy I with production shifting to B if $C_B < (1 + t_r) C_R$.

Now suppose that in the initial situation we have $C_A > C_B > C_R$ but $t_R > t_B > t_A$. Also, let

$$(2) \quad (1 + t_R)C_R > (1 + t_B)C_B > (1 + t_A)C_A$$

Thus X is produced in A which is inefficient. Policy change I now results in a shift in production from A to B, which is efficient. The same result follows from policies II and III. Additional initial situations and policies may be analyzed in this fashion, but these examples suffice to show that the outcome will differ (i.e. that results may be efficient, neutral, or inefficient) depending on the nature of the initial position and type of policy change.

DESTINATION TAXATION PRIOR TO UNION

Finally, we turn to the more usual case where the pre-union situation is one of destination taxation, the initial situation being thus efficient with regard to production

25. This is an arbitrary assumption. In the cases we consider the results will be the same if $t^* = t_b$, but if $t^* = t_A$ no production shifts will result from the various policies.

26. This policy is of special interest because it resembles the pattern to be adopted by the Common Market countries. However, the actual change will be from an initial destination base position, so that the results differ.

effects. Since countries are now largely on this basis (i.e. origin taxes are subject to the GATT adjustments), this is the initial situation from which tax policy changes instituted by the Common Market originate.

Agreement among A and B to equalize their destination rates leaves production efficiency unchanged, even though R's rate continues to differ. Differences in destination rates, as noted before, are not a source of production inefficiency.

Agreement among A and B to adopt equal origin rates while maintaining destination taxes toward the outside has the same result since equalized origin rates do not disturb production location. This is the coordination visualized under the proposed Common Market integration. Unlike the removal of internal tariffs while maintaining protection against the outside, the proposed tax integration would not cause inefficiency from a world point of view. Its significance, rather, is in permitting the removal of fiscal frontiers and eliminating imperfections that result in applying the GATT rules.

The situation would differ, however, if A or B were to apply the origin rate (without compensating credits) to exports to R as well. With R staying on a destination basis, production may now move from A or B to R, and production inefficiencies could result.

OTHER ASPECTS

This discussion of tax union effects was concerned with production effects only. But as noted before, elimination of production distortions by moving to a destination basis may be gained at the cost of consumption distortions. Tax unions, similarly, have both consumption and production effects. A tax union change which is neutral in its production effects may nevertheless create consumption distortions.[27] But as noted before, production inefficiencies are likely to be greater in magnitude and thus pose the primary problem.

Finally, our discussion of tax unions has been in terms of effects on *world* efficiency only. As before, a fuller analysis would have to add consideration of gains or losses that accrue to union countries as a group, or to individual member countries. As in the preceding discussion of national gains, this involves resulting changes in the terms and volume of trade, and may be dealt with as in the individual country case.

27. For a discussion of consumption and production effects and references to the relevant literature, see Dosser, "Economic Analysis of Tax Harmonization," *Fiscal Harmonization in Common Markets, 1,* as well as his earlier article, "Welfare Effects of Tax Unions," *Review of Economics Studies, 31* (3), no. 87 (1964). See also Mieszkowski, "Comparative Efficiency of Tariffs," *Journal of Political Economy, 74,* no. 6 (December 1966).

12 EXPENDITURE COORDINATION

I now turn to the other side of the coin, which is the coordination of public expenditures. This has to date been considered primarily as a matter of coordinating fiscal units within a country, but there is also growing concern with coordination at the international level. Both aspects will be considered.

In most instances, the regional organization of the fiscal structure has not been designed to yield an efficient pattern, but has grown as a by-product of historical development. In its international aspects, it dates back to the formation of nation-states and their modern boundaries; and in its structures within each nation, the pattern of fiscal federalism (decentralized or centralized) typically reflects the pre-nation-state basis of multiple political units. The division of fiscal responsibilities and resources among local governmental units similarly is the outgrowth of regional political development, with little relation to fiscal needs and capacities. The existing structure, therefore, was not designed to meet considerations of fiscal efficiency in the modern socio-economic setting. If regional government were made over in the image of fiscal efficiency, it would surely look very different from what exists today in most countries.

This is not to say that regional political structuring should involve nothing but fiscal considerations. The broader issues of territorial division between nations and of political centralization versus decentralization within a nation transcend fiscal considerations. Yet fiscal efficiency is an important factor, and there exists a degree of flexibility at the margin that permits improvement. This is the case especially for regional fiscal arrangements within nations. Conditions of rapid change in the regional patterns of living, such as the development of metropolitan areas in particular, permit or force a reconsideration of the fiscal structure. Beyond this, major changes in the structure of fiscal federalism are not out of the question. Such changes are now under debate in the United States and Canada, and continue in a fluid state in continental European countries such as Germany and Italy. Moreover, problems of expenditure coordination arise increasingly between nations, whether in the financing of international organizations such as the United Nations or NATO, in economic aid to developing countries, or in the Common Market type of union. To deal with these problems of change it is helpful to know what considerations enter into designing the spatial aspects of an efficient fiscal structure, even if we are forced to assume, for the time being, that nonfiscal factors can be disregarded.

In developing the regional aspects of the fiscal structure, it is again useful to distinguish between various fiscal functions, i.e. allocation, distribution, and stabilization. The allocation function involves the most direct relation to the regional problem: What spatial arrangement of fiscal organization is most efficient in rendering public services? Using United States terminology, which services should be financed at the federal, state, or local levels respectively? The question is wide open, and there is no general presumption for or against fiscal centralization.[1] The distribution function, on the other hand, we shall find to be primarily a mat-

1. On the concept of fiscal centralization, see Alan Williams, "Centralization and Decentralization in Public Finance with Special Reference to Central and Local Government in England and Wales," in *Centralization and Decentralization in Public Finance,* Travaux de l'Institut International de Finances Publiques (Proceedings of the 18th Congress), 1962.

ter of national rather than local policy. At the same time, important international aspects arise once the concerns of welfare policy are extended beyond the national boundary to a multinational level. The stabilization function, similarly, is national rather than local; but, as will be seen in the following chapter, there is an increasing need for international cooperation in this area as well.

ALLOCATION ASPECTS

As shown in Chapter 1, there are certain characteristics of social goods which bar their effective provision through the market mechanism. The basic reason is that such goods (as distinct from private goods) are nonrival in consumption, i.e. A's partaking in consumption does not interfere with benefits derived by B. Notwithstanding this difference, we argued that the fiscal structure should (subject to certain exceptions) provide for public goods or services in line with individual consumer preferences. Public services, that is to say, should be decided upon and their cost should be defrayed by the beneficiary group. The ideal tax pattern, insofar as the *allocation* function is concerned, is thus conceived in the spirit of benefit taxation. As noted before, this does not exclude the use of tax-transfer systems for income redistribution, or even interference with consumer preferences in exceptional instances where the "ruling group" considers this desirable.[2] Our principle, however, applies to the bulk of public services, evaluation of which is to be left to the individual voter-buyer, or consumer. It provides us with the basic concept from which a spatial theory of fiscal structure can be derived.

SPATIAL CHARACTERISTICS OF BENEFITS

The regional problem of fiscal structuring arises because benefits derived from public services are usually subject to spatial limitation. Our previous dictum that benefits from

2. See pp. 11, 24.

public services are available to all members of the group has to be restated.[3] Allowing for spatial limitations, we now find that benefits from public services rendered at a particular point in space are enjoyed in equal amounts by "all those present in this space." If we add the requirement that the supply of public services should be determined and their cost be defrayed by those who enjoy them, it follows that public services, the benefits of which accrue to people located in a particular region, should be decided upon and paid for by the people of that region.

This has far-reaching implications for the regional organization of the fiscal structure. Services may be divided into those with local, state, nationwide, or worldwide benefit regions. Services the benefits of which are worldwide (such as space exploration) should be financed on a worldwide basis; functions with nationwide benefits (such as national defense) should be performed by a nationwide agency, drawing on a nationwide service determination and tax base.[4] Services that are strictly local, such as streetlights for the houses surrounding a city square, will be provided for by a local service agency, with a correspondingly limited participation in service determination and tax base. Services that cover a wider region, such as transport arteries, will be determined and financed by the group of adjoining communities. Other functions such as education will be financed partly on a local and partly on a national basis, depending on labor mobility and so forth.[5]

The very logic of the approach thus provides the basis for

3. See p. 8.

4. For a discussion along these lines, distinguishing national, local, and international goods, see Albert Breton, "A Theory of Government Grants," *Canadian Journal of Economics and Political Science, 31,* no. 2 (May 1965), 175–87.

5. For an attempt to classify various services of urban government according to spatial incidence, see W. Hirsch, "Local vs. Areawide Urban Government Services," *National Tax Journal, 17,* no. 4 (December 1964), 331–39.

a regional theory of fiscal structure. The technical nature of the public service sets the benefit region, and the policy-determination and tax-base region should be adjusted to match it. The spatially limited nature of benefit incidence thus calls for a fiscal structure, composed of multiple service units, covering different-sized regions within which the supply of a particular service is determined and financed. Services with coinciding benefit region may be serviced by a single unit. While some services call for nationwide, others for statewide, and still others for metropolitan-area-wide or local units, this does not imply a hierarchical ordering of "higher" and "lower" level governments. Rather we are faced with coordinate units covering regions of different sizes.

TAPERING OFF OF BENEFITS

The spatial nature of benefit incidence would be greatly oversimplified if interpreted to mean that benefits are homogeneous within a given radius around the service center, and zero on the outside. It is more realistic to think of the problem as involving a tapering off of benefit intensity with increasing distance from the service center. A streetlight gives more protection close by than farther away and so forth. Our rule is restated to read that "benefits are enjoyed equally by all at a given location or point in the region." This does not change the principle that benefit and tax areas should coincide but it complicates its application.

If benefit intensity declines in successive rings around the center, so should cost assessments. Different rings, or locations, will then contribute at varying rates, corresponding to their declining benefit shares. Translated into a voting mechanism, residents of both the outer and inner rings should participate in the supply determination; but residents of the inner ring with a given taste and income will be called upon to contribute more than similar residents in the outer ring.

296

Expenditure Coordination

We have proceeded so far on the assumption that each type of public service is characterized by a specific benefit region, or spatial benefit incidence. Actually, the supply of any one service may be organized so as to cover a smaller or wider region. A block may be lit up by one large light in the middle of the block, or by several smaller lights spaced along the street; atomic development may be financed on a small scale by one nation alone or on a larger scale by a group of nations, and so forth. The choice of the benefit area thus becomes a variable in the policy decision and has important bearing on the cost at which the service is rendered. The supply of public services is subject to economies of scale, and the appropriate service region is one of the dimensions of this problem.[6]

Among the variables are the area of the service region R, the population density D, and the level of services to be provided L. Holding constant D and L, the cost of rendering the public service will vary with R.[7] As R is increased, more people participate in the service benefits, which (for any given total cost) reduces cost *per person*. But average cost (to the *group*) of rendering a given service level may vary as well. It may fall as the region to be serviced is increased up to a certain size, and rise if the region is expanded beyond this point. Sooner or later the latter factor may come to offset the gain from increased numbers, and

6. See Charles M. Tiebout, "An Economic Theory of Fiscal Decentralization," in *Public Finances: Needs, Sources and Utilization*, National Bureau of Economic Research (Princeton, Princeton University Press, 1961), pp. 79–97.

7. J. M. Buchanan in "An Economic Theory of Clubs," *Economica, 32* (February 1965), pp. 1–14, approaches the problem of increasing numbers in somewhat different terms, as the size of the group is entered as an argument in the consumer's utility function. This aspect does not enter into the present discussion, where only effects on costs are relevant.

per person cost begins to rise. If so, there is an obvious advantage in choosing the low-cost region and in adapting the number of service regions accordingly, depending on the size of the entire area to be covered. This consideration is of major importance in urban finance, where traditional districts may be too small for efficient supply of certain services and a metropolitan-area-wide unit is called for.

Another aspect of the scale problem appears if R and D are held constant while L is varied. The average unit cost of services may now decline as the service level L is increased, and rise if raised beyond this. Finally, holding constant R and L, the cost per person may be found to vary with D. As D is increased, the cost to any particular individual tends to fall because any given total cost is shared among more people. But as density increases beyond a certain point, the total cost of rendering the service may rise. Thus the cost per person will decline up to a certain level of density and may rise thereafter. Moreover, density if carried too far becomes a disutility in itself which must be weighed against possible reduction in per-individual cost of public services.

The determinants of the regional structuring of public services are thus twofold. Not only should the supply of particular services be organized in such a way that costs are allocated to and policy determination is made by those residing within the benefit region, but the size of the benefit region should also be determined so as to comply with lowest cost considerations.

EQUAL-TASTE COMMUNITIES

One further complication of the spatial characteristics of social goods remains to be noted. People's preferences for social goods, as for private goods, differ. But the significance of these differences is not the same. In the case of private goods it is to a person's advantage to share an economy with others whose tastes differ from his own, as this will enable him to obtain his desired goods at relatively lower prices. In the case of social goods, it is to his advantage to associate with others who prefer the same social goods and who value social goods more highly. They will then be prepared to pay more for such goods, and the cost share payable by him will be less. Also, if tastes are similar, there is less chance that compulsory budget decisions will offend his interests.

It follows, therefore, that it is efficient for people with similar tastes in social goods to reside together. Efficient location planning (in the absence of other overriding considerations) would encourage co-residency of people with similar tastes. Indeed there is a tendency for this result to come about automatically. The choice of communities becomes a device for recording preferences and, in a sense, acts as a substitute for the auction mechanism of the market.[8] Similarly, there are other forces at work that make for socially homogeneous neighborhoods, which in turn form efficient units of budget determination.

These considerations, to be sure, are more important in the setting of local finance, where fiscal factors may carry substantial weight in the choice of suburbs, than at the national or international level, where other considerations will be more important. Nevertheless, with increasing mobility fiscal considerations may come to enter even at that level. Certainly this may be so with regard to distribution policy, via either the deterring implications of progressive taxation or the attracting effects of welfare support.

BENEFIT SPILLOVERS

So far I have attempted to sketch the factors that enter into the regional design of an efficient public service structure. At a high level of abstraction, this calls for a de novo design of regional structures, without regard for the limitations imposed by existing political or fiscal institutions. I must now move toward a more realistic view and ask how

8. See Charles M. Tiebout, "A Pure Theory of Local Expenditures," *Journal of Political Economy, 64,* no. 5 (October 1956), p. 418.

the service function should be allocated among existing institutions. At this point, spillover problems become of central importance.

Such problems do not arise in a system where the service agency has jurisdiction over its benefit region and costs are assessed on the residents of the region. But problems of benefit spillover do arise once the regional unit in which the service supply originates and the taxes are imposed falls short of the entire benefit region covered by it. In the absence of joint ventures, governmental authority to assess cost contributions is typically limited to economic activity and to persons within its boundaries, and it cannot obtain direct contributions from those outside but benefiting from its services.[9] Thus benefit spill-out (i.e. out of the region of revenue jurisdiction) becomes an important factor in the fiscal picture.

Benefit spillovers may arise in various ways. One is through the outflow of services rendered by residents of region A to residents of region B. Thus flood control measures undertaken by upstream region A will be helpful to downstream region B; the development of a port in region C may be of vital importance for the economy of the adjoining regions D and E, and so forth. Another form of benefit spill-out operates through human investment and migration. Education services rendered in region A may be lost to that region through out-migration of the educated.[10] Still another mechanism is provided through residents of region B entering region A as workers or tourists, and partaking of A's public services. Yet they may neither be part of A's tax base nor have a voice in determining A's service levels. This involves a twofold offense against our basic rule

9. While exporting of tax burden may occur (see p. 306) this can be aimed at the foreign beneficiary only where the spill-out takes the form of intermediate expenditures on export goods.

10. See Burton Weisbrod, *External Benefits of Education: An Economic Analysis* (Princeton, Princeton University Press, 1964).

that public services should be determined and paid for by the beneficiary group.

Situations such as these lead to a malallocation of resources in public services unless cooperation between governmental units is provided for. First, let region A undertake services that involve a benefit spill-out to B but not vice versa. Region A, acting in isolation, will be interested in the benefits accruing to itself only and will equate its marginal cost with its marginal benefits. But benefits to the community as a whole $(A + B)$ are larger. Region B will allow for the spillovers from A and supplement them with its own output. An efficient solution will call for B to reduce its own output level and to pay A for supplying increased services. As a result of such cooperation, more services will be produced in A and less in B. Total consumption of such services will rise, as will total $(A + B)$ factor inputs into the service. Next, suppose that the benefit flow moves in both directions. Cooperation will again be to the advantage of both regions, and the location of factor inputs will again be shifted into the most efficient sites. Total consumption of the service will again rise. At the same time, total factor inputs may now decline, even though the benefit level rises.[11]

From an analytical point of view, the spillover problem of regional finance becomes similar to that of the usual social

11. J. M. Buchanan and M. Z. Kafoglis, "A Note on Public Goods Supply," *American Economic Review, 53,* no. 3 (June 1963). See also Alan Williams, "The Optimal Provision of Public Goods in a Theory of Local Government," *Journal of Political Economy, 74,* no. 1 (February 1966). Williams' different conclusion (that consumption may fall due to negotiation) arises because he compares the initial situation, in which no negotiation is allowed, with one where compensation must be paid rather than with one where compensation may be paid on a voluntary basis. Thus under his comparison one region's position may be worsened by negotiation, whereas this cannot be the case under the alternative comparison. See also W. C. Brainard and F. Trenery Dolbear, "The Possibility of Oversupply of Local Public Goods: A Critical Note," and rejoinder by Alan Williams, *Journal of Political Economy, 75,* no. 1 (February 1967).

goods case among a small number of individuals. The partners may bargain, and in the process preferences will be revealed, thus overcoming one of the basic difficulties encountered in the large number case. But bargaining imperfections block an efficient solution. Mediation now becomes an important factor in solving the problem.[12] This new function introduces a hierarchical element into the multiple-unit fiscal structure. While there would be no need for mediation if equality between benefit and service regions could be maintained, mediation becomes necessary once this fails to be the case. Short of rearranging service and assessment areas, the remedy is through cooperation between regions so as to secure a result that more nearly equals the efficient solution. Where the spillover is between governmental regions A and B, the government of a larger unit encompassing both A and B, and reflecting the interests of both, may be an effective mediator between them.

If the number of service units is large, the problem ceases to be one of mediation. Consider the case of elementary education in the United States where services are rendered by thousands of school districts, and important spill-outs into national benefits result. Since each district will consider its own benefits only, the consumption level of service will tend to be insufficient. Negotiation and mediation, which were possible among a small number of service units, now cease to be feasible. Adjustment might now be secured by a nationally financed matching grant, determined upon and paid for by the residents of all districts as a group, which reduces the cost of service supply to any one region and hence expands output. Thus each district finds that its own cost is equated with its own benefits at the margin, while the subsidy or matching grant accounts for the spill-out of benefits throughout the nation.

12. For a discussion of the bargaining problem, see J. G. Head, "Lindahl's Theory of the Budget," *Finanzarchiv, 23,* no. 3 (October 1964), 421–54.

But will the grant mechanism work even though numbers are large? If numbers are large, will not the own-input of services by any one district cease to be a significant factor of its own-benefit levels so that reliance is placed simply on benefit spill-ins from other regions? And if this analogy to the consumption of social goods by individuals holds, why does it not become necessary to provide for the service through a central, higher-level budget? Two explanations suggest themselves. One is that spill-out may well "dilute," or reduce, the benefit content. While supply of a certain service by A benefits B, B's benefit per unit of service is much less than it would have been if the service had been rendered in B. Thus own-consumption continues to depend significantly on own-input even though numbers (and hence sources of spill-out) are relatively large.

Another explanation may be that benefits obtained from spill-out may differ not only in quantity but in quality. They may satisfy a different want from that which is provided for by own-consumption. Providing education in district A gives benefits to the residents of A in the form of their own education. In addition, benefit spill-outs through migration, cheaper exports, or a better national electorate help the residents of B. But from their point of view, A's outlays meet a different need and do not replace the benefits derived by own-inputs in B. Parallel to the small number case, the government of the larger region over which spill-outs extend, again assumes a mediation function. But the appropriate tool in this case is a matching grant to the districts, financed on a multi-district basis.

DAMAGE SPILLOVERS: THE CASE OF WEAPONS

What has been said in the preceding section regarding benefit spillovers may, in reverse, be applied to the parallel case of damage spillovers. Such negative spillovers may be no less important. Thus strengthened police protection in ward A may cause the troublemakers to operate in ward B; upstream water use for irrigation may dry out downstream areas, and so forth. Damage spillovers of this sort may be on a narrow territorial scale (i.e. city wards) or on a national scale (i.e. river control). Or they may be on a worldwide scale, e.g. pollution of outer space by careless use of missiles.

The most striking case of damage spillover, of course, is to be found in the case of military outlays.[13] Let countries A and B be joined in an alliance against C and D. Defense expenditures by A and B will have mutually beneficial spillover effects, and so will those by C and D. But expenditures by A and B will have damage effects for C and D, and vice versa for expenditures by C and D. Indeed the very benefit to A and B is the damage to C and D, and vice versa. A rational solution would therefore be for A and B to pay C and D not to make such expenditures, and vice versa. With equal costs, payments would wash out and each group could put its resources to better uses. Given the possibility of inspection, which assures each party that the other side does in fact refrain from making such outlays, this would seem the obvious answer. The fact that it is not readily reached may be due to differences in the groups' ability to bear the cost, leading A and B to believe that they can exhaust C and D.

JOINT VENTURES AND BURDEN SHARING

An obvious, physical need for expenditure coordination arises where a given project cannot be undertaken, for physical reasons, unless construction proceeds in two or more political territories. Flood control, irrigation, and

13. The situation differs depending on whether the expenditures are for defensive, offensive, or mixed weapon systems. Outlays by A and B on purely defensive weapons would merely negate C's and D's outlays on offensive weapons but not call for defensive outlays on their part. Given an effective agreement not to build offensive weapons, there would be no need for defensive outlays. For a discussion of related problems of strategy see Thomas C. Schelling, *The Strategy of Conflict* (London, Oxford University Press, 1963).

highway construction are obvious examples. In such instances, the distribution of on-site costs may differ from the distribution of benefits, so that each must be measured separately. On the cost side, overhead costs may have to be allocated by some rule-of-thumb device, and so forth. Difficult problems of cost and benefit imputation arise; for instance, in the case of the St. Lawrence Seaway, the operation of which is the concern of both Canada and the United States.

More generally, the joint-venture approach arises not only where there exists a physical necessity for coordination, but may apply to functions that involve heavy benefit spillover and that may best be coordinated through a joint undertaking.[14] Military alliance, such as NATO, offers a good illustration. In determining how the cost shares should be allocated among the partners, two approaches may be taken. One is to allocate costs in line with benefits received, which from an allocation point of view offers an efficient solution.[15] The other is to consider the cost side by itself and—in analogy to most domestic tax-structure theorizing—aim at an equitable distribution of the cost.

This reopens the problems of the ability to pay theory, now at the international level. As this is basically a distribution issue and objective standards of interpersonal utility comparison are absent, especially at the international level, the answer is essentially a matter of value judgment. A variety of rate schedules may be used to compute per capita contributions of member countries and (multiplying by population) to set their total shares. Thus United Nations contributions are assessed by a proportional rate, subject to

14. Where the benefit spillover is to adjoining locations, the problem may be looked upon as a matter of spatial structuring of public goods supply, rather than of spill-out.

15. See M. Olsen and R. Zeckhauser, "An Economic Theory of Alliances," *Review of Economics and Statistics, 48*, no. 3 (August 1966), where it is argued that the larger partner tends to bear a "disproportionate" share.

a vanishing exemption at the lower end of the scale and a ceiling in the total cost share at the upper end.[16] More strongly redistributive schemes have been suggested for the financing of economic aid to developing countries, a matter that will be considered presently in connection with international redistribution.

TAX-BURDEN SPILLOVERS

Before proceeding, I return briefly to the tax side of the picture. If the spillover of expenditure benefits is a disturbing factor in efficient allocation, so is that of tax burdens.[17] The very premise that efficient allocation requires the cost of public services to be borne by the beneficiary group also demands that taxes should be borne by the community that imposes them. The rationale of regional finance breaks down when local public services are financed by taxes whose burden is shifted to another region. Only if benefit spill-out occurs is a corresponding burden export appropriate, provided that the export is to the region of benefit spill-in.

Taxes the burden of which disperses over a nationwide basis should thus be used to finance nationwide services. Others whose burden impact is local should be used to finance local services, and so forth. Within the nation, a strong case can be made for assigning taxes on corporate profits to national use, while property taxes are assigned to local use. Also a case can be made for using taxes on wages and salaries on a local basis, while reserving a sales tax to a regional, such as state or metropolitan-area base. A tax on cost payments, similarly, may be used at the state or local level to defray the cost of intermediate public goods, i.e.

16. See United Nations, *Report of the Committee on Contributions,* General Assembly, Official Records, 16th Session, Supplement no. 10 (A/4774); and 17th Session, Supplement no. 10 (A/5210).

17. For estimates of tax burden spillover among the states in the United States see Charles E. McLure, Jr., "Tax Exporting in the United States: Estimates for 1967," *National Tax Journal, 20,* no. 1 (March 1967).

goods that reduce the cost of production of resident business firms.[18] Not only do cost payments provide a better index for benefits received from such goods, but the tax also results in a justified burden export to the final beneficiaries of the local benefit input.[19]

The regional design of an efficient fiscal structure is thus a function of tax as well as expenditure policy. While the logic of the argument starts on the expenditure side, where the regional benefit incidence defines the appropriate burden area, implementation of the scheme requires that it be matched by taxes that in fact stay within the burden region. Nonexport of local tax burden (except for the intermediate expenditure case) is a prerequisite for a rational system of fiscal regionalism.[20]

EFFECTS ON FACTOR AND PRODUCT FLOWS

Actual fiscal structures do not succeed in securing a net balance between benefit and burden regions; and even where such balance is secured in some sense for beneficiaries and taxpayers as a group, substantial differentials may arise for individuals or subgroups within the region. This being the case, the imbalance between benefits and costs, reflected in a net gain or burden, becomes a distorting factor in economic activity. Indeed many of the problems noted in the preceding chapters in connection with tax policy also arise from the expenditure side.[21]

Factor Flows. Factor flows in response to expenditure differentials are especially important with regard to labor. Higher social security benefits and other transfer payments may attract labor where relative wage rates would not justify

18. See p. 239.
19. See p. 270.
20. See p. 283.
21. See R. Andel, "Problems of Government Expenditure Harmonization in a Common Market," *Fiscal Harmonization in Common Markets, 1,* Chap. 4.

movement. Similar effects may result from consumer services such as housing and health and education. Coordination between countries may be accomplished by adopting uniform service levels, by excluding temporary residents from transfers, or by charging on a benefit basis. The latter consideration, as noted previously, is in favor of letting tax allegiance for income tax purposes on work income be determined by residency;[22] but this is only a rough approximation, and in particular does not solve coordination with regard to social security payments.[23]

Capital flows, similarly, may be affected by expenditure policies, whether through the supply of intermediate goods, cost subsidies, availability of credit at preferential rates, or other. As noted before, such benefits should be allowed for in designing neutralizing tax adjustments, but are disregarded under prevailing GATT provisions.

Product Flows. Intermediate expenditures of government, i.e. expenditures that reduce the production cost of private firms, are equivalent to corresponding cost subsidies, and hence to negative origin taxes. The same argument, which applies with regard to distorting effects of origin taxes, thus also applies in reverse to such expenditures. Where taxes should be offset by an export credit, such outlays should be offset by an export tax. To the extent that taxes and such services are equal, both adjustments wash out. As noted before, origin taxation for intermediate expenditures is neutral.[24]

MERIT WANTS

The preceding line of reasoning provides us with the outlines of an efficient approach to the regional aspects of

22. See p. 259.
23. See R. Andel, "Problems of Harmonization of Social Security Policies in a Common Market," in *Fiscal Harmonization in Common Markets, 1,* Chap. 5.
24. See p. 239.

the fiscal operation. Provision for public services would be arranged in line with benefit areas, ranging from the national to the local in scope. Higher level governments (in the sense of governments encompassing wider regions) would mediate adjustments in benefit or burden spillovers, which lead to distorted decisions on the part of particular regions. And as will be shown later, the task of interindividual redistribution would be handled centrally, thereby obviating concern with interregional distribution.

This view of the matter is helpful in formulating the problem, but still overlooks a basic aspect of the broader issue of fiscal federalism. Individuals, while residents of particular regions, whether municipalities or states, also act as citizens of the larger national unit. As such, they may hold that minimum levels of certain public services (e.g. elementary education) should be available to all members of the larger group, independent of their particular place of residence within the nation. To assure these levels, the central government may decide to provide such services or, by way of subsidy (earmarked grants), induce lower level governments to provide them. Thus another aspect of fiscal federalism, not allowed for in the preceding discussion, enters the picture.[25] Central government, as it were, protects the national citizen against "inadequate" supply of local services as determined at the local level. In this sense, national government plays a centralist role which transcends the purely functional role ascribed to it in the preceding discussion.

ADJUSTMENTS IN DISTRIBUTION

We now turn to adjustments in income distribution, both within and between nations.

25. For a discussion along these lines see my "Approaches to a Fiscal Theory of Political Federalism" in *Public Finances: Needs, Sources, and Utilization*, pp. 97–122.

WITHIN NATION

The primary purpose of redistribution within the nation is to secure a proper state of distribution *among individuals*. This, clearly, is an appropriate concern of public policy, and to the extent that distributional adjustments are to be made, fiscal measures, including progressive taxation and transfer payments, are the proper tool. There is a strong case, however, for making this a national rather than a regional function. In the United States context, distribution policy should be on a national rather than state or local basis. Local policies of redistribution readily become a distorting element in location. Suppose first that the initial pattern of distribution and average income is similar in each region, but that redistribution policies differ. The poor will then move into areas where much redistribution occurs, and the rich will tend to leave such areas. As illustrated by the Poor Laws of Elizabethan England and the zoning ordinances of modern suburbs, they will try to keep the poor from following them. Similar movements result if redistribution policies are the same, but initial states of distribution or income levels differ. The poor will then move into high income areas, and the rich will tend to keep out the poor. Actually both types of variation apply, and local policy cannot cope with the problem.

While the regional grouping of people with similar tastes was shown to be a useful mechanism in securing an efficient provision of public services, location choice in line with distributional considerations serves no such purpose and distorts efficient resource use. Moreover, it is likely to result in a cleavage between rich and poor communities. Not only will these communities have unequal capacities for providing public services, but the need for welfare services and other distributional measures to take care of the poor will be high in precisely those communities in which average income is low. To illustrate: The higher income residents

310

leave the city center, thus reducing its tax base while the welfare burden grows. This phenomenon is typical for the fiscal problem of urban areas in highly developed countries such as the United States.[26] Similarly, lacking fiscal capacity is even more serious in urban centers of low income countries such as Lima or Calcutta, which are ill-equipped to deal with the large influx of agricultural surplus population.

It follows that distributional adjustments should be primarily a function of central finance.[27] This means that the progressive income tax, as the major instrument of high-income taxation, should be used primarily by central government, and that the use of income taxation at lower levels (in the United States, the state and especially the local level) should operate with a distinctly less progressive or even uniform rate structure. Also the financing of relief and welfare payments should be on a central or area-wide basis so as to eliminate benefit differentials that induce the poor to move to high benefit areas rather than to areas of good job prospects, as well as tax burden differentials that

26. See Harvey E. Brazer, "Some Fiscal Implications of Metropolitanism," in *Metropolitan Issues: Social, Governmental, Fiscal*, ed. G. S. Birkhead, Maxwell Graduate School of Citizenship and Public Affairs (Syracuse, Syracuse University Press, February 1962). See also Chap. 7 in Wilbur R. Thompson, *A Preface to Urban Economics* (Baltimore, Johns Hopkins Press, 1965).

27. J. M. Buchanan ("Federalism and Fiscal Equity," *American Economic Review, 40,* no. 4 [September 1950], 586–87) has argued that the federal government should engage in a tax-transfer scheme that will equalize a person's fiscal residue (excess of benefit over cost or vice versa) wherever he lives. I prefer to define a neutral situation as one where (1) measures to redistribute money income are undertaken nationally, and (2) public services are provided on a *marginal* benefit basis. This still permits difference in *total* utility derived from public services at various locations. Such differences may be accounted for in determining the proper state of distribution of money income, and their existence increases rather than decreases the efficiency of resource use. See also my "Approaches to a Theory of Fiscal Federalism," in *Public Finances: Needs, Sources, and Utilization.*

311

induce the rich to flee areas with high welfare obligations.[28]

Apart from the problem of securing a proper state of distribution among individuals, is there a further policy objective of redistribution *among regions?* If it could be assumed that interindividual redistribution was performed at the central (national) level, then there would be no further need for redistribution among regional governments. The philosophical foundation for concern with distribution —be it the egalitarian objective of reducing inequality or the humanitarian goal of assuring decent minimum incomes —relates to people and the family unit. It does not relate to differentials in average per capita income between regions. After a proper state of interpersonal distribution has been secured by central action—whether through a separate transfer system or a negative appendage to the income tax— there is no objection to such differentials in regional averages as may remain. Inequalities in fiscal strength, defined as the ratio of fiscal needs to resources, will have been leveled greatly by central assumption of responsibility for the redistribution (welfare) function; and though remaining differences in average incomes may still be reflected in different levels of public services, these, like differences in the average consumption of private goods, are merely a reflection of what interindividual distribution policy considers a tolerable degree of inequality.[29]

28. The problem may be met, to some extent, by enlarging the region, hoping that this will raise the average income of the enlarged region to the national level. (See Thompson, p. 271.) An alternative and more effective solution is to nationalize those fiscal functions (especially welfare) that are the primary cause of differentials in fiscal strength between regions.

29. It will still be true that for a given distribution of money income, welfare levels (including the consumption of public and private goods) will differ more if people segregate into high and low income regions than if they do not. But this is simply a factor to be allowed for in deciding what constitutes the proper distribution of money income.

312

At a more realistic level, it cannot be assumed, however, that the "proper" state of interpersonal distribution has been settled by central finance. In the United States, for instance, a vast poverty problem is left precisely with the regions that are least able to bear it. In this case, regional redistribution through central finance, transferring funds from strong to weak fiscal units, is needed although it offers only a second-best solution.

AMONG NATIONS

Concern with poverty, and the case for redistribution is a matter of value judgment.[30] But to the extent that such concern exists, the underlying humanitarian view can hardly be confined to the national boundary. The values—humanitarian or egalitarian—that provide the basis for concern are not such that they can be limited to the maladies of one's own nation. But though the principle of redistribution is readily extended (or calls for extension) to the international level, the fact remains that distribution policy on the international level is vastly more difficult to accomplish. For one thing, the inequalities are much greater, so that a much larger fraction of income would have to be surrendered by high income recipients to achieve even a modest result; for another, the organizational problem is much more complex because there is no "central government" on the worldwide level, so that distributional measures must be implemented via contributions and transfers between nations.

Magnitude of Problem. The inequality of income distribution on a worldwide basis is appalling.[31] The lowest

30. For a general introduction to this problem, see also Douglas Dosser, "Towards a Theory of International Public Finance," *Kyklos, 16,* Fasc. 1 (1963).

31. See also H. Theil, "Enige kwantitatieve aspecten van het probleem der hulpverlening aan onderontwikkelde landen," *De Economist, 2,* (1953); and Suphan Andic and Alan T. Peacock, "The International Distribution of Income, 1949 and 1957," *Journal of the Royal Statistical Society,* Series A, *124,* Part 2 (1961).

50 per cent of the world population receives less than 10 per cent of world income, while the highest 20 per cent receives 55 per cent, and the highest 10 per cent receives 30 per cent. This degree of inequality is much greater than that which prevails within countries, especially higher income countries. Moreover, there is reason to expect that per capita income in developing countries is rising more rapidly than in low income countries, so that the situation is worsening rather than (as tends to be the case with domestic distribution) improving over time.[32] Most appalling is the fact that about one-half of the world's population—including most of Asia, Africa, and the Middle East, and a good part of South America—subsists on a per capita income of $250 or less, the average per capita income for the lowest 50 per cent being little above $100. This compares with an average per capita income for the upper 50 per cent of over $1,300. With due allowance for the difficulties inherent in sweeping comparisons of this sort, the degree of inequality is staggering.

To be sure, if the given total income could be redistributed, a per capita income of $750 could be secured with total equalization. While low compared with the prevailing standards of advanced countries, this would involve a vast improvement for large parts of the world. But obviously, this could not be done while holding total income constant. Indeed, the contribution rate required from the higher income countries to achieve even a moderate adjustment would be exceedingly high.

In dealing with the financing of economic aid, it has been suggested that aid should be distributed in accordance with a pattern derived by applying, say, the United States personal income tax to the per capita income of developed countries,[33] and the suggestion has been made that shares be

32. See Gunnar Myrdal, *Economic Theory and Underdeveloped Regions* (London, Duckworth, 1951); and Andic and Peacock.

33. See P. N. Rosenstein-Rodan, "International Aid for Underdeveloped Countries," *Review of Economics and Statistics, 43*, no. 2

related to growth in per capita income. But the amounts involved have been very modest, and it is interesting to explore what would be required to secure more substantial results.

Redistribution Patterns. These relations are illustrated in Table 12–1, based on a fairly comprehensive sample, which included 86 countries and approximately two billion people, with the major omission of mainland China.[34] As shown in column 2, full equalization would level per capita income at about $750. This would involve contributions ranging from 74 per cent of GNP for the United States, 46 per cent for the United Kingdom, 34 per cent for the U.S.S.R., to 4 per cent for Italy. The corresponding shares in total contributions would be 59, 5, 14, and 0.22 per cent respectively. At the other end of this scale, India would receive an 816 per cent increase in its GNP and 46 per cent of total grants.

These magnitudes are startling and would be more so if China were included. Such vast redistribution would of course be economically self-destructive and is not useful to pursue. Lesser targets, however, are worth exploring. Col-

---

(May 1961), p. 110. A similar procedure is followed by Douglas Dosser, "Allocating the Burden of International Aid to Less Developed Countries," ibid., *45*, no. 2 (May 1963); and Douglas Dosser and Alan T. Peacock, "The International Distribution of Income with Maximum Aid," ibid., no. 4 (November 1964).

For further discussion see Irving B. Kravis and Michael W. S. Davenport, "The Political Arithmetic of Burden Sharing," *Journal of Political Economy, 71,* no. 4 (August 1963); John Pincus, *Economic Aid and International Cost Sharing* (Baltimore, Johns Hopkins Press, 1965); R. F. and H. J. Taubenfeld, "Independent Revenue for the United Nations," *International Organization, 18,* no. 2 (1964).

34. Based on population, gross domestic product at factor cost in U.S. dollars, and per capita GDP of 86 countries. United Nations, *Yearbook of National Account Statistics 1965* (New York, United Nations 1966), Table 9A, pp. 493–96. The GDP for the U.S.S.R., not there given, is estimated at $284 billion, with a per capita GDP of $1,144.

TABLE 12–1

Patterns of World Income Distribution*

	Before Equalization (1)	Full Equalization (2)	Floor of $150		Floor of $250	
			A Proportional (3)	B Progressive (4)	A Proportional (5)	B Progressive (6)
Per capita GNP, lower 50 per cent	$118	$751	$164	$166	$250	$250
Per capita GNP, upper 50 per cent	$1,366	$751	$1,321	$1,320	$1,238	$1,238
Per cent of per capita GNP contributed by (−), or received by (+)						
United States	—	−74	−3	−3.9	−9	−10.6
United Kingdom	—	−46	−3	−1.3	−9	−4.1
Sweden	—	−59	−3	−2.5	−9	−9.0
France	—	−47	−3	−1.3	−9	−4.2
U.S.S.R.	—	−34	−3	−0.9	−9	−3
Italy	—	−4	−3	−0.4	−9	−1.7
Japan	—	+27	−3	−0.2	−9	−0.7
Spain	—	+59	−3	—	−9	—
India	—	+816	+83	+82.9	+205	+204.9
Per cent of total subsidy contributed by (−), or received by (+)						
United States	—	−59	−35	−46.3	−38	−45.1
United Kingdom	—	−5	−5	−2.1	−5	−2.4
Sweden	—	−1	−1	−0.7	−1	−0.8
France	—	−5	−4	−2.0	−5	−2.2
U.S.S.R.	—	−14	−18	−5.4	−20	−6.9
Italy	—	−0.2	−3	−0.3	−3	−0.5
Japan	—	+2	−4	−0.2	−4	−0.3
Spain	—	+1	−1	—	−1	−0.3
India	—	+46	+68	+67.6	+60	+60.4

* For sources, see p. 315, n. 34

umns 3 and 4 show such a target, with grants sufficient to establish a per capita income floor of $150. In column 3 we assume these grants to be financed by a proportional tax on countries with per capita income above this level, the required rate being 3 per cent. This would involve a United States contribution of about $25 billion, or 3 per cent of GNP, and amount to 35 per cent of the total transfer. Under the progressive contribution schedule of column 4 the United States per cent of GNP would rise to 4 per cent, and its share to 46.3 per cent.[35] Columns 5 and 6 show corresponding approaches to a somewhat more ambitious target, setting the income floor at $250. The required proportional rate would now be 9 per cent, and the United States share would be somewhat lower.[36]

By the nature of the case, the United States share is extremely large, reflecting the combination of high per capita income and a large population. This, however, is not a very meaningful ratio. What matters is the respective shares in national income that would be absorbed in such contributions. But, as noted before, these shares are exceedingly high, compared to current levels of foreign aid, even if the implementation of relatively modest targets is considered. The negative income tax, international model, is a startling concept to contemplate.

Relation to Domestic Distribution. The problem of international distribution, as discussed in the preceding pages, was appraised in terms of average per capita incomes in various countries. But the basic objective is again distribution among individuals, not among countries, and the concern with average incomes is only an indirect means of

35. The progressive rates, used in col. 4 are: Per capita income up to $500 nontaxable, with rates of 1, 3, 5, 7 per cent applied to successive $500 increments in per capita income.

36. The progressive rates, used in col. 6 are: Per capita income up to $500 on nontaxable and rates of 4.5, 9, and 18.2 per cent applied to successive $500 increments in per capita income.

reaching this basic objective. This has two significant implications.

For one thing, receipt of aid by a country should be conditioned on its own effort to secure a modicum of internal redistribution on its own part. Similarly, there should be assurance that the aid will be used so as to raise incomes at the lower end of the internal income scale. To some extent this may be accomplished by giving the aid in kind, involving products of particular importance to low income budgets, but this offers no complete assurance, since foreign aid may then be substituted for domestic aid. If international concern is basically with distribution among individuals, it is only consistent to conclude that international policy should address itself as well to distribution within nations. In both cases, problems of national sovereignty (or international cooperation) are involved and, as yet, pose powerful obstacles to policy action.

For another, the scope of the redistribution problem greatly depends on the number of individuals whose income level is to be supported and hence is closely linked to population policy. Indeed, systematic attention to distribution policy would have to go hand in hand with population constraints, the latter being, as it were, a preventive policy of income maintenance.

REDISTRIBUTION AND GROWTH

As has been pointed out many times, distribution policy must not be considered only as a matter of redistributing slices in a given pie. Effects on the size of the pie, in particular the rate of economic growth, must be considered as well. If this holds for the case of national redistribution, it holds especially at the international level where the potential scale of distributional adjustment is so much larger. Nothing would be gained if the contribution of developed countries were pushed so far as to interfere with their economic ability to render continued aid.

It is generally said in this connection that the best way to render economic aid is to divert capital flows from high to low income countries. In the process, world output might be increased, as capital should be more efficient in countries where the capital to labor ratio is as yet very low; and there will be a redistribution of income from labor in high income countries (which then operate with less capital) to labor in low income countries whose productivity is increased by the rising capital to labor ratio.[37] If the process is not one of diverting capital flow but of adding to total capital formation (e.g. through tax-financed government grants) the incidence pattern within the high income country is less clear, but there will be an even greater relative gain in the position of the low income country.

Primary emphasis upon aid through capital formation thus has the advantage of economic efficiency, as well as of eventually substituting own-earnings for help from abroad, thus avoiding the "being on welfare" syndrome which is equally as disturbing in the international setting as it is in the domestic. Compared with these advantages, the disadvantage of burden incidence on labor in the capital exporting country may be minor, especially since it can be corrected (in its impact on the domestic size distribution of income) through appropriate tax policies.

At the same time, aid of this sort is limited by the absorptive capacity of low income countries. Estimated at from 3 to 5 billion dollars per annum, it is in excess of the aid (official or private capital flow) that has in fact been given by the developed countries but much below that which they can give without seriously depressing their own growth and rise in consumption levels. While emphasis upon capital aid

37. The suppliers of capital in the high income countries will not lose but gain as larger returns are obtained from investment in low income countries. Allowance must be made, however, for the greater risks that frequently accompany such investment, as well as for special tax incentives.

is in order, it should not be permitted therefore to interfere with setting adequate targets for overall aid.

The magnitude of the problem, as evidenced by prevailing inequalities, is staggering; and while it may be a pleasant oversimplification to argue that rising economic well-being assures peace, the logic of humanitarian concern surely cannot stop at the boundaries of well-to-do nations. The design of a workable if limited solution to the problem of international redistribution, though hardly perceived as yet, may well become the major task of a future system of international public finance.

13 FISCAL POLICY IN THE OPEN ECONOMY

The principles of stabilization policy in the closed economy are derived from and reflect the functional relationships that underlie the determination of national income. Stabilization policy in the open economy further depends on the mechanism, or lack thereof, by which adjustments in the balance of payments are brought about.

STABILIZATION POLICY WITH FIXED EXCHANGE RATES

We begin with fixed exchange rates and the income or employment effects of alternative expansionary or restrictive measures. Balance of payments effects are disregarded at the outset, with external balance added later as a second policy objective.

INTERNAL BALANCE

One-Country Model. Consider a simple Keynesian model, where investment is fixed and consumption is a function of disposable income. Unemployed resources are available, and the price level is assumed not to rise until full employment is reached. Writing for the closed economy

(1) $\quad Y = a + c(1 - t)Y + I + G$

(where $Y =$ income, $I =$ investment, $G =$ government expenditures, c = marginal propensity to consume, and t = proportional income tax rate) we have the familiar multiplier

$$(2) \quad \frac{dY}{dG} = \frac{1}{1 - c(1 - t)}$$

Applying this formulation to the setting of an open economy, equation 1 may be rewritten as

$$(3) \quad Y = a + c(1 - t)Y + I + G - m(1 - t)Y \\ - nG + E$$

where a and c relate to total consumption including imports, m is the marginal (assumed to equal the average) propensity to consume imports, and n is the fraction of government expenditures flowing into imports. The level of exports E is given independently. We then have

$$(4) \quad \frac{dY}{dG} = \frac{1 - n}{1 - (c - m)(1 - t)}$$

The multiplier is reduced by the leakage of government and consumer expenditures into imports. The larger n, m and t are, the less effective a device fiscal policy will be in controlling the level of income.

The balanced budget multiplier is similarly changed. Letting T stand for tax yield, we have

$$(5) \quad Y = a + c(Y - T) + I + G - m(Y - T) \\ - nG + E$$

and with $\Delta G = \Delta T$ we obtain

$$(6) \quad \frac{dY}{dB} = \frac{1 - c + m - n}{1 - c + m} < 1$$

where dB is a balanced budget change involving $\Delta G = \Delta T$. If $n = 0$, so that all government expenditures are domestic, the balanced budget multiplier remains 1, independent of the value of m.[1] If $n > 0$, the balanced budget multiplier falls below 1. It will then be smaller, the smaller m is[2] and the larger c is.[3]

Two-Country Model. We may now go a step further and correct the assumption of a constant value of E. Since one country's exports are another country's imports, income changes in trading countries are linked by the changes in their imports and exports.[4] Let us now write for country A

$$(7) \quad Y_a = a_a + c_a(1 - t_a)Y_a + I_a + G_a - m_a(1 - t_a)Y_a + m_b(1 - t_b)Y_b$$

which is similar to equation 3 except that country A's exports equal country B's imports, where subscripts a and b refer to countries A and B respectively. To simplify, we assume also $n = 0$ so that all G is domestic. Similarly we have for country B

$$(8) \quad Y_b = a_b + c_b(1 - t_b)Y_b + I_b + G_b - m_b(1 - t_b)Y_b + m_a(1 - t_a)Y_a$$

Solving equation 8 for Y_b and substituting for Y_b in equation 7, we obtain

1. The same import leakage applies to tax payers and expenditure recipients. Note that the symbols as used here do not represent the same variables as in the model of pp. 223–24.

2. The gain in income that is forfeited because of foreign spending will be greater if the income recipient imports little; hence the multiplier will be smaller.

3. If c is large, the multiplier effect of the domestic expenditure forgone will be large and the balanced budget multiplier will be small.

4. For a discussion of foreign trade multipliers, see Kindleberger, *International Economics,* App. C; and J. Vanek, *International Trade* (Homewood, Illinois, R. D. Irwin, 1962), Chap. 7.

$$(9) \quad \frac{dYa}{dGa} = \frac{1}{1 - (1 - t_a)\left[c_a - m_a + \dfrac{m_a m_b (1 - t_b)}{1 - (c_b - m_b)(1 - t_b)}\right]}$$

which shows the response of Y_a to an expenditure change in G allowing for interdependence with Y_b. The size of the multiplier for A is related positively to c_a, c_b, and m_b, and negatively to t_a, t_b, and m_a. The multiplier here shown is larger than that in equation 4, since the import leakage is now counteracted by a resulting rise in exports. But the multiplier will still fall short or at best equal that of the closed economy case of equation 1.

Similarly, we obtain the expression

$$(10) \quad \frac{dY}{dGb} =$$

$$\frac{m_b(1 - t_b)}{\left[1 - (1 - t_a)\left\{c_a - m_a + \dfrac{m_a m_b(1 - t_b)}{1 - (c_b - m_b)(1 - t_b)}\right\}\right]\left[1 - (c_b - m_b)(1 - t_b)\right]}$$

which shows the response of income in A to an expenditure change in B. While the multiplier under equation 10 is smaller than that under equation 9,[5] it is positive, subject to the usual stability condition. Fiscal expansion is mutually helpful and renders prosperity contagious. Such a policy thus stands in sharp contrast to one that aims at raising domestic income via the "export of unemployment," as implemented by import restriction or export subsidy.

Given the spillover of fiscal policy measures between the two countries, and assuming no offsetting countermeasures, it is evident that coordination of policies is crucial, especially for large economies with a high degree of trade involvement. For A to decide how much to expand, B's degree of expansion must be given, and vice versa. What is more, the degree of fiscal expansion in A should be such as to be

5. The two expressions would be the same if

$m_b(1 - t_b) = 1 - (c_b - m_b)(1 - t_b)$; but

$m_b(1 - t_b) < 1 - (c_b - m_b)(1 - t_b)$ since $c_b(1 - t_b) < 1$.

compatible with a full employment income in B, i.e. allow for a level of exports that equals full employment imports in B, and vice versa. Cooperation, therefore, not only involves protection against overshooting the mark on the part of either country, but also to seek that set of policies which will enable both to approach their objectives. This is not readily accomplished, partly because coordination is politically difficult, partly because the necessary information may be lacking, and partly because a country may be better off (due to terms of trade effects) if its full employment is combined with either unemployment or inflation abroad.

The preceding model, though instructive, remains very oversimplified. The first step toward a more realistic view is to make investment endogenous. If this is done by assuming investment to be a function of current income, we merely add a propensity to spend on investment to the propensity to spend on consumption and the formal argument remains the same.[6] If a fuller model is used, and an investment and liquidity preference function are added, the domestic multiplier becomes more complex, as does the corresponding influence of the trade factor.[7] But the essential nature of the argument (and the required process of mutual adjustment) is not greatly changed.

Monetary Policy. A new factor is added as capital movements and monetary policy are allowed for. The expansionary power of monetary policy, even more than that of fiscal policy, tends to be reduced in the open economy. The increase in investment, induced by monetary ease, is subject to a smaller multiplier, due to the import leakage; and though the import leakage generates export gains, these

6. Such a formulation is used, although in a somewhat different context, by Alan T. Peacock, "Towards a Theory of Inter-regional Fiscal Policy," *Public Finance/Finances Publiques, 20,* nos. 1–2 (1965).

7. See my *Theory of Public Finance,* p. 457, equation 19–7. Replacing equation 2 above by the more complex multiplier, corresponding expressions for equations 4, 9, and 10 may be derived.

fall short of the import loss. In addition, monetary ease now induces capital outflow, lowering interest rates abroad and tending to equalize rate levels. As is the case with fiscal expansion, monetary expansion in country A is thus shared by B; and while capital outflow tends to reduce the expansionary effect of monetary policy in A, part of the loss is recouped by the resulting income expansion in B, which has favorable repercussions on A's income. Proper policy determination again requires mutual adjustment, but both countries now enjoy a greater degree of freedom since each may vary its policy mix as well as its level of overall expansion.

Such is the situation for relatively large countries, as these are able to affect their domestic level of interest rates. If A is a small country and international capital markets are perfect, A may indeed be incapable of doing so, as domestic interest rates are fixed by the world market. Monetary policy will then be ineffective in raising employment, and sole reliance will have to be placed on fiscal measures.[8]

FOREIGN BALANCE

So far we have considered the employment effects of fiscal and monetary policy, and their interdependence between trading countries. We now turn to the associated effects on the balance of payments.

It is readily seen that expansionary fiscal policy has adverse effects on the balance of payments, i.e. reduces the surplus or increases the deficit. Income expansion in A raises A's imports. By raising B's exports, this will induce an expansion of B's income, with consequent rise of B's imports and A's exports, but the latter will fall short of the former, for otherwise no increase in B's income would oc-

8. See R. A. Mundell, "Capital Mobility and Stabilization Policy Under Fixed and Flexible Exchange Rates," *Canadian Journal of Economics and Political Science, 29,* no. 4 (November 1963), 479.

Fiscal Policy in the Open Economy

cur.[9] Expansion through monetary policy will have even more detrimental balance of payments effects, since capital outflow will be induced as well. In the long run, this is not a viable outcome. While countries can hardly be expected to solve balance of payments deficits by generating unemployment, they must strive to adjust policies so as to secure both internal and external balance. Our policies, therefore, must be reconsidered on this basis.[10]

Large Country. We begin with a situation where a country is sufficiently large, or capital flows are sufficiently imperfect, to permit it to influence the level of its own interest rates.

Suppose a country suffers unemployment, while its balance of payments is in balance. Fiscal expansion will raise employment but will tend to damage the balance of payments position via the import leakage.[11] Monetary expan-

9. Multiplier effects on the balance of payments P, giving an expression for dP_A/dG_A analogous to equations 4, 9, and 10, may be derived from the above systems. See also J. Vanek; and H. G. Johnson, *International Trade and Economic Growth* (London, George Allen and Unwin, 1958), Chap. 8, with references given there.

10. Important contributions to the basic literature in the field include Svend Laurson and Lloyd Metzler, "Flexible Exchange Rates and the Theory of Employment," *Review of Economics and Statistics, 32,* no. 4 (November 1950), 281–99; A. Harberger, "Currency Depreciation, Income, and the Balance of Trade," *Journal of Political Economy, 58,* no. 1 (February 1950), 47–66; and H. G. Johnson, "The Transfer Problem and Exchange Stability," *Journal of Political Economy 64,* no. 3 (June 1956).

Our discussion here draws heavily on the contributions by R. A. Mundell, including "Flexible Exchange Rates and Employment Policy," *Canadian Journal of Economics and Political Science, 27,* (1961), 509–17; "The Appropriate Use of Monetary and Fiscal Policy for Internal and External Stability," *International Monetary Fund, Staff Papers, 9,* (1962); and "Capital Mobility and Stabilization Policy," pp. 475–85.

11. See Mundell, "Appropriate Use," (1962). Measuring budget surplus (or deficit) on the ordinate and the rate of interest on the abscissa, Mundell draws two schedules, one showing full employment combina-

sion similarly may raise employment, but by inducing capital outflow will be even more detrimental to the balance of payments position. Thus a conflict between policy goals appears to exist. The goals may be reconciled, however, depending on the way in which employment and the balance of payments respond to the two policy tools. A solution exists if fiscal expansion has strong effects in raising employment but weak effects in creating a payments deficit, while monetary restriction has strong effects in improving the balance of payments but weak effects in reducing employment. Employment may then be raised without worsening the balance of payments if strong fiscal expansion is combined with some degree of monetary restriction, not sufficient to wipe out the employment effects of fiscal expansion, but enough to counter detrimental balance of payments effects. Similarly, a situation of payments deficit with full employment may be met by combining strong monetary restriction with some degree of fiscal expansion,[12] enough to offset the employment effects of monetary restriction, but not enough to cancel its balance of payments effects. In this sense, fiscal measures may be said to be the more strategic factor in combating unemployment, and monetary

tions and the other balance in the balance of payments combinations of fiscal and monetary policies. The latter schedule is steeper since, for a given employment gain, monetary policy causes a greater balance of payments loss than fiscal policy. The intersection of the two schedules defines the equilibrium position, and movement toward it is the path of stable adjustment.

If the initial position is one of correcting unemployment while the balance of payments is in balance, monetary expansion would lead to a balance of payments deficit at full employment; and budgetary restriction in an initial situation of balance of payments deficit would secure payments equilibrium at underemployment.

12. The precise roles of fiscal and monetary policies, and the appropriate combination of the two, depend on the values of the parameters in the system. See David J. and Attiat F. Ott, "Monetary and Fiscal Policy: Goals and the Choice of Instruments," *Quarterly Journal of Economics, 82,* no. 2 (1968).

measures in meeting a balance of payments deficit. More important, however, is the fact that in order to reach equilibrium on both counts, proper adjustment in both policies is needed.

The precise way in which the policies are to be combined will depend on the response parameters involved, and will also differ with the time period under consideration. While the above holds for the short run or over a fairly symmetrical cycle, it does not apply to the longer run. Here capital flows (via debt service) generate reverse effects on the balance of payments, thus reducing the freedom of policy choice and reintroducing the possibility of policy conflict. At the same time, the degree of policy freedom is greater than the preceding argument suggests. Quite apart from the possibility of exchange rate adjustments, it is a gross oversimplification to think of fiscal policy, and monetary policy as just two policy instruments. This is the case only if we exclude all but purely "general" fiscal and monetary measures.[13] Once selective policies are admitted, a much larger array of instruments becomes available. On the fiscal side, this includes differential taxation of traded goods, tax inducements or deterrents to capital movement, and so forth. On the monetary side, we have consumer credit controls, differential interest rates on foreign balances, and so on. This being the case, it is not necessary that the two policy instruments, needed to meet the two targets, be drawn from both the fiscal and monetary fields. Pairs of either fiscal or monetary tools may be found that will do the job.[14]

Whichever tools are chosen, the need for international coordination becomes greater if both external and internal

13. Moreover, it is not obvious just how "purely fiscal" and "purely monetary" measures should be defined, and whether the former can be applied without the latter. See my *Theory of Public Finance*, p. 528.

14. The difficulty of defining targets and instruments somewhat reduces the usefulness of the proposition that the number of instruments must equal that of targets. See J. Tinbergen, *On the Theory of Economic Policy* (Amsterdam, North Holland Publishing Co., 1952).

balance are considered. Countries with underemployment and balance of payments deficit will do well to rely on fiscal rather than monetary expansion to maintain high employment. But this policy can be successful only if other countries with balance of payments surplus pursue an opposite policy, i.e. rely on a combination of monetary ease with fiscal restriction. Unless this coordination can be achieved, fear of exchange losses will impede full employment policy in the deficit country, while the surplus country must choose between lesser growth (due to monetary restriction) or inflation.

Small Country. Stabilization policy is more difficult for a small country operating in a situation of easy capital movement and a well-developed capital market. Here the rate of interest is not subject to adjustment by domestic measures but determined by the rate that prevails in world capital markets. This being the case, expansionary monetary policy cannot be effective in raising domestic employment. Fiscal policy must be relied upon and other instruments must be used to deal with its balance of payments repercussions. As just noted, selective fiscal (or even monetary) instruments may be applied for this purpose. Alternatively, countries may seek to combine into a wider currency area so as to become master of their monetary setting.

INFLATION AND GROWTH

If the proper combination of fiscal and monetary policy can handle both the employment and the external balance targets, why do so many countries find it difficult to follow this apparently simple prescription? Certain complications, which have been overlooked so far, must be introduced to answer this question.

We have proceeded so far on the assumption that full employment can be reached without inflation. Actually, a rising level of employment tends to generate upward pressure on prices, be it temporarily because of bottlenecks or more permanently because of resulting changes in the setting of price and wage determination, making for more aggressive demands. In a fixed exchange rate setting, policies to raise employment or to maintain a high level of employment thus generate a trade deficit by raising prices. The inflationary dilemma of high employment policy, which arises even in the closed setting, becomes the more serious in the open setting, where it may also involve a payments deficit. "Modest" inflation may well be acceptable in the domestic context as a price of high employment, but balance of payments deficits have to be faced and dealt with. All this adds to the domestic case for price level stability (or rather, avoidance of domestic inflation in excess of that abroad) and makes it more difficult to maintain high employment. A further policy tool may be needed, such as guideposts for price and wage policies or other more or less mandatory forms of incomes policy which impose noninflationary limits on wage and price determination. Nothing need be said here about the well-known difficulties of such controls, but their effective implementation poses one of the major unsolved problems of economic policy in developed countries.

Further complications arise if we add the target of rapid growth to those of internal and external balance. To the extent that growth is a function of private capital formation, high employment must now be maintained through that mix of easy money and tight budget policy which secures the desired rate of capital formation. In the open setting, government may not be free to secure this growth-oriented fiscal-monetary mix, since a different mix is required by the combination of employment and balance of payments requirements. Again an additional instrument is needed if all three objectives are to be met.

This may take the form of selective fiscal inducements to private capital formation, inducements that (unlike monetary relaxation) will not generate capital outflow; or it may take the form of restrictions on capital outflow (or inducements to inflow) which will permit credit ease as an inducement to investment. Or the setting of the growth target may be changed by relying on public as distinct from private capital formation, in which case growth may be influenced by changing the composition of the budget without changing the fiscal leverage on aggregate demand. Finally, higher growth may be achieved by speeding up technical advance at a given rate of capital formation, in which case the general fiscal-monetary policy mix may again be reserved for achieving the internal and external balance targets.

But all this still leaves us with too easy a view of the problem. Theoretically, enough policies may be thought of to match the targets, but it is difficult to apply them in proper timing and proportions. Short-term capital movements are given to sharp fluctuations, adjustment lags in domestic and trade responses are difficult to predict, and the needed degree of international cooperation (as against retaliation) is hard to obtain. Thus it is exceedingly difficult to meet the needs of short-term adjustments which are called for in a highly variable and uncertain situation.

Similar difficulties arise in meeting more permanent types of maladjustment, i.e. positions of "basic disequilibrium" in the balance of payments. Closing a payments deficit may involve unemployment or retarded growth if domestic expansion cannot be disassociated from inflation. Use of certain policy instruments (i.e. tariffs or export subsidies) interferes with the flow of trade and thus reduces the efficiency of the world economy; use of others may do the same by interfering with efficient capital flow. The remaining alternative to the chronic deficit country is devaluation; but in order to work, devaluation must be supported by a fiscal policy which reduces disposable real income, reflecting the reduced use of resources available to the depreciating country and its worsened terms of trade.

332

STABILIZATION POLICY WITH FLEXIBLE
EXCHANGE RATES

Given these difficulties, the question arises whether the problem may not be solved more readily in a setting of flexible exchange rates. Stabilization policy may now be focused on internal balance only, since the balance of payments equilibrates automatically via exchange rate adjustments.

The role of *fiscal* expansion, again, depends on how the deficit is financed. If it is financed by a mix of money and debt issue that leaves the rate of interest unchanged, effectiveness will be increased relative to the fixed exchange rate case. The import leakage now gives rise to exchange depreciation, thereby checking imports and raising exports. Thus the expenditure multiplier is larger. If deficit finance involves a larger share of money creation so that the rate of interest is depressed, the effectiveness of fiscal expansion is increased further. Additional net exports are created due to depreciation resulting from capital outflow. If deficit finance involves a smaller share of money creation and upward pressure on the rate of interest develops, capital flows in and the exchange rate appreciates. Net exports fall and the rise in income is checked. The effectiveness of fiscal policy is reduced. The relative effectiveness of fiscal policy under the two systems thus depends on how the budget deficit is financed.

Monetary policy now can be effective even for a small country which cannot influence its own level of interest rates. But the modus operandi differs from the classical case of investment response to reduced rates of interest. As the money supply is increased in country A, the tendency for interest rates to fall induces capital outflow. This results in exchange depreciation and raises A's net exports, and hence income and employment. Monetary policy, working through exchange depreciation, is now capable of achieving internal balance, even though it could not do so in the fixed exchange rate case. If the country is in a position to influence its rate of interest, investment as well as exports will expand, and monetary policy will again be more effective than in the case of fixed exchange rates.

The problem of inflation also is less serious than in the fixed exchange rate setting. There the threat of inflation resulted in a potential conflict between internal and external balance. Under flexible exchange rates, domestic price rise does not interfere with equilibrium in the balance of payments, since it is met by offsetting adjustments in the exchange rate. Export prices will remain unchanged in terms of foreign currency, and import prices will rise along with domestic prices. The real terms of trade of the inflating country will thus be unchanged.

Addition of the *growth* target, similarly, may be accommodated more easily. A country that is sufficiently large to control its rate of interest may now choose that fiscal-monetary policy mix which yields the desired growth rate, without concern for its balance of payments. But a higher growth rate may still cause structural changes which raise the demand for imports relative to exports, and worsen the terms of trade; or if higher growth raises international competitiveness, the opposite may occur.

A country that is too small and too closely linked with world capital markets to affect its interest rates remains unable to influence investment via the mix of general fiscal and monetary policies. A further instrument is again needed —such as tax incentives to domestic investment or restraints on net capital outflow—to achieve both the growth and employment objectives. Alternatively, other vehicles of growth (government investment or promotion of technical progress) must be substituted for a higher rate of private capital formation.

In all, a system of flexible exchange rates facilitates the

task of domestic stabilization, as the problem of external balance is eliminated and only the domestic targets of internal balance and growth, and their implications for the terms of trade, are to be considered. Since the penalty of inflation is less severe, the severity of the potential conflict of high employment and growth versus price level stability is reduced. But these gains are obtained at the cost of throwing the major burden of adjustment to the international sector and of introducing a high degree of uncertainty and instability into foreign trade. Shifts in the trade sector in turn will require substantial structural adjustments and a high degree of flexibility in the domestic economies lest pockets of unemployment or overemployment develop as the size of the trade sector changes. The burden of such adjustments would be especially severe for developing countries that are characterized by a large trade sector, heavy reliance on capital imports for growth, and lack of internal flexibility. In all, the setting would be less favorable to trade and capital flow and less conducive to economic integration of the common market type as fixed exchange rates more nearly approximate a single currency situation. The greater ease of stabilization policy, therefore, is by no means the only consideration in comparing a regime of flexible and fixed exchange rates. A compromise solution, which reduces the traumatic effect of occasional exchange rate adjustment while normally preserving rate stability, would seem the better solution. The preoccupation of economists with international liquidity has had the unfortunate effect of diverting attention from the creation of such a mechanism.

DEVELOPING COUNTRIES

The preceding discussion of stabilization policy to secure the double target of internal and external balance was directed mainly at the position of developed countries. While the basic principles also apply to the case of less developed countries, these pose special problems which require qualification in the preceding discussion. Three aspects in particular should be noted.

LACK OF CAPITAL MARKET

The absence of a developed money and capital market, which is a general characteristic of less developed economies, renders it difficult to engage in the fine balancing of general monetary and fiscal policies that is feasible in the developed countries. In a country where capital markets and credit institutions are very limited in scope, it may be difficult or impossible to offset the detrimental balance of payments effects of a budget deficit by monetary restriction. Deficit finance may be more or less equivalent to borrowing from the central bank, and capital flows may not be responsive to interest rate differentials. As fiscal and monetary expansion proceed in unison, detrimental balance of payments effects may require other measures to maintain external balance. The extent to which such measures are needed depends on the composition of the output expansion. If the domestic expansion requires increased imports of capital goods, restraints on consumption imports may be needed; but if the expansion is led by export or import substitution industries, balance of payments effects may soon become favorable and relieve the need for countermeasures.[15]

EXTERNAL INSTABILITY

Less developed economies frequently have a large trade sector and depend heavily upon a limited range of export products. Changes in the level of foreign demand thus have an inordinate impact on the domestic economy and the foreign balance.[16] Changes in domestic supply conditions, in

15. The recent experience with economic expansion in South Korea strikingly illustrates this case.

16. See Alan T. Peacock and Douglas Dosser, "Stabilization in African Countries," *Public Finance/Finances Publiques, 17,* no. 3 (1962), where a basically Keynesian model is adapted to the low income country case.

the case of export products, play a similar role. Assuming such fluctuations to have some degree of regularity (forming a cyclical pattern rather than a secular development), the problem may be met, and a steady flow of imports be maintained, by countercyclical accumulation and disbursement of exchange reserves. This in turn calls for monetary and fiscal measures that will cushion the impact of these movements on domestic demand.

BALANCED GROWTH

Finally, we must introduce the requirement of external balance into planning for growth. This is important for two reasons. As the economy grows, new import demands are generated which call for an increased supply of foreign exchange. And for the economy to grow, increased imports of capital goods are needed, as the developing economy is usually not capable of supplying such goods domestically.

External Balance. Using the same notation as in our earlier model of growth in the developing economy,[17] we may state the condition of external balance as

$$(1) \quad \alpha(1 - s)(1 - t) + \beta c_g + \gamma kr - \bar{z} = \bar{f}$$

where α is the fraction of private consumption, β the fraction of government consumption, and γ the fraction of investment (public or private) which takes the form of imports. The symbol z equals exports and $\bar{f}$ equals net capital inflow (either government aid or private) both as a fraction of GNP. As before, s is the private propensity to save out of disposable income, t is the tax rate, c_g is government consumption as a fraction of GNP, k is the capital output ratio, and r is the growth rate, with $rk = i_t$ where i_t is total investment as a fraction of GNP. The coefficients z and f are assumed to be given exogenously. Equation 1 thus says that

17. See p. 223.

imports minus exports must equal capital inflow $\bar{f}$. From this condition we obtain

$$(2) \quad r = \frac{f + z - \alpha(1 - s)(1 - t) - \beta c_g}{\gamma k}$$

The growth rate r, which is compatible with external balance, will be larger the higher the exchange proceeds $\bar{f}$ and z are, and the smaller consumption imports of the private sector and of government are. Also, r will be larger, the smaller the import requirement for investment and the capital output ratio are. The maximum growth rate (with $t = 1$ and $c_g = zero$) equals $(\bar{f} + \bar{z})/\gamma k$. Alternatively, we may take r and t as given and solve for the required rate of capital inflow f.

Similarly, we may solve equation 1 for t and obtain the tax rate

$$(3) \quad t_{eb} = 1 - \frac{\bar{f} + z - \beta c_g - \gamma kr}{\alpha(1 - s)}$$

which is the tax rate required for external balance. It will be small if available exchange proceeds are large and if total import demands for consumption and investment are small.

Restating Internal Balance. The next step is to restate our earlier system of internal balance, given by equations 1–7 of Chapter 8, so as to make net imports endogenous.[18] We do this by adding the equation

$$(7a) \quad n = \alpha(1 - s)(1 - t) + \beta c_g + \gamma i - \bar{z}$$

Exports $\bar{z}$ are still assumed to be given exogenously, although this is not entirely correct, as the export share of output also responds to policy measures. Equation 8 of Chapter 8 now becomes

18. See p. 223.

$$(8a) \quad t_{ib} = \frac{c_g(1 - \beta) + r\left[k(1 - \gamma) - \dfrac{1}{v}\right] - s(1 - \alpha) + \bar{z}}{(1 - s)(1 - \alpha)}$$

where t_{ib} is the tax rate required to secure internal balance in the open system. For any given value of r, we may find the necessary t_{ib}. By using equation 7a, we may also determine the resulting level of net imports.

Combined Balance. It remains now to combine the conditions for internal and external balance. Since the required tax rate t is determined both by the external balance condition (3) and the domestic balance condition (8a), we must set the tax rate $\hat{t}$ so that $\hat{t} = t_{eb} = t_{ib}$. Equating t_{eb} as defined in equation 3 with t_{ib} as defined in equation 8a and solving for r, we obtain

$$(4) \quad \hat{r} = \frac{-\alpha + c_g(\alpha - \beta) + f(1 - \alpha) + \bar{z}}{\dfrac{\alpha}{v} + (\gamma - \alpha)k}$$

The equilibrium growth rate $\hat{r}$ will be larger if exports are large, and if the private sector propensity to import is small. A high rate of government consumption will be favorable or unfavorable, depending on whether the government's propensity to import consumer goods exceeds or falls short of the private propensity to do so. In thus defining $\hat{r}$, it must be kept in mind that the equilibrium tax rate $\hat{t}$ is assumed to apply, so that both foreign and domestic balance are assured.

Alternatively, equation 8a may be solved for r, and by equating with equation 2, the equilibrium rate of tax $\hat{t}$ may be determined.[19] We thus arrive at a pair of $\hat{r}$ and $\hat{t}$ which

19. The more complex expression for $\hat{t}$ becomes

$$\hat{t} = 1 - \frac{v}{\alpha(1 - s)}\left[\alpha k - c_g\left(\gamma k - \beta k + \frac{\beta}{v}\right)\right.$$
$$\left. - \bar{f}\left(k - \gamma k - \frac{1}{v}\right) - \bar{z}\left(k - \frac{1}{v}\right)\right]$$

satisfy the requirements of both internal and external balance.[20]

It is evident that stabilization policy for growth, with mutual allowance for both types of balance, is a complex matter. Even this simple discussion suggests that policy may make use of a variety of approaches, involving not only changes in t and c_g, but also measures aimed at affecting s and the foreign trade coefficients α, β, and γ.

20. In keeping the argument in fairly simple terms, we do not here proceed to explore the conditions under which a unique and stable equilibrium is achieved. For an intensive exploration of foreign balance and growth without specific attention to fiscal parameters, see H. B. Chenery and A. M. Strout, "Foreign Assistance and Economic Development," *American Economic Review, 56,* no. 4 (September 1966), Part 1, pp. 679–733.

14 FURTHER PROBLEMS

As noted at the outset, I have not undertaken to provide a comprehensive study in comparative fiscal analysis. Some aspects have been dealt with, others have been noted only briefly, and still others have been left out entirely. In concluding, it may be helpful, therefore, to sample certain additional problems which might have been covered in a more comprehensive study.

FISCAL CENTRALIZATION AND FEDERALISM

In the discussion of expenditure coordination, we saw that the economic criteria may be applied to the design of a regionally efficient fiscal structure. Existing institutions, however, were not constructed in this fashion, but reflect historical patterns of political development. The *fiscal* structure of a country is decentralized or centralized, depending on whether the *political* constitution is federalist or unitary, and not the reverse. No wonder then that fiscal structure differs vastly among countries, ranging from highly centralized systems such as the Netherlands and the United Kingdom to highly decentralized settings such as Australia, the United States, or Switzerland. At the same time, the regional pattern of the fiscal structure, as determined by historical-political forces, may be expected to bear significantly on the functioning of the fiscal system. This offers challenging prospects for comparative analysis.

To begin with, there is the question of how fiscal centralization or decentralization is to be measured, so that a comparison may be drawn among countries.[1] This may be looked at from either the revenue or the expenditure side. If revenues are considered, a distinction must be drawn between total and own-revenues, with intergovernmental transfers constituting the important difference. In considering expenditure centralization, allowance must similarly be made for the degree of central direction of local expenditures. Expenditures made at the local level may be not only centrally financed but also centrally directed. Local governments which act as central expenditure agents do not reflect expenditure decentralization in a meaningful sense, just as centrally collected but shared taxes do not constitute true revenue centralization. Thus various types of grants or transfers must be distinguished, depending on the extent to which central control of expenditures is involved.

Next, centralization may be measured as between various tiers of government. Thus a country may be relatively decentralized as between the top and middle levels of government but relatively centralized at the local level, or vice versa. Centralization, moreover, differs as between various expenditure functions, with the weight of defense finance a major factor in determining the overall degree of centralization.

Having measured the degree of revenue and expenditure centralization, one may then inquire how these bear on the level and structure of public services and receipts. Does a centralized system generate a larger public sector, and does it bias the expenditure structure in favor of services the benefit of which is nationwide, as against local type services? Moreover, how does the degree of centralization affect the

1. For the general theory of fiscal federalism, see the references given in nn. 1, 4, and 6 of Chap. 12.

variance of local service levels among localities? How will the resulting pattern of service differentials be affected by the regional distribution of income, and how are regional differences in service levels related to differences between fiscal ability and need?

Turning to the tax side, how does the prevailing degree of centralization or decentralization affect the composition of the tax structure? Certain taxes are imposed more appropriately and administered more readily at the central level, others at the state and local level. Therefore differences in tax centralization may be expected to bear on the equity of the tax structure, as well as on its effects on economic development and stabilization. Can it be concluded that the tax structure of centralized countries is more progressive, and can similar (or perhaps opposite) conclusions be drawn regarding the distributional results of the expenditure structure?

Given the prevailing structure of fiscal decentralization, interregional transfers may be used to secure some degree of fiscal equalization between regional governments (states and localities) as well as among levels of government (federal, state, and local). Distinct patterns of adjustment have evolved in various countries, including complex formulas of *Finanzausgleich* in Germany and Switzerland, need-oriented tax sharing devices as in Canada, an adjudicated system of revenue transfers between the states as in Australia, and so forth.[2] What are the comparative merits of these various

2. W. Bickel, "Der Finanzausgleich," *Handbuch der Finanzwissenschaft, 2* (1956), 730–88.

A description of the fiscal structure of various countries, including the relationship between levels of government and extensive literature references, may be found in the *Handbuch, 3* (1958), 140–583.

For a sample of further studies pertaining to particular countries, see: United States, Commission on Intergovernmental Relations, *Report to the President* (Washington, D.C., G.P.O., 1955); G. F. Break, *Intergovernmental Fiscal Relations in the United States* (Washington, D.C., The Brookings Institution, 1967); R. M. Burns, "Recent Developments

schemes, and how effective have they been in their political setting? Moreover, what use is made of various grant techniques (general versus earmarked, unconditional versus matching) in implementing intergovernmental transfers, and how successful have the grantor's efforts thereby been to influence the expenditure levels or patterns of the grantee?

For a variety of reasons—including political and administrative as well as economic factors—the optimal degree of fiscal centralization will vary with the state of economic development;[3] and it may be dominated, in other situations, by the scope of military expenditures, which are inherently central.

Finally, there are the implications of fiscal centralization (or lack thereof) for stabilization policy. The hypothesis to be tested is whether centralized systems have been more effective in fiscal stabilization, and in particular whether local fiscal behavior has been perverse in this respect. Thus the issue of fiscal centralization involves all aspects of fiscal policy and offers a fertile perspective for comparative fiscal analysis.

---

in Federal-Provincial Fiscal Arrangements in Canada," *National Tax Journal*, 15 (September 1962), 225–38; R. M. Kamins, "Democratic Centralism: Local Finance in the Soviet Union," *National Tax Journal*, 15 (December 1962), 353–67; Prest, *Public Finance in Theory and Practice*, Chap. 9; M. Newcomer, *Central and Local Finance in Germany and England* (New York, Columbia University Press, 1937); J. G. Head, "Financial Equality in a Federation, A Study of the Commonwealth Grants Commission in Australia," *Finanzarchiv, 26* (December 1967), 470–513; D. T. Lakdawala, "The Four Finance Commissions in India," *Indian Economic Journal, 13*, no. 4 (1966), 498–522; R. N. Biargava, *The Theory and Working of Union Finance in India* (London, Allen and Unwin, 1956).

3. For a study of development finance with emphasis upon local government see Hicks, *Development From Below*. Also see R. Bird, *Bibliography on Taxation in Developing Countries* (Cambridge, Mass., Harvard Law School, 1968), p. 17.

FISCAL POLICY DETERMINATION

The process of fiscal policy determination differs with the system of government, and the country's political structure. This applies to the composition and level of expenditure programs, and the determination of tax structure, as well as to the use of aggregate tax and expenditure measures in stabilization policy.

Expenditure determination involves the budgetary process and is generally the function of the executive (whether he is prime minister or president). Budget approval is the prerogative of the legislature. Auditing or expenditure control, assuring proper execution of legislated programs, may rest with either level or be the function of a third agency. Within this framework there is, however, a substantial difference in the degree to which the legislature is drawn upon in the formulation of the executive budget, and the extent to which the executive budget, once formulated, is subject to further modification by the legislature. The resulting structure of decision making in turn affects the cohesion and consistency of the expenditure plan, as well as the extent to which it must be responsive to immediate political pressure. This suggests comparison of how expenditure policy is determined in the tighter British or Canadian system of budget determination at the cabinet level, as compared to the United States system, where the budget is prepared at the Presidential level, but congressional budget adjustments play a larger role.[4]

4. A description of the budgetary structure of various countries will be found in *Handbuch der Finanzwissenschaft, 3.* For a sample of studies pertaining to particular countries, see H. Brittain, *The British Budgetary System* (London, Allen and Unwin, 1960); A. Smithies, *The Budgetary Process in the United States* (New York, McGraw-Hill, 1955); R. W. Davis, *The Development of the Soviet Budgetary System* (Cambridge, England, Cambridge University Press, 1958); A. B. Wildavsky, *Politics of the Budgetary Process* (Boston, Little, Brown, 1964).

Moreover, procedures at the legislative level differ in the degree to which the budget is examined and passed upon as an overall plan or is dealt with in a more piecemeal fashion. Again this will reflect upon the quality of budget determination. Beyond this, comparisons may be drawn between the methods followed in appraising particular budget programs, the use of program-budgeting or cost-benefit analysis, the forms of budgetary accounting and presentation, the time period over which the budget planning extends, the concepts of balance which are featured in the budget presentation, and so forth. While there is no readily available way in which to measure the quality of expenditure determination, a comparative analysis of planning practices would nevertheless be of interest.

Similar considerations apply to the determination of tax legislation. Under the parliamentary form of government, especially if combined with a high degree of party discipline, tax programs are introduced by the government and may be expected to be passed in essentially unchanged form. In other countries where tax policy is considered essentially a legislative prerogative (compare the House Ways and Means Committee of the United States Congress), the executive proposal is simply a point of departure for legislative tax considerations. As a result, the role and influence of economic and political groups in the determination of tax policy differs. This raises questions such as whether greater legislative influence leads to a more or a less progressive tax structure, whether it results in more or less comprehensive definitions of the tax base, or whether it makes for more frequent tax revisions.

Most important, perhaps, is the bearing of governmental organization upon the effectiveness with which fiscal policy may be used as a stabilization device.[5] This depends above

5. For a comparative analysis of stabilization policies in European countries, see a forthcoming study under the direction of Bent Hansen, to be published by the Organization for Economic Cooperation and Development, Paris.

all on the government's ability to take prompt action as changing needs require. A proposed change in the level of tax rates, called for by changing economic conditions, is more likely to be obstructed by the legislature if the fall of the government is involved than if the issue is merely the defeat of one particular administration bill.

This hypothesis may be tested by measuring the promptness of fiscal responses to changing conditions under various types of governmental arrangements. The frequency of fiscal adjustments in the United Kingdom, for instance, suggests a higher degree of flexibility than exists in the United States. Similar considerations may be applied to the government's ability to lower taxes when needed as well as to raise them when such action is called for. Writing in the spring of 1968, one cannot fail to be impressed with the promptness of restrictive action in Britain, following devaluation of sterling, as against the dismal tardiness of the United States Congress to implement a needed tax increase.

Social Security and Redistribution

One of the most striking fiscal developments of recent decades has been the rise and expansion of social security systems. While this has been a worldwide process, including low as well as high income countries, there exists nevertheless a wide variety in the structure of social security systems. How have these differences come about and what have been their economic and social consequences?

Coverage, benefits, and financing techniques differ widely among countries, and it is indeed difficult to give an internationally valid definition of what is meant by social security.[6] Most generally, it may be defined as a set of programs

6. For comparative analyses of social security systems see U.S. Congress, *European Social Security Systems, Economic Policies and Practices,* Paper no. 7, Joint Economic Committee, 89th Congress

347

providing for cash payments or curative services when deficiency in earnings or physical disability arises. A list of programs usually considered as belonging to social security includes programs for (1) old age, invalidity, and survivors, (2) sickness and maternity, (3) work injury, (4) unemployment benefits, and (5) family allowances. All five program categories have expanded rapidly in recent decades. Thus, covering the period from 1940 to 1960, the number of countries having category 1 programs rose from 33 to 64; the corresponding gains for category 2 were from 24 to 59, for category 3 from 57 to 110, for category 4 from 21 to 30, and for category 5 from 7 to 60.[7] Social security expenditures in the mid-sixties varied from 5 per cent of national income in the United States to over 14 per cent in Germany, with most Common Market countries above the 10 per cent level.[8] Indeed, the spread of such programs is even broader than these figures suggest, as, frequently, similar services are rendered outside of what is usually referred to as the social security system. Thus deductability of medical expenses for income tax purposes is analogous to cost benefits for sickness, exemption for dependents in determining the income tax base is analogous to family allowances, and so forth.

On the whole, three major approaches can be distinguished in how services or cash payments are provided. These include social insurance, social assistance, and public service. In the social insurance schemes, programs are financed mainly, if not entirely, from special contributions by employees and/or insured persons. Benefits to individuals are related to their contributions and the programs are usu-

---

(Washington, D.C., G.P.O., 1965) and U.S. Dept. of Health, Education and Welfare, *Social Security Programs Throughout the World*, Social Security Administration (Washington, D.C., G.P.O., 1961); J. H. Richardson, *Economic and Financial Aspects of Social Security: An International Survey* (Toronto, University of Toronto Press, 1960).

7. See *Social Security Programs Throughout the World*.
8. See *European Social Security Systems*, p. 11.

ally compulsory. Social assistance programs are financed mainly from general revenue sources, and benefits are related to the "needs" and "resources" of the recipient. Public service programs, similarly, are largely financed from general revenues, but the benefits are available automatically to all citizens falling within certain categories.

In the financing of old age, invalidity and survivors' insurance, the most common method is a system of contributions paid by insured persons, employers, and government. This is the case in Belgium, Germany, Great Britain, Italy, and Japan. In certain cases (e.g. France) the government makes only exceptional grants while in others (e.g. the United States, India, mainland China) the government does not contribute. In eastern European countries the funds are paid by the employer without contributions by the insured. Contribution and benefit levels vary greatly, and there is no readily discernible pattern.

Similarly, there is wide variation of the extent to which countries rely on the social insurance approach as against the public assistance and public service principles. Thus the insurance principle is emphasized in Germany, France, and Italy, and, to a lesser extent, in the United States. In Britain, on the other hand, emphasis is on the public assistance principle, with a correspondingly different financial structure. Among the most interesting recent developments has been the placing of social security payments on a flexible basis, both with regard to adjustments for inflation, and in order to permit pensioners to partake in productivity gains.

Comparative analysis again may address itself to a variety of problems. Of particular interest, from the point of view of economic development, is the effect of the social security system upon the community's propensity to save. Depending on who contributes and who receives the funds, income use may be shifted from saving to consumption. Such transfers, though desirable on distributional grounds, may thus retard growth. At the same time, saving may be increased in the case of funded programs, at least over the period of time needed for the system to mature. The role of social security finance as a factor in economic development is thus of acute interest.

Next, and no less important, is the extent to which social security does in fact contribute to income redistribution. Depending on how this question is formulated, different answers may be obtained. Thus the distribution problem differs whether related to size distribution either of current income or of lifetime income, or to distribution among other groups, such as old and young, healthy and ill, and so forth. In particular it would be of interest, for a comparative analysis, to test the hypothesis that the effect of social security has been largely to redistribute between subsections in the lower or middle income groups, rather than to equalize between income brackets.

More broadly, there is the question of the extent to which fiscal operations in various countries have in fact operated toward equalizing income, including not only the effects of the social security system, but of the entire tax and even expenditure structures as well. While research into this matter is hindered by the lack of distributional data in many countries, it is nevertheless of interest to develop a methodology of comparison and to apply it where feasible.[9]

Debt Policy

As a final illustration, drawn from a quite different aspect of public finance, the problem of debt policy and

9. For a comparative study of redistribution see Alan T. Peacock, ed., *Income Distribution and Social Policy* (London, Jonathan Cape, 1954). See also W. Irwin Gillespie, "Effect of Public Expenditures on the Distribution of Income," in *Essays in Fiscal Federalism,* ed. Richard A. Musgrave (Washington, D.C., The Brookings Institution, 1965).

management may be noted.[10] The ratio of public debt to GNP varies widely among countries. Countries which have experienced violent inflation and subsequent currency revolutions have typically low debt to GNP ratios, while countries with a more stable record have higher ratios. Among this group, the severity of past war finance is usually a decisive factor. Thus, the national debt to GNP ratio in the United Kingdom is over 100 per cent while that in the United States and Canada is about 50 per cent, followed by France with 25 per cent and Germany with less than 10 per cent. What are the implications of the resulting differences in the "burden" of debt, if such a concept may be applied? More important, what are the implications for the country's claim structure, for the functioning of the capital markets, the economic behavior of savings institutions, and the adaptability of the economy to economic change?

Not only are there sharp differences in the overall level of public debt, but debt structures differ as well.[11] Debts are divided differently between domestic and foreign, or publicly and privately held issues. Privately held domestic debt in turn differs by maturity, marketability, and other characteristics. While the term structure in some countries (such as the United Kingdom) has been traditionally much longer than in others (such as the United States), recent decades have generally witnessed a move toward shortening of maturities. Also, in some countries, such as France, heavy reliance is placed upon nonmarketable debt, or debt issued to particular bearers, while in others (including the United

10. See *Handbuch der Finanzwissenschaft, 3,* Parts 10 and 11, for description of debt structures and literature references.

11. For a discussion of comparative debt policies in Britain, France, and the Netherlands, see the issue on "Debt Management," *Public Finance, 16,* no. 1 (1961), 9–120; for further discussion of debt policies in European countries see European Economic Community, Monetary Committee, *The Instruments of Monetary Policy in the Countries of the European Economic Community* (Paris, 1962), p. 268.

States) primary reliance is placed on marketable issues. Where bearer debt is issued, yields may be differentiated to introduce redistributional objectives, and various incentives (be it tax advantages or lottery prizes) may be offered to render the debt more attractive.

Finally, there exist interesting differences in the role of debt management in relation to monetary and credit policy. In the United States, open-market operations involving dealings in public debt are the prime instrument of monetary policy, while British policy uses this instrument to a much lesser degree and even looks upon it with disfavor.[12] In France or Germany, open market operations have also been a less favored instrument of monetary policy, due partly to the lack of highly developed money markets in which such operations may be conducted readily. Also, practices differ with regard to treasury borrowing from the central bank, with direct reliance on the central bank being more acceptable in some countries (e.g. the United Kingdom) than in others (e.g. the United States). Comparative analysis of debt management thus leads to the broader issues of monetary policy and the structure of capital markets; and by extending the analysis to the role of public lending (i.e. the inverse of debt policy), a further, and in many countries vitally important, aspect of the fiscal structure may be drawn into the picture.

This list of illustrations might be extended readily into other aspects of the fiscal system. The very nature of the

12. For a discussion of British aspects, see United Kingdom, *Report of the Committee on the Working of the Monetary System*, Cmd. 827 (London, H.M. Stationery Office, 1959), referred to as the Radcliffe Report; and John H. Kareken in Chap. 2 of *Prospects of the British Economy*, ed. Richard E. Caves (Washington, D.C., The Brookings Institution, 1968). For discussion of U.S. policy, see the volumes, *Fiscal and Debt Management Policies* and *Stabilization Policies*, of The Commission on Money and Credit (Englewood Cliffs, N.J., Prentice-Hall, 1963).

fiscal process generates diversity of responses, conditioned by institutional, political, and ideological factors. The functions of tax and expenditure policy, as I have tried to show, differ with stages of economic development and political systems; adjustments in distribution, so close to the fiscal process, are inherently a controversial matter; and the very existence of externalities may be welcomed by some (including this writer) as testimony to the social conscience of nature, but deplored by others as a slip of creation, a mischievous barrier to reliance on independent individual action. No wonder then that a diversity of fiscal forms exists, and that comparative studies are of particular interest in this field. I hope that this volume will contribute to the pursuit of such work.

APPENDIX

APPENDIX TABLE 1

Composition of GNP

	U.S.S.R. 1962 billion R	United States 1962 billion $	United Kingdom 1962 million £	Federal Republic of Germany 1961 billion DM	Sweden 1961 billion KR
Consumption, privately purchased					
1. Retail sales to households	84.2	211.2	13,437	84.7	26.9
2. Housing	1.6	46.5	1,814	⎰102.0	⎰13.5
3. Other consumer services	10.8	98.0	3,394	⎱	⎱
4. Farm income in kind	12.5	1.0	45		
5. Total	109.1	356.7	18,690	186.7	40.4
Consumption, publicly provided					
6. Health care	5.6	7.4	927	8.7	2.0
7. Education	8.7	16.5	805	6.1	2.6
8. Internal security	1.5	4.0	173	20.2	3.6
9. Government administration + other, excluding defense	1.1	14.8	997		
10. Total	16.9	42.7	2,902	35.0	8.2
Gross investment (excluding defense)					
11. Private	2.5	79.1	2,815	76.1	15.8
12. Public	55.5	23.9	2,018	10.4	9.4

357

13. Total	58.0	103.0	4,833	86.5	25.2
14. Total (5 + 10 + 13)	184.0	502.4	26,425	308.2	73.8
Foreign sector					
15. Net exports	—	4.0	−1,742	6.8	—
Defense					
16. Pay and subsistence	4.8	2.8	400	⎰ 11.4	⎰ 1.4
17. Other	8.8	46.9	1,441	⎱	⎱
18. Total	13.6	49.7	1,841	11.4	1.4
19. GNP (14 + 15 + 18)	199.4	556.2	26,524	326.4	75.2
Further breakdowns (excluding defense)					
20. Total public purchases (10 + 12)	72.4	116.3	4,920	45.4	17.6
21. Total private purchases (5 + 11)	111.6	435.8	21,505	262.8	56.2
22. Total consumption (5 + 10)	126.0	399.4	21,592	221.7	48.6
23. Total investment (13)	58.0	103.0	4,833	86.5	25.2

The available distribution for the U.S.S.R. is taken as the pattern, and an attempt is made to adjust the data for the other countries accordingly.

U.S.S.R. Data are based on A. S. Becker, *Soviet National Income and Product, 1958–1962,* The Rand Corporation, Memorandum RM-4394-PR (June 1965).

Line 1: Includes purchases from state-cooperative trade and urban collective farm markets.

Line 2: Rents paid plus imputed rent.

Line 3: Fees of 1.1; other consumer services of 9.7, which include the following items: 0.8 for education and health, 1.2 for entertainment and culture, 3.7 for transportation, 1.1 for communication, 0.8 for public utilities, 2.1 other.

Line 4: Includes farm income and non-farm wages in kind. Excludes military subsistence.

Line 12: Includes 6.2 of increase in stocks, 45.9 of fixed capital formation, and 3.4 of research and development.

Line 16: Includes 1.3 of military subsistence recorded in household sector.

United States. Based on *Survey of Current Business* (Washington, U.S. Dept. of Commerce, July 1964). An attempt is made to enter items so as to match the pattern given for the U.S.S.R.

Line 1: Includes items I (excluding food consumed on farms), II, III, V, VII, XI, and XII of Table 14, p. 16.

Line 2: Item IV, Table 14, p. 16.

Line 3: Items VI, VIII, IX, X, XII, Table 14, p. 16.

Line 4: Item I-4, Table 14, p. 16.

Lines 6–10: Based on total purchases by groups shown in *Survey of Current Business*, p. 21, minus capital outlays by groups included in item XII.

Line 12: Includes capital expenditures of $35.2 billion (Census of Government, *Historical Statistics on Governmental Finances and Employment* [U.S. Bureau of the Census, Washington, G.P.O., 1962], p. 50) plus research and development expenditures of $4.2 billion.

United Kingdom. Source: Central Statistical Office, *National Income and Expenditure* (London, H.M.S.O., 1964).

Line 2: Includes rent, rates, water charges, maintenance, repairs, and improvements by occupiers.

Line 3: Includes 319 for entertainment, 1,205 for transportation, 155 for communication services, 84 for domestic services, 205 for insurance, and 1,426 for other services.

Line 4: Unspecified income in kind.

Line 12: Includes investment by public corporations.

Germany. Source: *Statistisches Jahrbuch* (Bonn, Statistisches Bundesamt, 1962); *Wirtschaft und Statistik, 63* (Bonn, Statistisches Bundesamt, 1963); United Nations, *Statistical Yearbook, 1963* (New York, United Nations); *Statistics of National Accounts, 1950–1961* (Paris, Organization for Economic Cooperation and Development).

Sweden. Source: *The Swedish Economy* (Stockholm, 1964), p. 140; United Nations, *Statistical Yearbook, 1963;* Statistika Centralbryau, *Statistisk Arsbök för Sverige, 1962; Statistics of National Accounts, 1950–1961.*

APPENDIX TABLE 2

Public Expenditure Structures

U.S.S.R., 1962[a]

	billion R	per cent of total	per cent of GNP
Current			
Education	8.7	8.7	4.5
Public health	5.6	5.7	2.8
Social security	11.5	11.6	5.7
Defense	12.4	12.5	6.2
Other current, including interest	8.6	8.9	4.3
National economy (capital outlay)	52.1	52.6	26.1
Total	98.9	100.0	49.6

U.S.S.R., 1961[b]

	billion new R	per cent of total
Current		
Education	11.3	14.5
Public health	5.2	6.7
Social security	10.6	13.7
Defense	9.3	12.0
Other current, including interest	7.3	9.4
National economy (capital outlay)	33.9	43.7
Total	77.6	100.0

Czechoslovakia, 1963[c]

	million Kč	per cent of total
Current		
Education, Public health, Social security	40.3	39.0
Defense	8.8	8.5
Other current, including interest	3.0	2.9
National economy (capital outlay)	51.3	49.6
Total	103.4	100.0

Poland, 1960[d]

	billion Zl	per cent of total	per cent of GNP
Current			
Education	19.5	9.7	4.8
Public health	14.2	7.1	3.5
Social security	23.5	11.7	5.7
Defense	14.9	7.4	3.6
Other current, including interest	15.3	7.6	3.7
National economy (capital outlay)	112.7	56.5	27.5
Total	200.1	100.0	48.8

United States, 1961[e]

	billion $	per cent of total	per cent of GNP
Current			
Education	19.4	12.4	3.7
Public health	7.0	4.5	1.3
Social security	25.7	16.4	5.0
Defense	25.8	16.5	5.0
Other current, including interest	47.8	30.5	9.2
National economy (capital outlay)	30.9	19.7	6.0
Total	156.6	100.0	30.4

Federal Republic of Germany, 1961[f]

	billion DM	per cent of total	per cent of GNP
Current			
Education	6.3	4.9	1.9
Public health	12.7	9.9	3.9
Social security	39.9	31.1	12.2
Defense	11.4	8.9	3.5
Other current, including interest	47.4	37.0	14.5
National economy (capital outlay)	10.5	8.2	3.2
Total	128.2	100.0	39.3

	United Kingdom, 1961[g]			Sweden, 1961[h]		
	billion £	per cent of total	per cent of GNP	billion KR	per cent of total	per cent of GNP
Current						
Education	1.2	13.0	4.5	1.9	10.6	2.5
Public health	.9	9.8	3.4	.6	3.4	.8
Social security	1.7	18.5	6.4	4.2	23.5	5.6
Defense	1.8	19.6	6.7	3.2	17.9	4.3
Other current, including interest	2.7	29.3	10.1	5.1	28.5	6.8
National economy (capital outlay)	.9	9.8	3.4	2.9	16.1	3.9
Total	9.2	100.0	34.5	17.9	100.0	23.8

a. A. S. Becker, *Soviet National Income and Product, 1958–62*, Rand Corp., Memorandum RM-4394-PR (June 1965), p. 12.

b. United Nations, *Statistical Yearbook, 1963*.

c. Ibid.

d. *Concise Statistical Yearbook of Poland, 1962*.

e. U.S. Dept. of Commerce, *Survey of Current Business*. The figure for defense includes national defense and atomic energy; that for "other" includes general government, agriculture, veterans' services, commerce, housing, natural resources, international.

f. Statistisches Bundesamt: *Wirtschaft und Statistik* (September 1962, September 1963); *Statistisches Jahrbuch* (1962); United Nations, *Statistical Yearbook, 1963*; Organization for Economic Cooperation and Development, *Statistics of National Accounts, 1950–1961*.

g. Central Statistical Office, *National Income and Expenditure* (London, H.M.S.O., 1962).

h. United Nations, *Statistical Yearbook, 1963*. Includes central government only.

APPENDIX TABLE 3

Revenue Structures in Socialist Countries

	Bulgaria 1963 million LV	Czechoslovakia 1964 thousand million Kčs	Poland 1964 thousand million Zl	U.S.S.R. 1964 thousand million R
1. Sales and turnover tax	1,738	50.3	128.4	35.2
2. Share in profits of state enterprises	602	26.3	64.7	29.5
3. Taxes on population	216	13.1	16.9	6.7
4. Other receipts from national economy	355	36.6	28.9 ⎫	20.5[a]
5. Other receipts	642	4.1	33.5[b] ⎭	
6. Total receipts	3,553	130.4	272.4	91.9
7. GNP[c]	5,676	169.5	497.0	181.5
8. Total receipts as per cent of GNP	62.6	76.9	54.8	50.6

Sources: Government receipts figures: United Nations, *Public Finance Yearbook, 1965* (New York, 1966). GNP figures: United Nations, *Yearbook of National Account Statistics, 1965* (New York, 1966).

a. For 1962, this item equals 20.3 billion rubles and is broken down as follows:

Income tax on collective farms	1.0
Cooperatives and organs of social organization	0.3
Social insurance fund revenues	4.5
Forest income	.3
Local taxes and fees	.7
Price differentials on agricultural machinery	1.5
Other	12.0
Total	20.3

For further details, see Becker, *Soviet National Income and Product*, p. 158.
b. Largely social insurance premiums.
c. Designated as "net material product."

APPENDIX TABLE 4

U.S. Government Expenditures (All Levels) by Function[a]

	Defense (1)	Public Debt (2)	Law, Order, and Administration (3)	Economic and Environmental Services (4)	Social Services (5)	Total (6)	Total (7)	GNP (8)
				Civilian				
1890	164	83	142	244	215	601	847	12.0
1902	306	97	225	431	391	1,047	1,660	21.0
1913	427	170	348	996	816	2,160	3,215	38.0
1922	1,378	1,370	643	2,642	2,603	5,888	9,297	74.0
1927	1,195	1,348	816	3,508	3,128	7,452	11,220	96.3
1932	1,649	1,323	950	3,519	3,671	8,140	12,437	58.5
1940	2,091	1,552	1,125	6,488	6,270	13,883	20,417	90.6
1948	20,001	4,722	2,049	8,056	14,901	25,006	55,081	239.0
1957	49,027	6,603	4,028	22,395	35,284	61,707	125,463	440.3
1962	57,449	9,173	5,513	33,597	58,291	97,401	176,240	530.0

a. Data for 1890 from Richard A. Musgrave and J. M. Culberson, "The Growth of Public Expenditures in the United States, 1890–1948," National Tax Journal, 6, no. 2 (June 1953), pp. 97–115. Data for 1902 to 1957 from Historical Statistics of the United States, U.S. Bureau of the Census (Washington, D.C., G.P.O., 1960), p. 723. The data are on budget basis and differ from the national account data used in Appendix Table 5. The various expenditure categories are allocated to match the grouping in Peacock and Wiseman, Growth of Public Expenditures in the United Kingdom. Items 439 (unallocable) and 440 (liquor store and utility expenditures) are included in col. 7 but not listed separately. Col. 1 includes items 414, 435; col. 2 is item 437; col. 3 includes items 428, 436; col. 4 includes items 416, 421, 429, 430, 431, 438; col. 5 includes items 417, 422, 426, 427, 433, 434, 441. Col. 7 includes amounts otherwise not itemized. For 1962 see U.S. Bureau of the Census, Historical Statistics on Governmental Finances and Employment (Washington, D.C., G.P.O., 1962), p. 33. The GNP data 1902–27 is based on Historical Statistics of the United States, p. 139.

U.S. Government Expenditures (All Levels) by Economic Category[a]
(Billion $)

	Purchases[b]			Transfers	Interest	Total
	National Defense	Civilian	Total			
1890	.1	.606	.7	.2	*	.9
1902	.2	1.1	1.0	.2	*	1.5
1913	.2	2.1	2.3	.3	*	2.6
1922	.6	5.4	6.0	.9	1.1	8.0
1929	1.3	7.2	8.5	.7	1.0	10.2
1932	1.5	6.6	8.1	1.4	1.1	10.6
1940	2.2	11.9	14.1	3.1	1.3	18.5
1948	11.6	22.9	34.5	12.0	4.5	51.0
1963	55.2	71.3	126.5	34.3	8.5	177.1

a. Figures for 1890–1922 from Musgrave and Culbertson, pp. 111–14.
Data from 1929 to 1963 are national income account figures, and thus
not strictly comparable with those of Appendix Table 4 which are on
budget basis. See U.S. Dept. of Commerce, *Survey of Current Business*
(August 1965).
b. Figures for Civilian and Total Purchases are residuals.
* Below 0.1.

Percentage Ratios—Samples A to D

		Y_e GNP at Factor Cost, Per Capita, US$ (1)	A			B		C	D	
			R/GNP (2)	T/GNP (3)	T_{id}/T (4)	T_s/N_Y (5)	S/N_Y (6)	T_Y/T (7)	CD/T (8)	I_{mp}/GNP (9)
Australia	(As)	1,270	0.25	0.23	0.49	9.8	9.1	0.28	6.7	2.7
Austria	(Au)	609	0.36	0.35	0.42	18.5	17.3	0.32	4.5	28.0
Barbados	(Ba)	235	0.19	0.18	0.61	—	—	—	17.0	65.7
Belgium	(Be)	785	0.23	0.22	0.42	17.3	16.2	0.25	4.8	35.5
Burma	(Bu)	48	0.18	0.17	0.69	—	—	—	30.0	24.1
Canada	(Ca)	1,584	0.27	0.24	0.52	10.0	8.6	0.20	6.8	22.3
Ceylon	(Ce)	—	—	—	—	3.8	4.0	—	—	—
Chile	(Ch)	385	0.18	0.18	0.46	11.4	9.5	0.33	12.0	11.9
China, N.R. of	(Ta)	87	0.20	0.17	0.85	0.9	1.0	0.05	—	—
Colombia	(Cb)	226	0.12	0.11	0.61	—	—	—	21.4	14.4
Congo	(Co)	101	0.21	0.18	0.51	—	—	—	—	—
Costa Rica	(Cr)	239	0.18	0.13	0.74	—	—	—	56.0	29.3
Denmark	(D)	1,046	0.26	0.24	0.47	11.9	11.9	0.42	—	—
Ecuador	(Ec)	152	0.19	0.15	0.71	—	—	—	33.0	18.9
El Salvador	(Es)	115	—	—	—	—	—	—	—	—
Finland	(Fi)	509	0.34	0.31	0.46	12.0	10.7	0.33	11.6	22.6
France	(Fr)	1,059	0.31	0.30	0.54	18.6	18.4	0.10	8.3	13.9
Germany, West	(WG)	936	0.36	0.33	0.45	21.0	19.3	0.19	2.7	19.3
Greece	(Gr)	254	0.20	0.19	0.61	—	—	—	18.9	20.0
Guatemala	(Gu)	—	—	—	—	3.0	3.0	—	—	—

Honduras	(Ho)	169	0.10	0.10	0.84	—	—	—	48.4	22.5
India	(In)	68	0.11	0.08	0.69	1.3	1.1	0.18	18.4	10.1
Indonesia	(Id)	69	—	—	—	10.8	10.5	—	—	—
Ireland	(Ir)	545	0.24	0.22	0.73	11.3	11.4	0.14	45.5	36.4
Italy	(It)	593	0.29	0.27	0.50	15.6	14.3	—	14.9	14.4
Jamaica	(Ja)	267	0.16	0.13	0.62	—	—	—	—	—
Japan	(Jn)	277	0.21	0.19	0.49	7.2	6.0	0.19	1.8	13.1
Korea, South	(SK)	90	0.11	0.08	0.71	—	—	—	17.8	14.6
Luxembourg	(Lu)	1,203	0.31	0.30	0.31	20.6	17.0	0.24	—	—
Mauritius	(Ma)	189	0.17	0.14	0.57	—	—	—	—	—
Netherlands	(Ne)	909	0.31	0.29	0.37	13.7	10.9	0.29	7.9	49.7
New Zealand	(NZ)	1,470	0.29	0.30	0.33	13.5	12.9	0.25	12.2	30.2
Nigeria	(Ni)	97	0.10	0.07	0.57	—	—	—	—	—
Norway	(No)	1,190	0.30	0.29	0.45	10.4	9.8	0.39	4.9	44.3
Panama	(Pa)	318	0.18	0.12	0.62	9.6	7.7	0.24	35.7	37.8
Peru	(Pe)	143	0.13	0.13	0.48	—	—	—	36.9	26.9
Philippines	(Ph)	102	0.11	0.10	0.74	—	—	—	8.0	14.4
Portugal	(Po)	238	0.18	0.17	0.48	8.6	6.3	0.10	18.7	24.4
Rhodesia	(Rh)	166	0.20	0.14	0.30	—	—	—	20.5	48.7
South Africa	(SA)	463	0.17	0.16	0.43	5.8	4.6	0.18	24.6	28.3
Sweden	(Sw)	1,345	0.33	0.29	0.32	12.9	12.5	0.47	3.8	28.8
Switzerland	(Sz)	1,207	—	—	—	11.3	8.3	—	—	—
Trinidad	(Tr)	396	0.18	0.15	0.51	—	—	—	—	—
Turkey	(Tu)	188	—	—	—	2.4	1.3	—	—	—
United Kingdom	(UK)	1,141	0.30	0.29	0.48	12.5	11.9	0.25	1.7	22.5
United States	(US)	2,202	0.26	0.25	0.33	6.6	5.8	0.34	.7	4.6
Viet Nam	(VN)	55	—	—	—	1.3	1.1	—	—	—

TABLE 6 (cont.)

Percentage Ratios—Samples E to J

	E		F	G		H	I	J
	$R - D/GNP$ (10)	D/GNP (11)	A_0/GNP (12)	T_{cp}/T (13)	T_p/T (14)	E_c/GNP (15)	$(E_c - D)/GNP$ (16)	E_T/GNP (17)
Australia	.22	3.3	.13	16.0	35	.30	.27	—
Austria	.29	1.2	.33	6.5	52	.28	.27	.34
Barbados	—	—	.07	22.2	17	.14	—	—
Belgium	.20	3.4	—	8.8	49	.21	.18	.25
Burma	.12	6.9	.42	—	—	.15	.08	.19
Canada	.21	6.2	.08	18.8	28	.22	.15	—
Ceylon	—	—	—	—	—	—	—	—
Chile	—	—	.14	18.5	36	.19	—	.21
China, N.R. of	—	—	.33	9.4	6	.18	—	—
Colombia	.10	1.8	.38	14.6	24	.07	.06	.38
Congo	—	—	.24	23.7	26	—	—	—
Costa Rica	.17	.6	.40	1.4	25	.11	.10	—
Denmark	.22	3.0	.09	5.6	48	.20	.17	.24
Ecuador	.17	2.6	.37	10.0	18	.15	.12	.16
Finland	.32	1.7	.22	11.5	41	—	—	—
France	.26	5.9	.11	6.9	39	.31	.30	.37
Germany, West	.33	2.9	.08	9.4	46	.28	.25	.19
Greece	.14	5.7	.34	2.9	37	.16	.11	.10
Guatemala	—	—	—	—	—	—	—	—
Honduras	.27	1.4	.49	7.8	8	.08	.07	—

367

Country								
India	.08	2.2	.50	5.0	25	.09	.07	—
Indonesia	—	—	—	—	—	—	—	—
Ireland	.22	1.1	.29	8.9	18	.21	.20	.27
Italy	.25	3.2	.21	—	—	—	—	—
Jamaica	—	—	.14	28.6	10	.11	.13	—
Japan	.40	1.7	.20	17.4	10	.15	.07	—
Korea, South	.10	6.2	.44	3.7	26	.13	.23	—
Luxembourg	.29	2.1	.09	18.0	51	.25	—	—
Mauritius	—	—	.33	24.5	19	.13	.17	—
Netherlands	.25	5.5	.11	13.6	49	.23	.19	.27
New Zealand	.26	2.2	.21	18.9	48	.21	.06	—
Nigeria	.10	.2	.63	—	—	.06	.21	—
Norway	.27	3.5	.13	7.2	48	.24	.14	—
Panama	.26	0.0	.28	14.3	24	.14	—	—
Peru	.11	3.1	.23	32.8	19	—	.07	—
Philippines	.09	1.7	.36	99.3	17	.09	.11	—
Portugal	.15	3.6	.29	21.5	31	.14	—	.17
Rhodesia	.20	.9	.21	52.2	17	—	.13	—
South Africa	.16	1.1	.13	31.6	26	.14	.20	—
Sweden	.28	5.1	—	12.4	55	.25	—	.32
Switzerland	—	—	.15	—	—	—	—	—
Trinidad	—	—	—	40.8	8	.15	—	—
Turkey	—	—	—	—	—	—	—	—
United Kingdom	.22	7.9	.04	16.0	36	.25	.17	.29
United States	.16	10.0	.04	20.0	47	.24	.14	—

Unless otherwise noted, averages for 1955–57 have been used throughout. Where not available, the closest available years were used.

GNP and GNP per capita, or Y_c

Averages of the two years 1953 and 1958 are used. They are based on gross national product at factor cost in each country and have been converted into current U.S. dollars by employing the parity (exchange) rates in the particular years. Source: United Nations, *Yearbook of National Accounts Statistics, 1963.*

Total Revenue R

R is total current revenue, tax and otherwise. To total current revenue given in the sources is added interest and capital transfers from corporations, households, and the rest of the world. Source: United Nations, *Yearbook of National Account Statistics, 1961* and *1963.*

Total Tax Revenue T

T is total tax receipts of combined government authorities. Source: United Nations, *Yearbook of National Account Statistics, 1961.*

Indirect Taxes T_{ia}

According to U.N. usage, T_{id} includes taxes on goods and services which are chargeable to business expense and taxes on the possession or use of goods and services by households. The main categories are: import, export, and excise duties, local rates, entertainment duties, betting taxes, business licenses, stamp duties, and motor vehicle and sales taxes. Real estate and land taxes are also included. Source: United Nations, *Yearbook of National Account Statistics, 1961.*

Corporation Taxes T_{cp}

T_{cp} includes direct taxes on corporations, i.e. taxes levied at regular intervals on profits, capital, and net worth. Corporate income and excess profits taxes, taxes on undistributed profits or on capital stock, are included. Source: United Nations, *Yearbook of National Account Statistics, 1961.*

Personal Taxes T_p

T_p includes direct taxes on households, including social security contributions from employers and employees. It also includes personal income taxes and surtaxes. Source: United Nations, *Yearbook of National Account Statistics, 1961.*

Defense Expenditures D

Sources: United Nations, *Yearbook of National Account Statistics* and *Statistical Yearbook, 1961* and *1963.*

Customs Duties CD

CD is customs duties received by the central governments of the respective countries. Source: United Nations, *Statistical Yearbook* for the years 1958–1963 for all countries except the United States and the United Kingdom. Source for the United Kingdom: Central

369

Statistical Office, *National Income and Expenditure* (London, H.M.S.O., 1962). Source for the United States: U.S. Dept. of Commerce, *U.S. Income and Output, A Supplement to the Survey of Current Business* (Washington, G.P.O., 1958).

Share of Agriculture Ag/GNP

Ag/GNP is the percentage of total GNP at factor cost originating in agriculture. Source: United Nations, *Statistical Yearbook, 1957, 1958, 1960, 1961.*

Social Security

T_s is total receipts of social security schemes. Source: International Labor Office, *The Cost of Social Security 1949–1957* (Geneva, 1961). It is the sum of (a) contribution from insured persons and employers, (b) special taxes, (c) state participation, (d) income from capital, (e) transfers from other schemes, (f) other receipts. Schemes included are: social insurance and assistance; family allowances; public employees, military and civilian; public health services; public assistance and assimilated schemes; benefits for war victims; administrative expenditures not allocated above.

S is total social security expenditures including the above categories; same source.

National Income NY

National income obtained by subtracting from GNP at market prices (a) indirect taxes, (b) depreciation. Source: United Nations, *Yearbook of National Account Statistics, 1961 and 1963.* For most countries averages of 1955, 1956, and 1957 were taken. Depending on the availability of the other variables, the years were shifted slightly to be consistent with the other data.

Income Taxes T_Y

T_Y is obtained by subtracting social security tax receipts from personal taxes T_p. In the case of most non-European countries, T_p is given in United Nations, *Yearbook of National Account Statistics, 1961.* The social security tax receipts are from I.L.O., *The Cost of Social Security 1949–1957* (Geneva, 1959). They include contributions from insured persons and from employers and apply to the categories (1) social insurance and assimilated schemes, and (2) public employees. This method was used for the following countries: Australia, Chile, Taiwan, Finland, India, Japan, New Zealand, Panama, South Africa, the United States. The figures for the other countries were obtained from the Office for Economic Cooperation and Development, *Statistics of National Accounts 1950–1961* (Paris, 1964). Again averages of 1955–57 were used.

Current Expenditures E_c

As given in United Nations, *Yearbook of National Accounts Statistics, 1963.* Includes all levels of government. Averages for 1955–57.

Total Expenditures E_T

Capital expenditures as given in United Nations, *Statistical Yearbook, 1961,* for central government are added to E_c.

370

APPENDIX TABLE 7

U.S. Tax Receipts—All Levels of Government*

(million $)

	Individual Income Tax and Death Duties	Corporation Profits Tax	Excise and Sales Tax	Customs	Property	Employment	Other	Total
1890	—	—	201	230	443	—	31	905
1902	4	—	295	254	706	—	147	1,406
1913	—	35	372	319	1,332	—	255	2,313
1922	2,207		1,312	356	3,321	—	837	8,033
1932	548	709	1,540	328	4,487	—	554	8,166
1940	1,566	1,303	4,253	349	4,430	834	874	13,742
1950	15,647	11,440	13,307	423	7,349	2,645	2,721	56,532
1960	49,035	23,359	25,291	1,123	16,405	11,159	7,836	134,208

* Sources: For federal receipts see U.S. Bureau of the Census, *Historical Statistics of the United States, Colonial Times to 1957* (Washington, D.C., G.P.O., 1960), pp. 697–700, 712–13. Also U.S. Treasury Dept., *Annual Report* for the fiscal year 1963 (Washington, D.C., G.P.O., 1963). For state and local receipts: U.S. Bureau of the Census, *Census of Governments, 1962* (Washington, D.C., G.P.O., 1963) *6*, no. 4; *Historical Statistics on Government Finances and Employment* (Washington, D.C., G.P.O., 1964).

APPENDIX TABLE 8

Great Britain—Central Government Receipts plus Local Rates in England, Scotland, and Wales[a]

(million £)

	Individual Income Tax and Death Duties[b]	Corporation Profits Taxes[c]	Excises, Motor Vehicle Duties, Stamp Taxes	Customs	Rates	Other	Total
1880–81	17.4	—	29.7	19.2	25.7	15.6	107.6
1890–91	22.9	—	35.2	19.8	31.0	18.6	127.5
1900–01	39.9	—	40.9	26.3	47.5	33.1	187.7
1910–11	89.1	—	49.9	33.1	72.0	31.8	275.9
1920–21	441.9	219.9	234.2	134.0	169.9	395.0	1,595.9
1930–31	406.4	3.0	172.5	121.4	169.5	154.5	1,627.3
1940–41	686.8	104.0	275.8	304.9	231.2	142.8	1,739.5
1950–51	1,710.7	267.7	822.3	905.2	323.9	451.3	4,481.1
1960–61	2,858.1	263.1	1,149.2	1,457.0	754.2	616.5	7,097.8

a. Sources: Great Britain, Central Statistical Office, *Annual Abstract of Statistics*, nos. 88, 99; Great Britain, Board of Trade, *Statistical Abstract for the United Kingdom*, nos. 54, 77; *The Statesman's Yearbook* (London, 1892, 1942, 1951, 1961); B. R. Mitchell, *Abstract of British Historical Statistics* (London, Cambridge University Press, 1962), pp. 394–95.

b. Includes income tax and surtax.

c. Includes national defense contribution, excess profits tax, and excess profits levy.

Germany—Tax Receipts at All Levels of Government[a]
(in million RM/DM)

Fiscal Year	1913–14[b]	1925–26[c]	1930–31	1938–39	1950–51[d]	1959–60[d]
Income and inheritance tax						
Income tax	1,390.2	2,271.6	2,789.4[h]	5,903.1[h]	3,646.2	14,922.7
Inheritance tax	61.0	27.3	79.0	104.2	24.6	115.1
Subtotal	1,451.2	2,298.9	2,868.4	6,007.3	3,670.8	15,037.8
Corporation tax		186.6	450.0	2,416.6	1,528.5	5,157.5
Excise and sales tax						
Use tax	775.2	1,611.2	2,235.6	3,102.1	4,107.5	8,382.6
Turnover tax		1,403.2	1,002.4	3,356.7	4,920.0	14,808.0
Automobile taxes[e]	45.4	384.7	521.1	483.7	586.3	1,952.4
Stamp taxes[f]	394.5	514.9	492.1	569.2	292.3	1,132.6
Subtotal	1,215.1	3,914.0	4,261.2	7,511.7	9,916.1	26,275.6
Customs	640.5	590.4	1,082.9	1,818.0	706.7	2,472.5
Real estate taxes[g]						
Real estate tax	435.5	871.5	1,420.9	1,629.0	1,052.3	1,595.5
Business tax	179.3	514.3	952.2	1,709.6	1,177.5	6,547.7
Subtotal	614.8	1,445.8	2,373.1	3,338.6	2,229.8	8,143.2
Other taxes						
Property tax	78.8	270.4	450.1	390.6	109.1	950.1
Burden equalization					1,702.8	2,231.5
Other taxes	45.4	1,413.1	2,006.1	1,572.9	684.6	373.4
Subtotal	124.2	1,673.5	2,456.2	1,003.7	2,495.5	3,555.0
Total, all taxes	4,045.8	10,119.2	13,481.8	23,055.7	20,538.4	60,641.6

a. Derived from: *Einzelschriften zur Statistik des Deutschen Reiches*, no. 10 (Berlin, 1930); *Statistik des Deutschen Reiches*, 437 (Berlin, 1933); *Statistisches Jahrbuch für das Deutsche Reich 1942; Statistik der Bundesrepublik Deutschland, 57 and 58* (Wiesbaden, 1953); *Finanzbericht 1962* (Bonn, 1962).

b. Territory of 1913.

c. Territory of 1925.

d. Includes West Berlin.

e. Beförderung- und Kraftfahrzeugsteuer (transport and automobile tax).

f. Kapitalverkehrsteuern, Grunderwerb-, Versicherung-, Wechsel-, Rennwett- and Lotteriesteuer (stamp tax on sale of securities, purchase of real estate, insurance, debt contracts, racing, and lottery).

g. Accrues to local government.

h. Inclusive Bürgersteuer (citizen's tax).

BIBLIOGRAPHY

The following is not designed to be a comprehensive bibliography, but consists largely of works to which reference is made in the text. For further sources, the reader is referred to the collections of readings and bibliographies listed under the relevant subject headings.

THE PUBLIC SECTOR AND ECONOMIC ORGANIZATION

Andic, Suphan, and Jindrich Veverka, "The Growth of Government Expenditures in Germany Since the Unification," *Finanzarchiv*, N.F., *23* (January 1964).

Bergson, Abram, *The Economics of Soviet Planning*, New Haven, Yale University Press, 1964.

———, "Socialist Economics," in *A Survey of Contemporary Economics*, ed. Howard Ellis, Philadelphia, Blakiston, 1948.

Buchanan, J. M., "Fiscal Institutions and Efficiency in Collective Outlay," *American Economic Review, 54,* Papers and Proceedings (May 1964).

Canada, Royal Commission on Taxation, *Report of the Royal Commission on Taxation* (Carter Commission), Ottawa, Queen's Printer, 1966.

Clark, Colin, "Public Finance and Changes in the Value of Money," *Economic Journal, 55* (December 1947).

Eckstein, Otto, "A Survey of the Theory of Public Expenditure Criteria," *Public Finances: Needs, Sources and Utilization,* National Bureau of Economic Research, Princeton, Princeton University Press, 1961.

Gerloff, W., *Steuerwirtschaft und Sozialismus*, Leipzig, 1922.

Goldscheid, Rudolf, "A Sociological Approach to Problems of Public Finance," in *Classics in the Theory of Public Finance,*

ed. Richard A. Musgrave and Alan T. Peacock, London and New York, Macmillan, 1958.

Head, J. G., "Public Goods and Public Policy," *Public Finance/ Finances Publiques, 17* (1962).

Hedtkamp, Gunter, "Das Steuersystem im Dienste der Sowjetischen Staats und Wirtschaftsordnung," *Finanzarchiv,* N.F., *20* (1960).

Holzman, F. D., *Soviet Taxation,* Cambridge, Mass., Harvard University Press, 1955.

International Institute of Public Finance, Papers Contributed to Prague Congress 1967, published in *Public Finance/Finances Publiques, 23* (1968).

Johansen, Leif, "Some Notes on the Lindahl Theory of the Determination of Public Expenditures," *International Economic Review, 4* (1963).

Kalecki, M., *An Outline of the Theory of Socialist Growth,* Varsava, PWN, 1963.

Kaemmel, E., "Das Finanzsystem der Deutschen Demokratischen Republik," in *Handbuch der Finanzwissenschaft, 3,* ed. W. Gerloff and F. Neumark, 2d ed., Tübingen, Mohr, 1958.

Kurowski, L., and R. Szawlowski, "Das Finanzsystem und der Stattshaushalt Polens," *Handbuch der Finanzwissenschaft, 3,* ed. W. Gerloff and F. Neumark, 2d ed., Tübingen, Mohr, 1958.

Lange, Oskar, "On the Economic Theory of Socialism," in *On the Economic Theory of Socialism,* by Oskar Lange and Fred M. Taylor, ed. B. E. Lippincott, Minneapolis, University of Minnesota Press, 1938.

Menz, Gertraud, *Die Entwicklung der Sowjetischen Besteuerung unter Besonderer Berucksichtigung der ordnungspolitischen Funktionen,* Berlin, Duncker and Humblot, 1960.

Musgrave, Richard A., "Provision for Social Goods," in *The Economics of the Public Sector,* ed. J. Margolis, International Economic Association, forthcoming.

———, *The Theory of Public Finance,* New York, McGraw-Hill, 1958.

Pechman, Joseph A., *Federal Tax Policy,* Washington, D.C., The Brookings Institution, 1966.

Prest, Alan R., *Public Finance in Theory and Practice,* 3d ed. London, Weidenfeld and Nicholson, 1967.

Pryor, Frederick L., "East and West German Governmental Expenditures," *Public Finance/Finances Publiques, 20* (1965).

Bibliography

——, *Governmental Expenditures in the Soviet Union and the United States,* publication forthcoming.

Samuelson, P. E., "The Pure Theory of Public Expenditure," *Review of Economics and Statistics, 36,* no. 4 (November 1954).

Schumpeter, J. A., *Capitalism, Socialism and Democracy,* New York, Harper and Co., 1942.

——, "The Crisis of the Tax State," in *International Economic Papers,* no. 4 (1954).

Solow, Robert, "A Contribution to the Theory of Economic Growth," *Quarterly Journal of Economics, 52* (February 1956).

Timm, Herbert, "Steuern im Sozialismus," in *Beiträge zur Finanzwissenschaft und zur Geldtheorie,* Festschrift für Rudolf Stucken, ed. Fritz Voigt, Göttingen, Vandenhoeck and Ruprecht, 1953.

PUBLIC EXPENDITURE DEVELOPMENT, THEORY AND EMPIRICAL EVIDENCE

Andic, Suphan, and Jindrich Veverka, "The Growth of Government Expenditures in Germany Since the Unification," *Finanzarchiv,* N.F., *23* (January 1964).

Copeland, M., *Trends in Government Financing,* National Bureau of Economic Research, Princeton, Princeton University Press, 1961.

Gupta, S. P., "The Size and Growth of Government Expenditures," doctoral dissertation, University of York, England, 1965.

——, "Public Expenditure and Economic Growth," *Public Finance, 22,* no. 4 (1967).

Hicks, Ursula K., *British Public Finances 1880–1952,* London, Oxford University Press, 1954.

Lewis, W. Arthur, *The Theory of Economic Growth,* Homewood, Ill., R. D. Irwin, 1955.

——, and A. M. Martin, "Patterns of Public Revenue and Expenditure," *The Manchester School of Economic and Social Studies, 24* (September 1956).

Musgrave, Richard A., and J. M. Culbertson, "The Growth of Public Expenditures in the United States, 1890–1948," *National Tax Journal, 6,* no. 2 (June 1953).

Nurkse, R., *Problems of Capital Formation in Underdeveloped Countries,* Oxford, Basil Blackwell and Mott, 1958.

Oshima, H. T., "Share of Government in Gross National Product

377

for Various Countries," *American Economic Review, 47* (June 1957).

Peacock, Alan T., and Jack Wiseman, *The Growth of Public Expenditures in the United Kingdom,* National Bureau of Economic Research, Princeton, Princeton University Press, 1961.

Rosenstein-Rodan, P. N., "International Aid for Underdeveloped Countries," *Review of Economics and Statistics, 43,* no. 2 (May 1961).

———, "Problems of Industrialization of Eastern and Southeastern Europe," *Economic Journal, 53* (June 1943).

Thorn, Richard, "The Development of Public Finance during Economic Development," *The Manchester School of Economic and Social Studies, 35* (January 1967).

Timm, Herbert, "Das Gesetz der Wachsenden Staatsausgaben," *Finanzarchiv,* N.F., *21* (1961).

United Nations, *Statistical Yearbooks,* New York, United Nations.

———, *Yearbooks of National Accounts,* New York, United Nations.

United States Bureau of the Census, *Historical Statistics on Governmental Finances and Employment,* Washington, D.C., G.P.O., 1962.

Wagner, Adolph, *Finanzwissenschaft,* 3d ed. Leipzig, Winter, 1883.

———, *Grundlegung der politischen Oekonomie,* 3d ed. Leipzig, Winter, 1879.

Wicksell, K., *Finanztheoretische Untersuchungen,* Jena, Fischer, 1896, translated and reprinted in Richard A. Musgrave and Alan T. Peacock, eds., *Classics in the Theory of Public Finance,* London and New York, Macmillan, 1958.

Williamson, J. G., "Public Expenditure and Revenue: An International Comparison," *The Manchester School of Economic and Social Studies, 29* (January 1961).

TAX STRUCTURE DEVELOPMENT, THEORY AND EMPIRICAL EVIDENCE

Aaron, Henry, "Some Criticism of Tax Burden Sharing," and comment by R. M. Bird, *National Tax Journal, 18,* no. 3 (September 1965).

Bird, R. M., *Bibliography on Taxation in Developing Countries,* Cambridge, The Law School of Harvard University, 1968.

———, "A Note on Tax-Sacrifice Comparisons," *National Tax Journal, 17,* no. 3 (September 1964).

Bibliography

————, and O. Oldman, eds., *Readings on Taxation in Developing Countries,* Baltimore, Johns Hopkins Press, 1967.

Dosser, Douglas, "Indirect Taxation and Economic Development," in *Government Finance and Economic Development,* Alan T. Peacock and Gerald Hauser, eds., Paris, Organization for Economic Cooperation and Development, 1965.

Due, John, *Taxation and Economic Development in Africa,* Cambridge, Mass., M.I.T. Press, 1963.

Goode, Richard, *The Individual Income Tax,* Washington, D.C., The Brookings Institution, 1964.

————, "Taxation of Savings and Consumption in Underdeveloped Countries," in *Readings on Taxation in Developing Countries,* R. M. Bird and O. Oldman, eds., Baltimore, Johns Hopkins Press, 1967.

————, George E. Lent, and P. D. Djha, "Role of Export Taxes in Developing Countries," International Monetary Fund, *Staff Papers, 13* (1966).

Harberger, A., "Issues of Tax Reform for Latin America," in *Fiscal Policy for Economic Growth in Latin America,* Joint Tax Program of the Organization of American States, Baltimore, Johns Hopkins Press, 1965.

Hicks, Ursula K., *Development from Below: Local Government and Finance in Developing Countries of the Commonwealth,* London, Oxford University Press, 1961.

Higgins, B., *Economic Development, Principles, Problems and Policies,* New York, Norton, 1959.

Hinrichs, H. H., "Determinants of Government Revenue Shares Among Less Developed Countries," *Economic Journal, 75* (September 1965).

————, *A General Theory of Tax Structure Change During Economic Development,* Cambridge, Mass., The Law School of Harvard University, 1966.

Joint Tax Program of the Organization of American States, *Fiscal Policy for Economic Growth in Latin America,* Baltimore, Johns Hopkins Press, 1965.

Kaldor, N., *An Expenditure Tax,* London, George Allen and Unwin, 1955.

————, "The Expenditure Tax in a System of Personal Taxation," in *Readings on Taxation in Developing Countries,* Bird and Oldman, eds., Baltimore, The Johns Hopkins Press, 1967.

————, "Tax Reform in India," in ibid.

Lotz, Joergen R., and Elliott R. Morss, "The Influence of Selected

Factors on Tax Levels in Developing Countries," unpublished manuscript.

————, "Measuring Tax Effort in Developing Countries," International Monetary Fund, *Staff Papers, 14* (1967).

Marx, Karl, and Friedrich Engels, "The Communist Manifesto," in *Handbook of Marxism,* New York, International Publishers, 1935.

Naharro, J. M., "Production and Consumption Taxes and Economic Development," in *Fiscal Policy for Economic Growth in Latin America,* Joint Tax Program of the Organization of American States, Baltimore, Johns Hopkins Press, 1965.

Peacock, Alan T., and Gerald Hauser, eds., *Government Finance and Economic Development,* Paris, Organization for Economic Cooperation and Development, 1965.

Pigou, A. C., *A Study in Public Finance,* 3d ed. London, Macmillan, 1951.

Prest, Alan R., *Public Finance in Under-developed Countries,* London, Weidenfeld and Nicholson, 1962.

Wald, Haskell, *Taxation of Agricultural Land in Underdeveloped Economies,* Cambridge, Mass., Harvard University Press, 1959.

World Bank, Mission to Colombia, "A Graduated Land Tax," in *Readings on Taxation in Developing Countries,* R. M. Bird and O. Oldman, eds., Baltimore, Johns Hopkins Press, 1967.

COMPARISON OF TAX STRUCTURES

Bittker, B. I., "A Comprehensive Tax Base as a Goal of Income Tax Reform," *Harvard Law Review, 80* (1967) and response by Richard A. Musgrave in *Harvard Law Review, 81* (1967).

Eckstein, Otto, and Vito Tanzi, "Comparison of European and United States Tax Structures and Growth Implications," *The Role of Direct and Indirect Taxes in the Federal Revenue System,* The Brookings Institution, Princeton, Princeton University Press, 1964.

Eliasson, Gunnar, *Investment Funds in Operation,* Stockholm, National Institute of Economic Research, 1965.

Forte, Francesco, "Comment on Schedular and Global Income Taxes," in *Readings in Taxation in Developing Countries,* R. M. Bird and O. Oldman, eds., Baltimore, Johns Hopkins Press, 1967.

Gerloff, W., and F. Neumark, *Handbuch der Finanzwissenschaft,* 2d ed. Tübingen, Mohr, 1958.

Haig, Robert Murray, "The Concept of Income—Economic and

Bibliography

Legal Aspects," in *The Federal Income Tax,* ed. Haig, New York, Columbia University Press, 1921.

International Program in Taxation, The Law School of Harvard University, *World Tax Series* (Boston, Little, Brown), describing tax systems of a large number of countries.

Musgrave, Peggy B., "Direct Business Tax Harmonization," in Carl S. Shoup, ed., *Fiscal Harmonization in Common Markets, 2,* New York, Columbia University Press, 1967.

Musgrave, Richard A., "How Progressive Is the Individual Income Tax?" *Tax Revision Compendium, 3,* U.S. Congress, House Committee on Ways and Means, Washington, D.C., G.P.O., 1959.

———, "The Role of Social Insurance in a System of Social Welfare," *The U.S. Social Security System,* ed. F. Harbeson, Princeton, Princeton University Press, 1968.

———, and Tun Thin, "Income Tax Progression, 1929–48," *Journal of Political Economy, 56,* no. 6 (December 1948).

Pechman, J., "Individual Income Tax Provisions of the Revenue Act of 1964," *Journal of Finance, 20* (May 1965).

Schanz, Georg, "Der Einkommensbegriff und die Einkommenssteuergesetze," *Finanzarchiv, 13* (1896).

Simons, H. C., *Personal Income Taxation,* Chicago, University of Chicago Press, 1938.

United Kingdom, *Royal Commission on the Taxation of Profits and Income, Final Report,* Cmd. 9474, London, H.M. Stationery Office, 1955.

J. A. Stockfisch, "International Comparisons on Direct and Indirect Taxes," in *Excise Tax Compendium,* United States Congress, Washington, D.C., G.P.O., June 15, 1964.

THE CHANGING FUNCTION OF FISCAL POLICY

Chenery, H. B., "The Application of Investment Criteria," *Quarterly Journal of Economics, 67* (February 1953).

———, "Comparative Advantage and Development Policy," *American Economic Review, 51* (March 1961).

Djha, P. D., and V. V. Bhatt, "Income Distribution: A Case Study of India," *American Economic Review, 54* (September 1964) and comments by Eva Mueller, I. R. K. Sarma, and S. Swamy in *American Economic Review, 55* (December 1965).

Eckaus, R. S., "The Factor-Proportions Problem in Underdeveloped Areas," *American Economic Review, 45* (September 1955), reprinted in D. N. Agarwala and S. P. Singh, *The*

Economics of Underdevelopment, London, Oxford University Press, 1958.

Eckstein, Otto, "Investment Criteria for Economic Development and the Theory of Intertemporal Welfare Economics," *Quarterly Journal of Economics, 71* (February 1957).

Galenson, W., and H. Liebenstein, "Investment Criteria, Productivity and Economic Development," *Quarterly Journal of Economics, 69* (August 1955).

Hansen, B., "Tax Policy and Mobilization of Earnings," in Alan T. Peacock and Gerald Hauser, eds., *Government Finance and Economic Development,* Paris, Organization for Economic Cooperation and Development, 1965.

Heller, W., "Fiscal Policies for Underdeveloped Countries" in R. M. Bird and O. Oldman, eds., *Readings on Taxation in Developing Countries,* Baltimore, Johns Hopkins Press, 1967.

Higgins, B., "Financing Accelerated Growth," in Alan T. Peacock and Gerald Hauser, eds., *Government Finance and Economic Development,* Paris, Organization for Economic Cooperation and Development, 1965.

Joint Tax Program of the Organization of American States, *Fiscal Policy for Economic Growth in Latin America,* Baltimore, Johns Hopkins Press, 1965.

Kaldor, N., "The Role of Taxation in Economic Development," in ibid.

Krishnaswamy, K. S., "The Evolution of Tax Structure in a Development Policy," in Alan T. Peacock and Gerald Hauser, eds., *Government Finance and Economic Development,* Paris, Organization for Economic Cooperation and Development, 1965.

Krzyzaniak, Marian, "Effects of Profits Taxes: Deduced from Neoclassical Models," in M. Krzyzaniak, ed., *Effects of Corporation Income Tax,* Detroit, Wayne State University Press, 1966.

Kuznets, Simon, *Modern Economic Growth,* New Haven, Yale University Press, 1966.

————, "Quantitative Aspects of the Economic Growth of Nations: VIII. Distribution of Income by Size," *Economic Development and Cultural Change, 11,* no. 2 (January 1963), Part II.

Lewis, W. Arthur, "Economic Development with Unlimited Supplies of Labor," *The Manchester School of Economic and Social Studies, 23* (May 1955); reprinted in D. N. Agarwala and S. P. Singh, *The Economics of Underdevelopment,* London, Oxford University Press, 1958.

Bibliography

————, *The Theory of Economic Growth,* Homewood, Ill., R. D. Irwin, 1955.

Rao, V. K. R. V., "Investment, Income and the Multiplier in an Underdeveloped Economy," *Indian Economic Review* (February 1952); reprinted in D. N. Agarwala and S. P. Singh, *The Economics of Underdevelopment,* London, Oxford University Press, 1958.

Richman (Musgrave), Peggy B., *Taxation of Foreign Investment: An Economic Analysis,* Baltimore, Johns Hopkins Press, 1963.

Sato, R., "Fiscal Policy in a Neo-classical Growth Model: An Analysis of Time Required for Equilibrating Adjustment," *Review of Economic Studies, 30,* no. 1 (February 1963).

Shoup, Carl S., "Production from Consumption," *Public Finance/Finances Publiques, 20,* nos. 1–2 (1965).

Solow, Robert, "A Contribution to the Theory of Economic Growth," *Quarterly Journal of Economics, 70* (February 1956).

United States, *Report of the President's Commission on Budget Concepts,* Washington, D.C., G.P.O., October 1967.

TAX COORDINATION

Dalton, Hugh, *Principles of Public Finance,* 9th ed. London, Routledge and Kegan Paul, 1936.

Dosser, Douglas, "Economic Analysis of Tax Harmonization," in Carl S. Shoup, ed., *Fiscal Harmonization in Common Markets, 1,* New York, Columbia University Press, 1967.

————, "Theoretical Considerations for Tax Harmonization," in *Comparison and Harmonization of Public Revenue Systems,* Luxembourg Congress of the International Institute of Public Finance, 19th Session, September 1963, published 1965.

————, "Welfare Effects of Tax Unions," *Review of Economic Studies, 31* (3), no. 87 (1964).

European Economic Community, "Report of the Fiscal and Financial Committee on Tax Harmonization in the Common Market," reprinted in *Tax Harmonization in the Common Market,* Chicago, Commerce Clearing House, 1963.

Johnson, H. G., "Optimum Tariffs and Retaliation," *Review of Economic Studies, 21* (2), no. 55 (1953–54).

Jones, Ronald W., "International Capital Movements and the Theory of Tariffs and Trade," *Quarterly Journal of Economics, 81,* no. 1 (February 1967).

Kaldor, N., "A Memorandum on the Value-Added Tax," *Essays in Economic Policy, 1,* London, Duckworth, 1964.

Kindleberger, Charles P., *International Economics,* 3d ed., Homewood, Ill., R. D. Irwin, 1963.

Lipsey, R. G., "The Theory of Customs Unions: A General Survey," *Economic Journal, 70* (September 1960).

McLure, Charles, "Commodity Tax Incidence in Open Economies," *National Tax Journal, 17,* no. 2 (June 1964).

Mieszkowski, Peter M., "The Comparative Efficiency of Tariffs and Other Tax-Subsidy Schemes as a Means of Obtaining Revenue or Protecting Domestic Production," *Journal of Political Economy, 74,* no. 6 (December 1966).

Musgrave, Peggy B., *United States Taxation of Foreign Investment,* International Tax Program, Cambridge, Mass., The Law School of Harvard University, forthcoming.

Musgrave, Richard A., "Effects of Business Taxes Upon International Commodity Flows," in Marian Krzyzaniak, ed., *Effects of Corporation Income Tax,* Detroit, Wayne State University Press, 1966.

————, and Peggy B. Richman, "Allocation Aspects, Domestic and International," in *The Role of Direct and Indirect Taxes in the Federal Revenue System,* Princeton, Princeton University Press, 1964.

Owens, Elisabeth A., *The Foreign Tax Credit,* International Tax Program, Cambridge, Mass., The Law School of Harvard University, 1961.

Scitovsky, T. de, "A Reconsideration of the Theory of Tariffs," *Review of Economic Studies, 9,* no. 2 (1942).

Shibata, Hirofumi, "The Theory of Economic Unions: A Comparative Analysis of Customs Unions, Free Trade Areas, and Tax Unions," in Carl S. Shoup, ed., *Fiscal Harmonization in Common Markets, 1,* New York, Columbia University Press, 1965.

Shoup, Carl S., "Taxation Aspects of International Economic Integration," *Papers of the International Institute of Public Finance,* 9th Session, Frankfurt, 1953, The Hague, W. P. Stockun, n.d.

————, ed., *Fiscal Harmonization in Common Markets,* New York, Columbia University Press, 1965.

United Kingdom, *The Report of the Committee on Turnover Taxation,* Cmd. 2300, London, H.M. Stationery Office, 1964.

United States, Report of the Special Sub-Committee on State Taxation of the Committee of the Judiciary, *State Taxation*

Bibliography

of Interstate Commerce, 88th Congress, 2d Session, House Report no. 1480, Washington, D.C., G.P.O., 1964.

Viner, J., *The Customs Union Issue,* New York, Carnegie Endowment for International Peace, 1950; reprinted Washington, Anderson Kramer Associates, 1961.

PUBLIC EXPENDITURE COORDINATION

Andel, R., "Problems of Government Expenditure Harmonization in a Common Market," and "Problems of Harmonization of Social Security Policies in a Common Market," both in Carl S. Shoup, ed., *Fiscal Harmonization in Common Markets,* New York, Columbia University Press, 1965.

Andic, Suphan, and Alan T. Peacock, "The International Distribution of Income, 1949 and 1957," *Journal of the Royal Statistical Society,* Series A, *124,* Part 2 (1961).

Brainard, W. C., and F. T. Dolbear, "The Possibility of Oversupply of Local 'Public' Goods: A Critical Note," and rejoinder by Alan Williams, *Journal of Political Economy, 75,* no. 1 (February 1967).

Brazer, Harvey E., "Some Fiscal Implications of Metropolitanism," in G. S. Birkhead, ed., *Metropolitan Issues: Social, Governmental, Fiscal,* Syracuse, Syracuse University Press, 1962.

Breton, Albert, "A Theory of Government Grants," *Canadian Journal of Economics and Political Science, 31,* no. 2 (May 1965).

Buchanan, J. M., "An Economic Theory of Clubs," *Economica, 32* (February 1965).

———, "Federalism and Fiscal Equity," *American Economic Review, 40,* no. 4 (September 1950).

———, and M. Z. Kafoglis, "A Note on Public Goods Supply," *American Economic Review, 53,* no. 3 (June 1963).

Dosser, Douglas, "Allocating the Burden of International Aid to Less Developed Countries," *Review of Economics and Statistics, 45,* no. 2 (May 1963).

———, "Towards a Theory of International Public Finance," *Kyklos, 16,* Fasc. 1 (1963).

———, and Alan T. Peacock, "The International Distribution of Income with Maximum Aid," *Review of Economics and Statistics, 46,* no. 4 (November 1964).

Head, J. G., "Lindahl's Theory of the Budget," *Finanzarchiv,* N.F. *23* (October 1964).

385

Hirsch, W., "Local vs. Areawide Urban Government Services," *National Tax Journal, 17*, no. 4 (December 1964).

Kravis, Irving B., and Michael W. S. Davenport, "The Political Arithmetic of Burden Sharing," *Journal of Political Economy, 71,* no. 4 (August 1963).

McLure, Charles E., Jr., "Tax Exporting in the United States: Estimates for 1967," *National Tax Journal, 20,* no. 1 (March 1967).

Musgrave, Richard A., "Approaches to a Fiscal Theory of Political Federalism," *Public Finances: Needs, Sources and Utilization,* National Bureau of Economic Research, Princeton, Princeton University Press, 1961.

Myrdal, Gunnar, *Economic Theory and Underdeveloped Regions,* London, Duckworth, 1951.

Olsen, M., and R. Zeckhauser, "An Economic Theory of Alliances," *Review of Economics and Statistics, 48,* no. 3 (August 1966).

Philip, Kjeld, *Intergovernmental Fiscal Relations,* Copenhagen, Institute of Economics and History, 1954.

Pincus, John, *Economic Aid and International Cost Sharing,* Baltimore, Johns Hopkins Press, 1965.

Rosenstein-Rodan, P. N., "International Aid for Underdeveloped Countries," *Review of Economics and Statistics, 62,* no. 2 (May 1961).

Schelling, Thomas C., *The Strategy of Conflict,* London, Oxford University Press, 1963.

Scott, A., "The Economic Goals of Federal Finance," *Public Finance/Finances Publiques, 19,* no. 3 (1964).

Taubenfeld, R. F. and H. J., "Independent Revenue for the United Nations," *International Organization, 18,* no. 2 (1964).

Theil, H., "Enige kwantitatieve aspecten van het probleem der hulpverlening aan onderontwikkelde landen," *De Economist, 2* (1953).

Thompson, Wilbur R., *A Preface to Urban Economics,* Baltimore, Johns Hopkins Press, 1965.

Tiebout, Charles M., "An Economic Theory of Fiscal Decentralization," in *Public Finances: Needs, Sources and Utilization,* National Bureau of Economic Research, Princeton, Princeton University Press, 1961.

———, "A Pure Theory of Public Expenditures," *Journal of Political Economy, 64,* no. 5 (October 1956).

United Nations, *Report of the Committee on Contributions,* General Assembly, official Records, 16th Session, Supplement no. 10 (A/4774), and 17th Session Supplement no. 10 (A/5210).

———, *Yearbook of National Account Statistics, 1965,* New York, United Nations, 1966.

Weisbrod, Burton, *External Benefits of Education: An Economic Analysis,* Princeton, Princeton University Press, 1964.

Williams, Alan, "Centralization and Decentralization in Public Finance with Special Reference to Central and Local Government in England and Wales," in *Centralization and Decentralization in Public Finance,* Travaux de l'Institut International de Finances Publiques (Proceedings of the 18th Congress), 1962.

———, "The Optimal Provision of Public Goods in a Theory of Local Government," *Journal of Political Economy,* 74, no. 1 (February 1966).

FISCAL POLICY IN THE OPEN ECONOMY

Chenery, H. B., and A. M. Strout, "Foreign Assistance and Economic Development," *American Economic Review, 44,* no. 4 (September 1966).

Harberger, A., "Currency Depreciation, Income, and the Balance of Trade," *Journal of Political Economy, 56,* no. 1 (February 1950).

Johnson, H. G., *International Trade and Economic Growth* (Cambridge, Mass., Harvard University Press, 1958), chapter 8.

———, "The Transfer Problem and Exchange Stability," *Journal of Political Economy, 64,* no. 3 (June 1956).

Kindleberger, Charles P., *International Economics* (3d ed., Homewood, Ill., R. D. Irwin, 1963), Appendix C.

Laursen, Svend, and Lloyd Metzler, "Flexible Exchange Rates and the Theory of Employment," *Review of Economics and Statistics, 32,* no. 4 (November 1950).

Mundell, R. A., "The Appropriate Use of Monetary and Fiscal Policy for Internal and External Stability," International Monetary Fund, *Staff Papers, 9* (March 1962).

———, "Capital Mobility and Stabilization Policy Under Fixed and Flexible Exchange Rates," *Canadian Journal of Economics and Political Science, 29* (1963).

———, "Flexible Exchange Rates and Employment Policy," *Canadian Journal of Economics and Political Science, 27* (1961).

Musgrave, R. A. and P. B., "Fiscal Policy," in R. E. Caves, ed.,

Britain's Economic Prospects, Washington, D.C., The Brookings Institution, 1968.

Peacock, Alan T., "Towards a Theory of Inter-Regional Fiscal Policy," *Public Finance/Finances Publiques, 20,* nos. 1–2 (1965).

———, and Dosser, Douglas, "Stabilization in African Countries," *Public Finance/Finances Publiques, 17,* no. 3 (1962).

Tinbergen, J., *On the Theory of Economic Policy,* Amsterdam, North Holland Publishing Co., 1952.

Vanek, J., *International Trade,* Homewood, Ill., R. D. Irwin, 1962, Chap. 7.

FURTHER PROBLEMS

Biargava, R. N., *The Theory and Working of Union Finance in India,* London, Allen and Unwin, 1956.

Bickel, W., "Der Finanzausgleich," in W. Gerloff and F. Neumark, eds., *Handbuch der Finanzwissenschaft, 2,* 2d ed. Tübingen, Mohr, 1956.

Break, G. F., *Intergovernmental Fiscal Relations in the United States,* Washington, D.C., The Brookings Institution, 1967.

Brittain, H., *The British Budgetary System,* London, Allen and Unwin, 1960.

Burns, R. M., "Recent Developments in Federal-Provincial Fiscal Arrangements in Canada," *National Tax Journal, 15* (September 1962).

Commission on Money and Credit, *Fiscal and Debt Management Policies and Stabilization Policies,* Englewood Cliffs, N.J., Prentice-Hall, 1963.

Davis, R. W., *The Development of the Soviet Budgetary System,* Cambridge, England, Cambridge University Press, 1958.

European Economic Community, Monetary Committee, *The Instruments of Monetary Policy in the Countries of the European Economic Community,* Paris, 1962.

Gillespie, W. Irwin, "Effect of Public Expenditures on the Distribution of Income," in Richard A. Musgrave, ed., *Essays in Fiscal Federalism,* Washington, D.C., The Brookings Institution, 1965.

Hansen, Bent, *Comparative Analysis of Stabilization Policy in O.E.C.D. Countries,* Paris, Organization for Economic Cooperation and Development, forthcoming.

Head, J. G., "Financial Equality in a Federation, A Study of the

Commonwealth Grants Commission in Australia," *Finanzar-chiv*, N.F., *26* (December 1967).

Kamins, R. M., "Democratic Centralism: Local Finance in the Soviet Union," *National Tax Journal, 15* (December 1962).

Kareken, John H., "Monetary Policy" in Richard E. Caves, ed., *Prospects of the British Economy*, Washington, D.C., The Brookings Institution, 1968.

Lakdawala, D. T., "The Four Finance Commissions in India," *Indian Economic Journal, 13*, no. 4 (1966).

Musgrave, Richard A., ed., *Essays in Fiscal Federalism*, Washington, D.C., The Brookings Institution, 1965.

Newcomer, M., *Central and Local Finance in Germany and England*, New York, Columbia University Press, 1937.

Peacock, Alan T., ed., *Income Distribution and Social Policy*, London, Jonathan Cape, 1954.

Prest, Alan R., *Public Finance in Theory and Practice* (3d ed. London, Weidenfeld and Nicolson, 1967), Chapter 9.

Richardson, J. H., *Economic and Financial Aspects of Social Security: An International Survey*, Toronto, University of Toronto Press, 1960.

Smithies, A., *The Budgetary Process in the United States*, New York, McGraw-Hill, 1955.

United Kingdom, *Report of the Committee on the Working of the Monetary System* (Radcliffe Report), Cmd. 827, London, H.M. Stationery Office, 1959.

United States, Commission on Intergovernmental Relations, *Report to the President*, Washington, D.C., G.P.O., 1955.

———, Department of Health, Education and Welfare, Social Security Administration, *Social Security Programs Throughout the World*, Washington, D.C., G.P.O., 1961.

———, Joint Economic Committee, 89th Congress, *European Social Security Systems, Economic Policies and Practices*, Paper no. 7, Washington, D.C., G.P.O., 1965.

Wildavsky, A. B., *Politics of the Budgetary Process*, Boston, Little, Brown, 1964.

INDEX

Index

Index

Index

Profit taxes (*cont.*)
parison of, for developed countries, 200–02; coordination of, 261; integration of, 268; and level of income, 152; shifting of, 252

Profits tax coordination: and deferral, 266; and efficiency, world basis, 248, national basis, 249; and equivalent rates, 269; and origin of income, 261; and shifting, 252; and types of investor, 264–67

Progressive taxation: and burden sharing, 317; and capital gains, 197; and capitalism, 132; comparisons of, 180

Pryor, F. L., 39 n.

Public debt, 350

Public sector, size of, 34

Purchase tax, 205

Rao, V. K. R. V., 209 n.

Retail sales tax, and destination principle, 276

Richardson, J. H., 348 n.

Ritvo, H., 19 n.

Rosenstein-Rodan, P. N., 76, 314 n.

Royal Commission on the Taxation of Profits and Income, Report of, 189

Samuelson, P. E., 8 n.

Sarma, I. R. K., 212 n.

Schanz, G., 189

Schelling, T., 304 n.

Schumpeter, J., 3 n., 132 n.

Shibata, H., 287 n.

Shoup, C. S., 203 n., 238 n.

Simons, H. C., 189

Singh, S. P., 209 n.

Smithies, A., 345 n.

Social security systems, 347

Social security taxes: direct or indirect, 174; and finance of benefits, 347; and GATT rules, 279; and per capita income, 155

Social wants: under capitalism, 8; nature of, 8–11; under socialism, 10; spatial aspects of, 294

Socialist system: and distribution, 25; and expenditure structure, 35; and fiscal functions, 31; and incentives, 23–26; and merit wants, 13; and role of taxation, 14; and social wants, 10, 13, 40; and stabilization, 30; tax reform in, 54; tax structure of, 42

Solow, R., 57 n., 228 n.

Stockfisch, J. A., 168 n.

Strout, A. M., 338 n.

Subsidies, 19

Surplus land, taxation of, 215

Swamy, S., 212 n.

Sweden: expenditure structure of, 36, 38, 41; investment credit in, 203; tax structure of, 44, 62, 168, 205

Switzerland, fiscal centralization in, 341, 343

Tanzi, V., 168 n.

Taubenfeld, R. F. and H. J., 315 n.

Tax allegiance, place of, 258

Tax coordination: compatibility of efficiency and equity aspects, 251; and efficiency, world basis, 248, national basis, 249; and equity, among persons, 244, among countries, 246; for income taxes, 258–61; model solution for, 239; for product taxes, 271–90; for profits taxes, 261–69; in tax union, 250–87

Tax legislative process, 346